MAKING **GROWTH** HAPPEN IN **INDIA**

A ROAD MAP FOR POLICY SUCCESS

V. KUMARASWAMY

ATLANTIC

PUBLISHERS & DISTRIBUTORS (P) LTD

ATLANTIC
PUBLISHERS & DISTRIBUTORS (P) LTD
7/22, Ansari Road, Darya Ganj, New Delhi
Tel.: +91-11-4077 5252, 2327 3880
E-mail: orders@atlanticbooks.com
Web: www.atlanticbooks.com

This edition published in 2025 by Atlantic Publishers & Distributors (P) Ltd.

Previous edition published by SAGE Publicationss in 2014

Registered Office and Editorial Office
Atlantic Publishers & Distributors (P) Ltd.,
7/22 Ansari Road, Darya Ganj, New Delhi-110002, India

Library of Congress Cataloging-in-Publication applied for

ISBN 978-8-126-94362-3

For details of our editorial offices, customer service, and more information about Atlantic Publishers and Distributors (P) Ltd. Products, visit us at www.atlanticbooks.com

Printed and bound in United States of America

Advance Praise

The book gives a fresh insight into several aspects that have a huge relevance at the moment. What is creditworthy is the lucid way in which the author handles these issues. For example on the NREGA issue, he gives a nice example of how 'NREGA is like giving excessive grace marks to a student who keeps failing his exams repeatedly'. This is an interesting take on the subject and I doubt whether any economist, whatever be their ideological leanings, will disapprove this. Mr Kumarswamy's agenda and blueprint for 12 per cent growth is just the potion India needs at this hour to reach the heights we all aspire to.

—Professor Abraham Koshy
Professor of Marketing,
Indian Institute of Management, Ahmedabad

Mr Kumaraswamy has applied his deep knowledge of consumer behaviour, developmental issues and programmes to come up with a suitable design for accelerating our growth. If India is to rightfully claim its place amongst the world's leading economic powers and provide employment opportunities to its citizens, its policy makers would do well to seriously consider the author's proposals.

—Harsh Pati Singhania
Director, JK Organization

The book blends data, anecdotes and analysis in a way that makes it both insightful and interesting—a combination rare in books on Indian economy.

—Rohit Saran
Editor-at-Large, India Today Group

There is no doubt that a well-implemented good strategy is better than a perfect strategy that is poorly implemented. Mr Kumaraswamy's book provides a very refreshing non-economist's perspective into the design and delivery of economic programmes rather than focussing on the relevance of reforms as a fundamental economic strategy. In doing so, it seeks to search for ways to improve their effectiveness and suggests new programmes aimed at enhancing the country's growth rates.

—Rohit Walia
Executive Chairman
Alpen Capital (ME) Limited

This is an important book, written with a fresh perspective on the vital issues facing the country. Even though Kumaraswamy claims to be a non-economist, he has sufficient insights into the broad economics behind significant policy decisions to warrant a close reading by the policy makers and implementers. A must read for every Indian interested in the future of the country.

—Professor S. Manikutty
Professor (Retired)
Indian Institute of Management Ahmedabad

Mr Kumaraswamy's insights into the drivers of change in India need to be widely absorbed. A timeless book at a strategic inflection point when India will certainly get rerated.

—Shailesh Haribhakti
Managing Partner
Haribhakti & Co.

To
the inquisitive economist lurking in each of us
by
a non-economist

Contents

List of Tables

List of Abbreviations

2G	Second generation
ADR/GDR	American/global depository receipt
AIIMS	All India Institute of Medical Sciences
B2B	Business to business
B2C	Business to consumer
BOP	Balance of payments
BOT	Build, operate and transfer
BPL	Below poverty line
BRIC	Brazil, Russia, India and China
CCEA	Cabinet Committee on Economic Affairs
CAD	Current account deficit
CAG	Comptroller and Auditor General
CACC	Capital Account Convertibility Committee
CCI	Competition Commission of India (or) Controller of Capital Issues
CEA	Chief Economic Advisor
CIA	Central Intelligence Agency
CACP	Commission for Agricultural Cost and Prices
CPI	Consumer price index
CWG	Commonwealth Games
DGCA	Director General of Civil Aviation
DPCO	Drug Price Control Order
DTC	Direct tax code
EEFC	Exchange earner's foreign currency
ELSS	Equity linked savings scheme
FCI	Food Corporation of India
FDI	Foreign direct investment
FMCG	Fast moving consumer goods
FRBM	Fiscal responsibility and budget management
FTA	Foreign tourists arrival

GDP	Gross domestic product
GDS	Global distribution system; also gross domestic savings
GMRC	Good manners and right conduct
GOI	Government of India
GST	Goods and services tax
HDI	Human Development Index
ICOR	Incremental capital output ratio
IIFT	Indian Institute of Foreign Trade
IIM	Indian Institute of Management
IIT	Indian Institute of Technology
IPL	Indian Premier League
IRR	Internal rate of return
ITI	Industrial Training Institute
LARR	Land Acquisition and Rehabilitation and Resettlement Bill
MHRD	Ministry of Human Resource Development
MSP	Minimum support price
NGO	Non-governmental organisation
NHAI	National Highways Authority of India
NHDP	National Highways Development Project
NIFT	National Institute of Fashion Technology
NID	National Institute of Design
NPV	Net present value
NREGA	National Rural Employment Guarantee Act
OPEC	Organisation of Petroleum Exporting Countries
PDS	Public distribution system
PPP	Public–private partnership
PSU	Public sector undertaking
RBI	Reserve Bank of India
ROCE	Return on capital employed
ROI	Return on investment
RTE	Right to education
SSA	Sarva Shiksha Abhiyaan
SEBI	Securities and Exchange Board of India
SLR	Statutory liquidity ratio
SME	Small and medium enterprises

TTCI	Travel and Tourism Competitiveness Index
VAT	Value added tax
WDR	World Development Report
WGC	World Gold Council
WHO	World Health Organisation
WTTC	World Travel and Tourism Council
WPI	Wholesale price index
WTO	World Trade Organisation

Foreword

For the India of 1.2 billion people, growth is not a choice but an imperative. Without adequate growth the very fabric of the nation is at risk. The tens of millions that join India's workforce must either receive gainful employment or the nation risks severe social disorder and unrest. Further, the inequality of the growth that has occurred so far presents another challenge which must be addressed if the country is to see a peaceful path to prosperity. This is the complex context around which Kumaraswamy has crafted an extremely readable and interesting analysis of the problems that hold India back and how they might be addressed. This is an extremely ambitious and equally laudable undertaking.

As the author notes, 'economic reforms have three important and, to a large extent, inter-dependent legs on which its success rests, namely (1) appropriate strategy or economic policy at the macroeconomic level, (2) translation of these into meaningful plans and programmes at the segment or sectoral level and (3) effective delivery or implementation thereof.' By targeting this book at the second and third of these levels, Kumaraswamy does a valuable service. Too often is evaluation and review targeted at the policy level. Yet, whether the policy has any impact is eventually dependent upon what he calls ground realities. For a reform policy to have an effective impact on the people that it targets, it should be ground into reality of the institutional context—something often not considered deeply by policy makers. Kumaraswamy's book, at the broadest level, is a call to draw attention to this often underemphasized but extremely important component of the economic transformation process.

Equally noteworthy is the fact that Kumaraswamy has written a book that looks at economic issues but explicitly as a non-economist. This is laudable because it is helping us broaden the discourse from the ivory towers of academia which often have limited exposure to ground realities, and bringing it to the level of the lay (albeit thoughtful and informed) person who has lived those realities and been exposed to them deeply. The book is full of thoughtful analysis, and contains many plausible critiques; it is, however, also likely to generate disagreement as all books that address complex topics do. Many of the problems of programme delivery that Kumaraswamy addresses are open to multiple different interpretations with consequently different solutions. Kumaraswamy's fresh thinking demands our attention even if we may not agree with all his diagnoses and recommended solutions. I think this book should be an important read for all policy makers and social programme designers who are hoping to enhance and improve the life of the average Indian. I have found it to add many layers to my own understanding of the common programmes that we have seen implemented.

Gautam Ahuja
Professor, University of Michigan
Ann Arbor, USA

Preface

HISTORY OF INDIAN REFORMS

The initial seeds of reforms were first sown by our late Prime Minister Rajiv Gandhi. Useful changes in indirect taxation took place during the succeeding regime. The short-lived regime of late Prime Minister Chandrasekhar faced an acute crisis on the forex front and came up with some path-breaking measures. However, the full-blown implementation of those measures got derailed prematurely due to political events. It was only in 1991 that the government of late Prime Minister Narasimha Rao through Dr Manmohan Singh introduced several initiatives which paved the way for increased role of private sector. There was without doubt much more depth to the various initiatives during their tenure and several measures were taken for the first time in our country. The successive governments in the last two decades have, by and large, followed up on those measures.

India's socialism of the first 40 years since Independence did have its purpose. It was not as mindless as in many other countries. It was blended with democracy judiciously. It created some demand, made up for lack of investments and entrepreneurship at a crucial juncture. However, looking at our own progress and the kind of progress many of the East Asian economies had achieved in the period since 1965, it would be naïve to argue that we should have continued with our socialistic approach. The government and agencies involved in reforms have an obligation to calibrate the reforms so as not to repeat the failures of the past. In several reform policies, there seems to be a fair degree of consensus by now. With the benefit of experience, initial objections and apprehensions seem to have settled down. Whatever shrillness is there in the debates these days seems more about political posturing.

COMPONENTS OF REFORMS

Economic reforms have three important and to a large extent interdependent legs on which its success rests, namely (1) appropriate strategy or economic policy at the macroeconomic level, (2) translation of these into meaningful plans and programmes at the segment or sectoral level and (3) effective delivery or implementation thereof. This is graphically illustrated in the box below.

To illustrate the difference—increased literacy may be the socio-economic objective while the programme to deliver it can be Sarva Siksha Abhiyaan; removal of hunger and poverty may be the macro social objective which is delivered by public distribution systems through fair price shops and NREGA; increased tax efficiency may be the end-goal achieved through GST, DTC, etc.

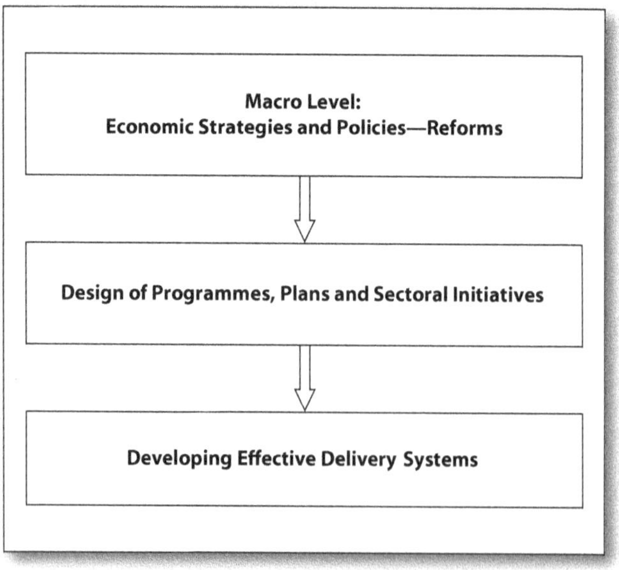

THE FOCUS OF THIS BOOK

This book is more about stages 2 and 3—i.e. design of programmes and delivery thereof and less about the macroeconomic policies and strategies. This book is not about fiscal deficits,[1] WTOs, balance of payments, Gini-coefficients,[2] Phillips curves,[3] finance commissions, plan approach papers, etc. This is more about the programmes like NREGA, GST, DTC, MSPs, PDS and fair price shops, food subsidies, land acquisition initiatives, etc. that are designed to translate overall objectives at macro level into specific initiatives at micro level. The book seeks to identify the lacunae in them and a search for ways to improve their effectiveness and suggest new programmes aimed at enhancing the country's growth rates.

There are specific reasons for my bias towards programme design and delivery systems while I lay far less emphasis on the relevance of reforms as a fundamental economic strategy. *Firstly*, there are several books on reforms as a strategy from the macroeconomic perspective and there is very little a non-economist can add to the existing available literature. *Secondly*, there is fair degree of consensus amongst the economists (surprising indeed!) on the need and efficacy of reforms. This is backed by sound theories which have been shown to work in other countries that have achieved sustained growth over a period of time. *Lastly*, not many can fault the lofty ideals behind many of the reform policies like employment guarantees, MSP, food or education subsidies. There can be few valid arguments against support for people who have

[1] Fiscal deficit is the amount by which the government's expenditure exceeds its income.

[2] Gini-coefficient is a measure of equality of income distribution. A co-efficient of '0' means perfect distribution where everyone has the same income and '1' means where all income is concentrated in one person.

[3] Phillips curve is a curve showing the relationship between unemployment and inflation—usually inverse—a higher inflation being associated with lower unemployment.

starved for decades, denied equal opportunities and have taken (or have been forced to take) permanent residence below poverty line. That we have failed to solve our basic problems even after six decades of independence speaks poorly of our implementation efficiencies.

While macroeconomic reforms may be well intentioned, many programmes and plans seem to falter more due to ill-fitting designs. They seem to ignore ground realities, end-user reception, social conditioning of people at the receiving end of social services and interventions, suffer bad sequencing and surprisingly in a lot of cases overlook even basic economic principles. The book will illustrate this in several places.

The book by Nobel laureate Joseph Stiglitz (*Globalization and Its Discontents*) examines how economic policies are framed wrongly in countries after countries ignoring ground realities; how they are designed to serve the donors' interest rather than donees' requirements, and how such policies have had to fail. This book examines several places where there is clear disconnect between policies and strategies at the broad level and the plans, pronouncements designed to implement them, between action plan and follow-up, mix up between cause and effect, and programmes laid ineffective due to design defects. This particular leg of reforms seems to have escaped serious scrutiny from economists in India, or at least not analysed to the depth it deserves.

To summarise, this book is less of a critique of reforms as an economic strategy and more of a selective look about its faulty planning, the pitfalls, lessons to be learnt, ways to correct them and the ways (even if unconventional) ahead.

ORGANISATION OF THE BOOK

Part I of the book looks at the current reform programmes and their effectiveness. It delves into how reforms may be the cause of some social problems and the need for adjustments in such areas in order to avoid alienating people or large sections of them and examines the reasons why some of our flagship programmes are failing. Chapter 3 of Part I looks at some essential actions or systemic changes necessary to get better results from the government's policies and plans.

Part II is about an alternative growth path. It combines the learning from the analyses in Part I with new growth initiatives for suggesting a strategy and a set of new programmes for achieving 12 per cent growth rates. It looks at the need to develop appropriate market structures, deliberate actions needed to create employment besides re-orienting our education to facilitate meaningful employment creation.

The sequence does not follow the normal sectoral flow that economists follow; it is not organised as agriculture, industry, service, banking, fiscal matters, human resource development, etc. The flow and placement of topics have more to do with the unrealised potential, their criticality to the success of reforms and their ability to deliver growth the way the country wants.

INTENDED AUDIENCE: NON-ECONOMIST ECONOMISTS

There is an economist in each one of us—whether we are a homemaker, student given to serious debating, professional, businessman, politician, journalist, etc. We all think of economic issues all the time in our own ways based on our comprehension and what affects or appeals to us most. The book is intended towards these 'non-economist economists'.

It is for those who want to understand the issues and perspectives, the whys and wherefores without getting too academic about it. Academics, policy planners and programme designers who are looking for feedback on ways to improve design and delivery efficiencies of programmes would also be interested.

There is no claim or pretence of elaborate statistical proofs, academic rigour and tightness, or conclusions based on rigorous sampling, tabulation and analysis of data gathered by interviewing such samples to arrive at conclusions.

CAVEAT

There is a thick air of despondency for the last 3–4 years about India, its polity, its economy, law and social order, etc. Some of the economic woes can be attributed to external global factors but much of it is also due to the nature of our democracy. The prevailing mood is such that even an honest evaluation of our programmes might sound like a critical assault on the institutions.

If the book appears negative in its earlier sections, it is purely incidental. In the latter part, the attempt is to build effective programmes and growth engines to step up growth rates and achieve better distribution of income in a socially inclusive manner. The air of cynicism would hopefully give way to hope in these parts.

Acknowledgements

No book can be written without the active and passive co-operation of the family. I would wish to thank my wife Sharada and my daughter Akhila for being supportive of this venture.

I owe a lot to my employers, the JK Group, for giving me opportunities to travel and witness several parts of the world during the course of my work. Several observations and case studies quoted in the book would not have been feasible but for these opportunities.

Many thanks to Professor Dr Ahuja for agreeing to write the Foreword inspite of his heavy academic load.

I owe a lot of thanks to Yogendra Khurana, Vallur Sundar Raman, Sharada and Ramesh who have helped me in reading the manuscript and offering suggestions in several places to make the book more readable. Their forthright observations were of immense help and guidance.

Thanks are due to Professor Abraham Koshy, Professor of Marketing Area, IIM Ahmedabad, Chandu Nair and Li'l Ram for their valuable encouragement at crucial times and not allowing me to give up. Thanks are also due to M.K. Subramaniam, Adi Saravanan, Professor S. Manikutty, M.K. Chandrasekar and Dr Saha for their help.

Many ideas explored in this book have been published in some form in economic dailies like *Business Line* and *Business Standard* over the last over a decade and a half. Thanks are due to them in large measure in honing my writing skills and for their necessary permissions. However, it should be mentioned that this book is in no way a reproduction; all ideas explored in the published articles have been re-visited and re-written in the current context.

Evaluating the Current Reform Programmes

PART I

Every public action which is not customary is either wrong or, if it is right, is a dangerous precedent. It follows that nothing should ever be done for the first time.

—F.M. Cornford
in *Microcosmographia Academica* (1908)

India has had some success with reforms. The table on the next page summarises India's progress in select social and economic parameters. Even if in some parameters we could have done better, by and large, the 20 years under reforms have delivered far better results than the 40 years before. Several large states have also shown significant improvement in their growth rates during 20 years reforms as compared to the decade preceding reforms as will be seen later.

However, India's achievements with reforms have not been as consistent or impressive as in many other Asian countries during similar phase of growth. There are several countries which have achieved double-digit growth rates more regularly without much noise while India is yet to clock a single double-digit growth year. This can be partially attributed to Indian lethargy, lack of cohesion, preference for raucous debates, and the peculiarly dysfunctional strain of democracy afflicting India. Any comparative study of India with East Asian countries and China will clearly illustrate that there is plenty of latent scope to increase the yields from reforms.

India Before and After Reforms—Select Indicators							
S. No.	**Indicators**		**Before Reforms**			**After Reforms**	
			1950–51	**1970–71**	**1990–91**	**2000–01**	**2010–11**
1	Size of economy—GNP at factor cost	Current ₹ Cr	9,995	44,098	524,268	1,969,249	7,078,512
2	Per capita income (₹)—NNP	Current	264	763	5,621	17,295	53,331
3	Decadal growth rates	Previous 10 yrs	–	4.0	5.6	5.6	7.4
4	Life expectancy (female)	Yrs	31.7	44.7	59	63.3	64.2
5	Literacy	%	18.3	34.4	52.2	64.8	74
6	Unemploy-ment (regd job seekers)	Million	*0.3*	*5.1*	*36.3*	*41.3*	*$$ 38.9*
7	Road network	000 km	400	915	2,331	3374	$$ 4,110
8	Availability of pulses+ cereals	g/person	*394.9*	468.8	510.1	416.2	438.6
9	Forex reserves	$ billion	1.9	0.6	2.2	39.6	274.6

Source: Economic Surveys. Figures in italics are from Statistical Outline of India, Tata Services Limited.
Note: $$ data is for 2007–08.

Reform supporters are quick to come up with explanations like 'strong consensus for weak reforms' or claim that dosage is inadequate and hence advocate more reforms as the answer. Quite often, our democracy and fractured mandate in legislatures serve as the punch bag for the relative low success of reforms or difficulties in implementation.

However, there are some cracks in the design of several (not all) of our programmes and policies which are not strictly accounted for by defective political system, culture, social order, lax administration or snail-paced justice delivery.

Part I mainly looks at these aspects. If reforms are to succeed and win over more people to its side and deliver better benefits to people, they have to be designed appropriately. The designers have to keep in mind the target population, their needs and aspirations, current consumption pattern, absorption capability (mentally, physically, culturally, socially, besides economically), social conditioning, education levels, immediate priorities and motivations, practices prevailing, family values and sensitivities, etc. Not all factors may be relevant in all cases, but it is essential to know the crucial and relevant ones in a given case. There are reasons to doubt whether our policies, plans and programmes reflect such understanding. Even in macro policies, one has to think through the chain of causation and the impediments it is likely to face in percolating to field level and the effects on people.

Chapter 1

ECONOMIC REFORMS, SOCIAL FISSURES

Democracy means government by discussions but it is only effective if you can stop people talking.

—Clement Attlee (1957)

The pursuit of reforms seems to have led to some social problems. Firstly, there are now various forms and degrees of *disaffection* with the state and some of its policies. The disaffection ranges from naxalism at one extreme end to voting out governments which are considered reform oriented but have not delivered on creating employment. The country is witnessing increasing aggression against land acquisition for industrial development, violent demonstrations against petrol price revisions or foreign direct investment in retail, etc. Industrial strikes that were dormant for a couple of decades are rearing their head once again. Secondly, there is a *mutual and reflexive slavishness* between the voters and the voted at the political level. Thirdly, *corruption* levels are high which are accompanied by extreme political apathy. Fourthly, there is a refusal to analyse and address (and/or take advantage of) the potential problems from increasing *migration* from rural to urban areas. There are also some other social problems like the failure of justice systems, breakdown of many institutions and lack of independent institutions of integrity. But these are not the focus of this book.

Reforms seem to have contributed to some of these in varying degrees. Economic policies are not made in a vacuum and have to be developed within the social context and have to serve citizens in the way they want; perception gaps if any have to be plugged by including the disgruntled in the reform process, by creating stakes in its success and by designing convincing action programmes.

1.1 Reforms as a Source of Disaffection

EXPECTATIONS

The efficiency of our administration in compensating the victims or refugees of development is dismal and credibility is near nil, from Bhagra Nangal to Bhopal. Even today the design of compensation structure to people who are asked to give up resources for general benefit lacks understanding of their anxieties and fears. Continuing fears are sought to be compensated with one-time pay-offs. Loss of livelihood and sense of loss on how to survive (since they have no skills other than their traditional ones) are sought to be compensated monetarily for people who do not know how to manage money.

When reforms were initiated, there were high hopes of employment generation which would have solved problems at the micro level—family and individual. Instead of utilising labour (a surplus resource in India), the government has been cutting down its own staff strength. As will be seen in Chapter 5, between 1990 and 2010, public sector employment as a percentage of population fell from 2.15 per cent to 1.46 per cent. By not creating employment, the government is both promoting discord and reducing potential demand in the economy.

Two fundamental failures (compensation related and employment related) have led certain sections to growing disaffection of various kinds, including rising naxalism (which looks like more an economic problem than of law and order). Singur and Nandigram, reactions to several mines in

Odisha (such as Vedanta and Posco) and Koodankulam serve as examples. Through the ballot box itself, most of the governments which came to symbolise reforms between 1991 and 2004 (for example, Telugu Desam Party in Andhra Pradesh and the Congress [1996] and NDA in 2004) were thrown out quite unexpectedly signifying, besides other things, the reception to the reforms they pursued.

SACRIFICE WITHOUT COMMENSURATE COMPENSATION

Given our dismal track record, any fresh attempt to conscript resources from one section to benefit another or the nation in general was bound to be met with scepticism and resistance. Government would have done well to set its record straight and thus created confidence before further such initiatives.

The social agenda that India pursued for 40 years before reforms was more potent in stifling entrepreneurship and less successful in creating opportunities and redistributing income and wealth more equitably. Naturally, those people who were expecting 'independence dividend' but did not get to participate in it would have felt most hopeful for being the first beneficiaries of reforms. It is questionable if these were the first target beneficiaries of reforms, although of late through several social intervention programmes, the government seems keen on making up.

Let us take the example of Koodankulam where the state came up with the country's twenty-first nuclear power plant. It calls for the nearby residents to sacrifice for the greater good of the state's residents. The land required for the plant itself was not much, but for the people in the nearby areas, constant fear of living in danger—fatal or otherwise—is real.

These fears need to be overcome through (i) education of facts, safeguards, first aids and procedures to be adopted during emergencies; (ii) creation of confidence that the state would adequately deal with future contingencies (unlike Bhopal); and (iii) financial compensation—one time and continuing. If the fear and risk are continual and persistent, the residents should ideally be compensated on a continuing basis. The amount of compensation payable should be recovered from user-beneficiaries through user charges. One-time compensation for a continuing risk is poor psychology/economics. Patriotism (the satisfaction that one derives by giving up something for a larger group and nation) is not an adequate compensation anymore. Given the corruption levels, the state's failure in many respects in meeting citizen's expectation, the failure of justice systems, un-helpful behaviour of most officials towards citizens and the dilution in political standards, it would be foolish to even expect people to be patriotic.

Most of the cases calling for selective sacrifice for larger good have led to protests, litigation, and in some cases outright violence and strong official counter measures have served as poor advertisements for reforms. In select areas, people, who have not gained anything in the past and whose interests have generally been neglected, are asked to sacrifice now without 'adequate compensation' and/or training for alternative survival skills. For them, the offering of naxalist leaders seems far more appealing than the official alternative. The more our reforms encroach on such geographical areas, the more militant the reactions could be, given our current approach.

EMPLOYMENT

The government by creating 2 crore primary jobs at lower skill/salary levels which would have led to secondary employment of 5–6 crore could have won far more votes than achieving 7–9 per cent growth rates. Probably, if we had kept the employment intensity the same as before reforms, by now India could have solved its unemployment problems. We would not have needed debatable programmes like National Rural Employment Guarantee Act (NREGA) or Food Bill.

Reforms, as is examined elsewhere, have generally been facilitative of a capital-oriented growth in preference to employment creation. The introduction or facilitation of contemporary technology in commercial banking, for example, may have delivered visible benefits to its customers, improved service levels, cut down on time delays, facilitated 24-hour connection to their account through the internet. However, if the news reports of the time were to be believed, it had also thrown 400,000 people out of jobs even if by voluntary separation accompanied by compensation. People in other sectors may not have been as lucky with the quantum of compensation for their separation. In any case those aspiring for a job in these sectors would have faced disappointment.

The net effect has been that the fruits of reforms seem to have been delivered to a select few (in percentage terms)—a sad state in which although the gainers' gains have far exceeded the losers' losses, the gainers seem far fewer in number than the relative losers. Free electricity, cycles and promise of reservations, NREGA and subsidies get more votes than promise of reforms. This is discernible from the voting patterns.

1.2 Mutual Servitude or Reflexive Slavery

This is perhaps a case where social fissures and political milieu have an effect on economic policies rather than the other way around.

A peculiar situation seems to have emerged of late where both the elected and the electors seem helpless against each other. Once elected, the combined might of people, the opposition, moral values, constitutional niceties, and the justice and audit systems are not enough to rein in those elected. Even the parties themselves look powerless vis-à-vis their own legislators. A serious course correction seems vital for curing this.

With a political system and government which has delivered less and less, where both performance and approach look lackadaisical and insensitive, the voters have come to expect less and less. Short-term sacrifices for long-term benefits do not seem to hold any promise anymore even if the people sacrificing and the intended beneficiaries are the same (e.g. stalled slum re-development efforts in Mumbai). Where the sacrificers and beneficiaries are different, matters can be far worse. Short-term gain is the only thing that they have come to expect (or have been forced by experience to expect).

Since the political class has learnt this, they have also learnt to feed the citizens with short-term measures. Unless they continue to do this, their political continuance is in jeopardy. Short-term measures differ from place to place, people to people, region to region, class to class, religion to religion, caste to caste, etc. in a diverse society and the political legislatures capture this reality and we end up with an indecisive system. Thus, we have a political system which has power only to concoct measures that deliver more and more entitlements, subsidies and largesse. The majority party within ruling coalition is subordinate (or even helpless) to other smaller parties and collectively all of them to the people in general.

1.3 Corruption

IMPROPER PRICING—A MAJOR CONTRIBUTORY

In the last 2–3 years, there have been several cases of alleged corruption surfacing such as CWG, 2G and coalgate. Like in all economic transactions, corruption also has both demand and supply sides—the giver and the taker—both of whom are guilty to an extent even if due to differing compulsions. Poor institutional mechanisms to identify the corrupt and punish them within definitive effective time frames help spread of corruption. But it is only a facilitating factor; the main causes seem to be economic. Improper price discovery process has been responsible for the spread of corruption at the wholesale level (in transactions of political decision involving the government, political parties and businesses). Reform-induced income inequality has caused the corruption levels to spread rapidly at the retail level (in regular day-to-day transactions between the citizens and the various government departments or agencies).

Corruption is an agency problem that exists because the value at which government sells/allocates its services/resources is much less than its monetary value to the user/purchaser. Or where the government is the buyer, the price it pays is more than the cost to the supplier or its usual market price. The difference is the kitty available for sharing between the agent and the purchaser or seller and bribe (the price of corruption) settles somewhere in between. Corruption can exist in private sector too (such as out of turn allotments in cars and educational seats), but is normally corrected quickly by price revisions by alert entrepreneurs.

At the wholesale level, resources (spectrum, air–space, natural resources such as coal, minerals, etc.) that were previously being exclusively developed by the government or its agencies were freed up for use/development by private sector. There was no issue of pricing these resources so long as the state was the sole dispenser of services based on these. Before reforms, where private enterprise was allowed it was largely based on licensing but government did not bother with recovering proper economic values in return; nevertheless, it provided a system of rules, however badly designed.

PRICE DISCOVERY MECHANISM NOT PUT IN PLACE

The existing order was changed, licensing dispensed with and natural (tangible and intangible) resources were freed up for development by private sector under reforms. This required institution of a proper price discovery mechanism to ensure that the government got its due value in return. The private sector has generally moved faster and proved smarter in discovering the true values of such opportunities; the government and the regulators have been found grossly inadequate in assessing the values or evolving systems. People who discovered the true values faster and had the right connections shared a portion with those vested with the authority and made away with the rest. Some set up the down-stream enterprises and for others (many with political connections) acquisition at a cheaper price and downloading the same at proper market price by itself became the main enterprise.

Unsettling the existing order of things without putting in place, robust price discovery process is the main villain (besides lax vigilance and diluted moral standards) for several giant-sized corruptions erupting in rapid succession in the last few years.

But corruption at wholesale level may not be as debilitating to the common man as corruption at day-to-day level at each touch-point between the citizens and the state. With the former, there are fewer parties involved as either giver or receiver and it pinches neither at a personal level. Such corruption is more fodder for the media, source of satisfying work for Comptroller and Auditor General (CAG), grist for scoring political points and a missed opportunity for plugging fiscal deficits. It does not compromise the general moral standards of the vast majority like retail corruption does.

If we look carefully, there is a high degree of inappropriateness in pricing of most government services which are a major source of corruption. If a service is heavily underpriced, it results in corruption and bribery: the official dispensing it will take part of the difference, particularly if the vigilance is lax. If it is overpriced (like stamp duty in real estate), it results in tax evasion and black money or corruption to induce the law enforcer to turn a blind eye.

The price that a retail consumer wants to pay depends on the perceived value to him. This will depend upon his income level, personal urgency, time and demand–supply balance which may alter from time to time, lot size, place, quality and consistency of product or service.

An illustration: The monetary value of a Shatabdi ticket for a last-minute traveller will vary from person to person: some are more moneyed and some are likely to be more desperate. No matter what the price of 'tatkal' tickets there will be someone willing to pay more, which a smart ticket examiner can 'extract' as bribe. This factor has been very well exploited by the low-cost airlines (at least those operating in the Western world) who have fine-tuned programmes of harvesting the entire value so much so that they are the only ones in airline industry making money consistently.

Cost of production is just one criterion and in many cases a weak consideration from the buyer's side for determining price to pay. The government has priced its services (or goods) mainly based on 'costs to serve' or 'cost of production'. This is true even where the target users are likely to be rich, like 1stAC passengers in Rajdhani trains or airlines. The government has followed this pricing (in fact much less than cost) in higher education such as IITs, IIMs, AIIMS where the recipient is bound to enter the rich- or middle-income class on completion irrespective of whether he starts poor or rich. There is a near total disregard for the other factors on which the recipient values them.

Inevitably there are gaps between the government's pricing and the value to its recipients. *In general, it is highly unlikely that anyone will pay a bribe when there is no gap between the value to him and the price being charged.* If corruption has to disappear, it is essential for the government to adopt a pricing based on the value created for the consumers and close these gaps. If such gaps are greatly reduced, vigilance has a far better chance to succeed and with lesser work load as will be seen in Chapter 3.

UNEQUAL GAINS AND MORAL DEGRADATION

Pricing gaps (they have existed even before reforms) and lax vigilance alone do not sufficiently explain the sudden spurt in corruption levels during the last few years. This can be explained only by the increased moral degradation (as much of the giver as of the taker). The increase in disparity of incomes and inequality and liberalisation of salaries which facilitated these have had unintended adverse consequences.

Studies by psychologists and behavioural economists have concluded that an average person would prefer earning $60,000 amongst peers who earn $50,000 to earning $90,000 in a neighbourhood where others earn $100,000.[1] It is the relative (to others) income that counts more than the absolute levels.

While reforms may have benefitted most people, it benefitted some people much more than others. Emerging opportunities aided in some people gaining more and faster than others. Rapid liberalisation of salaries and steep cuts in income tax rates aided this. These led to several people improving their income levels and life styles way faster relative to those with fixed incomes or government employees and those working in mature industries which could not keep pace. This left the slow gainers and non-gainers with heart burns, grudges or possibly a feeling of personal inadequacy—a salubrious condition for re-examining one's own moral standards and values and gradual onset of dilution in the same. Once the baby steps of corruption are taken, there may be no going back and each act is the justification for the next one which only gets bigger in size. With a lax enforcement system, corruption thrives and spreads.

But what can explain the higher (hopefully perceived not actual) level of corruption in the various arms of administration and government. The emoluments of public sector undertaking (PSU) employees (using it as a surrogate for all government employees) have gone up much more than the national average since independence. It has risen more rapidly

[1] J.S. Duesenberry. 1949. *Income, Saving and the Theory of Consumer Behaviour.* Cambridge: Harvard University Press. Also see Alan Greenspan. 2013. *The Map and the Territory*, pp. 24–25.

during reforms. Average PSU salaries from being 8.7 times per capita income when reforms began are 12.5 times by 2012.[2] (In comparison, the average income of a government employee in the US is about 2.8 times the national per capita income.) It appears that the reference point for comparison to feel good or inadequate is not the national average but the immediate neighbourhood of other family members, colleagues, relatives, fellow professionals, neighbours, etc.

Reforms have thrown up just enough examples of people who have made rapid progress and serve as reference points for many of their neighbours to feel jealous. While it is foolish to argue that reforms should stifle individual initiative by regulating salaries, it could have graduated the process by liberalising it far more slowly and moderating tax cuts over a longer period of time.

WILL STATE FUNDING HELP?

It is often argued that state funding of elections would be an effective antidote to corruption. Given the causality of corruption, without closing pricing gaps, tightening vigilance, addressing income inequalities and putting in place a robust price discovery mechanism, state funding will be a limp, ineffectual, wasted effort. It might become one more way of lining the politicians' pockets.

In mid-2011, the chief of Thailand's Securities Commission had to resign for facilitating a meeting between two groups of shareholders in a listed shipping company where he owned 100 shares. The staff cried conflict of interest capable of tarnishing the image of the regulator and refused to work till he actually resigned. This is feasible only because people are not numb to corruption, societal values bring about a sense of

[2] *Source:* Appendix Tables 1.1 and 3.2 of Economic Survey, 2012–13 which give per capita income of India and PSU employees, respectively.

shame and exerts a moral pressure, laws are strict and enforcement is swift, certain and without fear or favour and influence peddling is impossible.

1.4 Migration Issues

India is largely an agrarian society where bulk of the population lives in rural areas. But as the country grows, it is inevitable that India will face two kinds of migration—activity migration and geographical migration. The first refers to shifting from existing activity to another vocation, profession or source of income. This may or may not be accompanied by the second kind of migration.

Agricultural production cannot grow beyond a point since the land that can be brought under cultivation is limited. Some kinds of productivity improvement by improved seeds, irrigation, better farming practices may be feasible. But from the consumption side, India, despite its poverty and hunger, is not exactly food deficient in terms of availability of cereals and grains and calories required as will be seen in Chapter 2. Increasing agricultural productivity has its own risks and can easily induce what can be termed *immiseration*.[3] As we grow, agriculture will have to release a huge number of people into the other sectors—service or industry. There is no way agriculture can absorb them. Is the rest of economy prepared or being readied to make this possible? This relates to activity migration.

Geographically, our rural areas which support 60 per cent or more of the population will not be able to support the growth aspirations either. For inclusive growth and more equitable distribution of income, either the economic activities in rural areas have to increase commensurately or the

[3] After a similar phenomenon suggested by the well-known economist and trade theorist Jagdish Bhagwati in the context of foreign trade.

rural population have to move into urban areas. Are our policies creating enough opportunities for jobs or demand in rural areas so that they find local employment and continue to prosper where they are. There is hardly any evidence that this is happening. On the contrary, mere mention of any economic activity being moved to tribal land or acquisition of rural land for economic activity has become contentious and through overzealous protective policies almost become economically unviable.

Our continued growth aspirations would require large-scale migration into urban areas and migration to non-traditional jobs and vocations—occupations which are non-traditional to the individuals or even to the society. Agriculture and rural areas have an income of 15–20 per cent but are supporting 55–60 per cent of population. Even if they release one-fourth of 'excess', it is 10 per cent or 12 crore people—a huge number who have to be retrained and re-housed in cities.

This is an area which is either forgotten or not addressed adequately. We have only seen the first crop of migrants of land sellers—people who have sold their land at unexpectedly high prices—irrespective of whether they are rich or poor. Their (especially those who have no personal perspective plan) migration into cities is creating major problems in our cities. This may have also added to the crime rates which have increased significantly. Our cities' policing and administration have no action plan on coping with this emerging crisis due to budget constraints and the pressure to reduce manpower. The administration does not have enough budget allocation—government seems too busy fighting budget deficits and keen on fighting its electoral battles with king-sized subsidies.

Countering these problems requires growth and development of cities, re-orienting migrating people and a plan for absorbing them, re-orienting their skill sets, expansion of government services and staff in line with growth, and moderating the migration of economic activity to rural areas. Without these, our strength in numbers which should give us demographic dividends and be the chief source of competitive advantage could become a major source of worry.

* * *

The net result is a grossly under-performing system which has to be improved by better design of programmes that communicate, demonstrate and actually deliver benefits. We also need some actions to induce greater accountability from the ruling and the elected.

Chapter 2

LAUDABLE GOALS YET DEFECTIVE PROGRAMMES

Amateurs think of tactics; Professionals talk of logistics.
—A saying within the American army

POSITIVE THINGS ABOUT INDIA

India is a complex and diverse country with multiplicity of languages, religions and differences in climatic conditions and history of various regions. Despite such administrative difficulties, we have managed to coexist and develop peacefully unlike many other countries with such diversity.

Our election systems, the way Mumbai sub-urban rail system works daily, the way we respond to crises such as tsunami and earthquakes certainly make us stand out in the comity of nations. Our Green Revolution, the way Reserve Bank of India (RBI) has generally managed the monetary systems, our army's track record in ensuring peace without getting over ambitious are all worthy of celebration.

Our stock market systems and the way it is administered by SEBI is perhaps the best in the world today. The immigration systems at IGI Airport in Delhi, particularly contrasted with what was before, appear comparable to any other modern airport in the world.

Despite all the negative publicity that preceded it, the Common Wealth Games were well organised. The largest congregation on earth—*Kumbh Mela*—gets organised flawlessly by the political system.

Golden Quadrilateral[1] has improved the road networks considerably. Sikkim has become the first state to achieve toilets in all houses. The way our Mumbai Airport handles its traffic volumes in such a narrow patch is amazing.

Thus, there are many things that go right which are worthy of celebration. However, it is only when we dare to be self-critical that we can put in place corrective actions to make things better. As mentioned in the Preface, this book is about the few flagship programmes on which a lot depend but are not working well on the ground and not delivering results that they should.

CRACKS IN PROGRAMMES

There are some cracks in the design of several (not all) of our programmes and policies which are not strictly accounted for by our political system, culture, social order, lax administration or snail-paced justice delivery.

The designers have to keep in mind the target population, their needs and aspirations, current consumption pattern, absorption capability (mentally, physically, culturally, socially, besides economically), social conditioning, education levels, immediate priorities and motivations, practices prevailing, family values and sensitivities, etc. Not all factors may be relevant in all cases; but it is essential to know the crucial and relevant ones in a given case. There are reasons to doubt whether our policies, plans and programmes reflect such understanding. Even in macro policies, one has to think through the chain of causation and the impediments it is likely to face in percolating to field level and its effect on people.

[1] Golden Quadrilateral is a highway network in the shape of irregular quadrilateral formed by connecting Delhi, Kolkata, Chennai and Mumbai and connecting several major cities, towns and centres of industrial, cultural and agricultural importance.

2.1 National Rural Employment Guarantee Act (NREGA) and Food Bill: Can Derail Long-term Growth in Rural Areas

Through Green Revolution, we managed to reach production levels capable of satisfying the total demand almost four decades ago. India is a unique case where there is excess demand (unsatisfied hunger where one-third is below poverty line [BPL]) for food. There is also excess supply of food—the buffer stock the government holds is two and half times the norms. These are ideal conditions where market mechanisms should have worked. Yet we are struggling to find a market mechanism to put the excess demand and excess supply together. NREGA and Food Bill seem an apologetic overture to hide this failure. The Food Bill repeats the failures of the past and does not create a sustainable model.

EFFECT ON THE INDIVIDUAL MOTIVATIONS

The design of both NREGA and Food Bill reflects the government's failure to understand the individual motivations, responses and social conditioning that affects the beneficiaries and the basic lessons in consumer behaviour at the micro level. Collectively, we may not have learnt appropriate social or economic lessons from NREGA operations.

One would have assumed that the NREGA recipients would adopt it as supplementary employment opportunity besides their usual employment, instead of giving up their regular occupation, especially given the widespread under-employment in rural areas.

A government's actual infusion of ₹35,000–40,000 crore per annum through NREGA should have created an additional primary employment for about 1 crore people assuming ₹35,000 (including wages, leakage and material) per person. Given the low savings level in the rural areas—our national average household savings is 18–19 per cent and in rural areas much less—and hence a very high level of consumption, the income multiplier should be very high. Even if one assumes a much more sober employment multiplier of 3, it should have created 3 crore jobs in the rural areas—capable of substantially impacting unemployment and the associated problems such as hunger and malnutrition. But there is hardly any evidence of such big-bang impact in the rural areas.

Instead, there is greater than expected increase in absenteeism from regular employment—organised and unorganised—and consequent increase in wage levels in traditional vocations. Instead of working additional hours and enhancing incomes and climbing aspirational ladders, the rural recipients seem to have given up (in various degrees) their regular occupation and chosen to be satisfied with their current levels of income and consumption. Observations and experience at field level seem to strongly indicate that such people are either in majority or a substantial (not ignorable) minority. Sure, there will be exceptions. And when one is talking of a population of 120 crore, even the exceptions can be in multiples of crore.

INCOME–LEISURE TRADE-OFF: THE INDIAN PARADOX

This highly unanticipated and counter-intuitive outcome of NREGA needs to be understood at least in retrospect and lessons built into such interventions in the future. If Keynes theorised that wages are sticky downwards, it appears that consumption habits are also sticky upwards to a great degree.[2] It is an uphill task to change social behaviour and personal habits of people beyond a certain age and even aspirations and desires seem to solidify with advancing age.

[2] And any large-scale unexpected receipt of incomes which the recipient has not planned or anticipated seems to induce wasteful expenditure compared to incomes which are regular in nature.

Demand for products depends on aspirations and desires, availability and exposure to temptations (products and services), and peer pressure. Clearly, peer pressure amongst the rural poor is feeble to begin with, and the penetration level of many products in our rural areas except for shampoos, soaps, toothpastes, mobile phones and sweetmeats, is very low. Desires have been marinated at very low levels for ages of poverty and under-nourishment. Given this social conditioning, rural people seem to have preferred greater leisure (than what policy planners or any other economist would have expected) than work for additional incomes to finance their aspirational spending. Leisure is not a privilege of the rich alone; even the poor fancy such pursuits especially since the benefits of giving up their leisure for work is so insignificant, given the low wage levels. Most of the NREGA wages have hence invaded just food, causing high food inflation.

The Food Bill does not seem to incorporate the lessons from this social dynamics—low aspirations resulting in substitution of employment instead of supplementing it, leading to rising wage levels in traditional occupations and food inflation.

POSSIBLE NEGATIVE SIDE EFFECTS

NREGA is like giving excessive grace marks to a student who keeps failing his exams repeatedly. It might provide short-term succour; but in the long term, they tend to damage the system as well as stymie individual growth and eagerness to work. There are other possible side effects.

Firstly, if the farm labour take the benefits of food security and 'shrink' their work to a corresponding extent, we could have a steep increase in agrarian labour costs. Our agriculture which is already ailing for want of public or private investments or research (the last significant breakthrough came about four decades ago) could hardly cope with a crisis on the key input—labour costs or availability.

Secondly, when a large 'employer' like NREGA enters the rural market with such high 'effective' wages, the wage level is bound to increase. Rural industrialisation may suffer a setback.

Thirdly, and perhaps the most dreadful is the long-term consequence. Like aspirations, desires and lifestyle even lethargy and leisure can be hard-coded into personal DNA. Easy money from NREGA and Food Bill could easily lead to long-term lethargy in people who are already used to un/under employment induced work inertia. This is perhaps the biggest drawback in the NREGA design.

Any development or poverty reduction depends as much on individual desire and initiative as on external help and intervention. Such a development of lethargy (even if it afflicts a section of the people) will blunt the effectiveness of future developmental initiatives.

There is a need to understand the individual responses, consumer behaviour and motivations at micro level to programmes like NREGA instead of the macroeconomic cause–effect studies that are normally done. Without designs which properly incorporate lessons therefrom, we may end up with a serious social and economic monster which is not retractable resulting in a huge dent on government finances, lethargic attitudes and a costly labour resulting in poor comparative advantage.

FOR A MORE MEANINGFUL INTERVENTION

The government may not be able to recover commensurate value in return for NREGA wages from the target beneficiaries but can always use it for achieving its other social objectives. Government has social intervention schemes such as family planning, spread of literacy and health care at the personal level and road construction, water harvesting and micro irrigation, etc. at the village or regional level. By making NREGA a *quid pro quo* for specific targets in its social interventions at individual levels, the government can reach better implementation efficiencies. Some examples are as follows:

Effect of Net Effective Wages of NREGA—Not Adequately Researched or Understood

Most of the targeted beneficiaries of NREGA are at and below poverty level and when they find work in nearby rural industries, it is at prescribed 'minimum wages' or often lower. But they may have to put in full 8 hours of work or more to earn their 'minimum wages'. With the lack of accountability in NREGA work, the actual work component is much less. In some places, work may only be on paper and wages may be more for signing registers and marking token presence. The effective work put in may not be more than 1–2 hours. For this, the target beneficiaries get paid minimum wages.

The effective per hourly wages in non-NREGA jobs are about ₹20 per hour assuming ₹150 per day of 8 hours. In NREGA, it is ₹50–60 per hour (say ₹150 per day of 2–3 hours working). Thus, in effective terms, NREGA pays 3–4 times wages compared to other rural jobs.

How can an individual, who is facing this situation, sustain his motivation where 1 day he has work (NREGA) which effectively pays ₹50 per hour but on other than NREGA days he has to work for ₹20 per hour. If the higher 'net effective wages' alternative (NREGA) is not capable of completely absorbing his time, would he be able to sustain motivations towards the lesser 'paying' job for the balance of time? It only stands to reason that he will slowly dilute his motivation, presence, etc. to existing non-NREGA jobs and try to equalise his 'effective per hourly wages'.

This will start with higher absenteeism, refusal to take up work or higher collective bargaining if not militant ways. If a person refuses normal work due to diluted motivations and goes for only NREGA, his total individual income may also go down, since NREGA does not provide full-time employment.

1. The schemes can be restricted to women only. Women are more likely to spend it on the family needs rather than spend it in wasteful ways than men. With NREGA income, mothers may depend less on children to generate family income and hence more likely to make their children study up to higher classes. This will help in achieving better enrolment at primary and maybe even secondary school levels. It will contain undue wage inflation in rural industries if men are excluded from NREGA.
2. For males, time spent in skill development programmes (by any of the recognised vocational training providers whether by private or public agencies) can be made eligible for NREGA reimbursement. This will build skills and reduce the effective cost (adjusted for enhanced

productivity) of labour and the rural area's share in production. If it does happen, it would wean away people from NREGA to other gainful employment and reduce NREGA outlay over a period of time.

3. For families with two or more children at a certain cut-off date, it can be made contingent on adoption of family planning and liable to be stopped if they contravene the conditions. For others when they reach the desired family size of two, continuation can be conditional on family planning. This will help achieve better results in our family planning initiatives.

Social security to cover cyclical unemployment or temporary unemployment between jobs, like in the West, may be alright. But it may be an inappropriate medicine for solving chronic unemployment, which can be solved only with expansion of rural manufacturing/industrial employment opportunities.

2.2 The Politics of Minimum Support Prices (MSPs)

WHY MSPs AT ALL

The objectives of MSPs may be either to increase in production or to boost farmers' income. In the developed world, most subsidies are for boosting farm incomes. India does not have a trade surplus and hence will not be able to finance huge food imports. Hence sustaining production is the prime interest, although of late boosting incomes have started assuming greater importance. Production, amongst various things, depends on the prices the farmers get at their farm gate. In recent years, agricultural prices have generally been buoyant. If these had reached the farmers, then it would have ensured greater and increasing farm production. However, most of distribution in India is in the hands of middlemen who corner a far greater share of the end consumer price inflation. This distorted structure does not allow the increase in end consumer prices to reach the farm gates.

It becomes necessary therefore to design alternatives including direct method of incentivising the farmers like MSPs. With better farm gate prices, hopefully we should sustain production and productivity so that we are self-sufficient on the food front.

THE POLITICS OF INDIA'S MSPs

The Cabinet Committee on Economic Affairs, Government of India, determines the MSPs of various agricultural commodities in India based on the recommendations of the Commission for Agricultural Cost and Prices keeping in view factors such as increase in cost of production, demand and supply situation, inter-crop parity, and trend of domestic and international market prices.

Lessons from Thailand: Rice Pledge Programme

The rice pledge scheme of Thailand has been under operation since the latter half of 2011. It provides all the lessons to anyone looking for evidence of the kind of all-round mess that a politically motivated and badly designed farm produce price support scheme can create.

Thailand was the largest exporter of rice for over 30 years before the scheme started. Ostensibly to support its rural vote bank, the scheme was started by their ruling party whereby farmers could deposit their rice harvest with the government agencies at a fixed price of about $450 a tonne when the ruling world price was around $430 per tonne and was way over the domestic ruling price. The authorities perhaps thought that if Thailand controlled supplies to the world market, prices would rise steeply (like in Oil) benefitting the local farmers.

But market forces took a different turn. India and Vietnam quickly filled the gap and steeply increased their share and in India's case it was accompanied by a quick upgradation of production facilities to get better quality as well. A year or so after the programme started, Thailand Government was sitting on nearly 17 million tonnes of stock nearly two-thirds its annual production. Given the international prices, it was impossible to get rid of the stocks without a huge loss since the minimum costs for preparing and shipping are in the range of $125–150 per tonne.

(Box Continued)

(Box Continued)

Holding stocks would entail gradual rotting involving a possible write off of more than $4 billion. It is almost impossible to withdraw such populist programmes without incurring the wrath of the people and risk losing their votes.

Given that only about 1.1 million families are involved in rice production in Thailand compared to 3.7 million households engaged in farming sector, the scheme has raised the prices of rice, their staple food, to unsustainable levels for the balance families as well as those who are not in agri-sector.

The Thai Rice pledge programme has played out the effect of ill-conceived market interventions in a compressed period and illustrates the possible long-term risks from some of the recent moves in India's programmes.

Note: Readers are referred to (1) 'Rice pledging poses long-term risks' by Sutapa Amornvivat in *Bangkok Post* (19 September 2012) and (2) 'The price of populism and hoarding grain' by Tejinder Narang in *Businessline* (5 September 2012).

Political compulsions in 2009 and 2013 seem the more dominant logic for announcing erratic price increases than costs or the need to ensure sustained supplies, or developing and sustaining an efficient market structure. As a direct consequence, the objective has of late been changed to 'fair and remunerative price' from 'MSP'. Let us see how the price announcements—the quantum, manner and periodicity—can cause us harm in the long run.

CONSEQUENCES

Firstly, Table 2.1 (which traces the history of MSPs since reforms) reveals forcefully the dominant cause of the current (2010–12) rate in agricultural produce prices and hence the general inflation and the cause of the farmer suicides earlier. In just 1 year (2008–09), MSPs of most food grains were increased by 30–75 per cent. Prior to that, MSPs stayed stuck for nearly 5 years. Why it was kept at nearly the same level is a mystery. Surely, costs of living in rural areas would have gone up between 2002–03 and 2007–08. Even the costs of farm inputs, transport costs of marketable surplus would have gone up. This inaction of

Table 2.1 Minimum Support Prices of Key Crops (₹/Quintal)

	Paddy	Cotton (f414)	Jowar	Moong Dal	Ground-nut	Soyabean	Sesamum (from 1995–96)
1990–91	205	620	180	480	580	350	850
2007–08	645	1,800	600	1,700	1,550	910	1,580
2008–09	850	2,500	840	2,520	2,100	1,350	2,750
2010–11	1,000	2,500	880	3,170	2,300	1,400	2,900
2011–12	1,080	2,800	980	3,500	2,700	1,650	3,400
2012–13 (announced)	1,250	3,600	1,500	4,400	3,700	2,250	4,200
CAGR Incr (%) (annualised)							
Between 1990–91 and 2007–08 (annualised)	7%	6%	7%	8%	6%	6%	5%
2008–09 alone	32%	39%	40%	48%	35%	48%	74%
Between 2008–09 and 2010–11 (annualised)	9%	0%	2%	13%	5%	2%	3%
2011–12 alone	8%	12%	11%	10%	17%	18%	17%
2012–13 alone	16%	29%	53%	26%	37%	36%	24%

Sources: 1. Economic Survey 2011/12 Appendix Table 5.5 (page A67) for all years except 2012–13. 2. 2012–13 prices have been taken from GOI notifications.

not adjusting the MSP is condemnable especially since the officialdom has not allowed independent markets to develop in the rural areas and the farmers have come to heavily rely on subsidies, MSPs and public distribution systems (PDS) for their sustenance. The fall in real incomes year on year for nearly half a decade should be the chief suspect for rural suicides.

Secondly, the Buffer Stocks with the government have been steadily increasing over the years and have reached nearly 220 per cent by January 2012. The pace of build up while nowhere near Thailand's is still alarming and this 'cornering' may itself be a dominant reason for the high food inflation especially harsh on those who are not beneficiaries of MSPs.

The pace of net addition to stocks is far ahead of current release, implying that procured stocks spend an ever increasing time in the godowns—an ideal condition for rotting stocks. If an impartial and apolitical physical audit of stocks is conducted, then it might reveal the true extent of physical damage.

Thirdly, surely there are other more productive investment avenues available with the government for investing its scarce monies than in 'sure to rot' PDS stocks implying capital wastes and failure to earn minimum return on investments. The investment in excess stock of rice and wheat alone as on January 2012 is about ₹36,000 crore, the interest on which at the government's borrowing rate of 8 per cent itself is about ₹3,200 crore—enough to feed about 12 lakh people permanently right through the year, assuming ₹75 per day is sufficient per person for meeting food needs. This is for people with zero income; if the top-up requirement alone is taken into account, the potential may be more.

Fourthly, not all crops are covered under MSPs. Nor are the increases equal and proportionate. It does not seem to be benchmarked to cost increases either. Such arbitrariness will definitely make some feel cheated and make way for political patronage and over a period of time lead to needless polarisation.

Fifthly, the decisions of farmers while rustic are based on native intelligence and perhaps most often logical to take care of the weather, monsoon, inter-cropping and crop rotation needs. All these creative instincts might make way to political lobbying and unproductive mind reading games. Given the farmers' level of desperation, they have been observed to cut crops mid-way through their cycle to replace them with crops that seem most attractive on the newly announced prices.

This has been seen recently in cotton and wood plantation. Their desperate decision may prove false if the prices announced in the ensuing season are not according to their expectations leading to a sense of needless deceit.

IS MSP A MISPLACED SOLUTION

Is India really short of production or is the problem of poverty and hunger due to distribution failures and wastes? If it is due to production shortfalls, increasing MSPs to induce more production may be justifiable. Shortfall and surplus will have to be decided based on the total requirement based on the calorific value of production and the aggregated calorific energy requirements of the population. Table 2.2 shows the per capita calorific value available from select items of consumption.

The calorie requirement varies based on so many factors with an average of about 2250 calories per person. As per the Economic survey, the per capita availability of just the eight items listed in Table 2.2 itself is about 2150 calories per day,

Table 2.2 India: Per Capita Availability Per Day 2010–11

S. No.	Item	Net Per Capita Availability g/No. (eggs)	Cal/100 g or No.	Total Calories
1	Cereals	407.0	345	1,404.15
2	Pulses	31.6	340	107.44
3	Sugar	46.6	400	186.30
4	Vanaspati	2.7	650	17.81
5	Edible oil	37.3	550	204.93
6	Eggs (No.)	0.15	173	25.12
7	Fish	19.2	91	17.45
8	Milk	281.0	65	182.65
	Total			2,145.85

Source: Appendix Tables 1.17 and 1.19 and pages 192–194 of Economic Survey, 2011–12 for per capita availability. Calorific values are from the Internet.

which meets 96 per cent of the average requirement. If other primary items such as meat, poultry, palm oil (even if imported), fruits and vegetables are included, India should be largely deemed self-sufficient on the production side. Sure, there are other claimants for the available calorie, but buffer stocks would not be piling up if these were indeed in net deficit situation.

The Food and Agricultural Organisation's recommended availability per capita per day is about 440 g of cereals and pulses. India has been maintaining this level for most of the last 50 years. The production has fallen short in just 12 out of the last 50 years[3] that too by very marginal amounts in the years of shortfall. Due to increasing diversification in consumption seen of late, even 440 g seems superfluous.

India's poverty and hunger seem more the result of failure of systems at the distribution end and of market mechanism and high proportion of wastes; production shortfalls seem the least of the issues. The steep hikes in MSPs (not benchmarked to costs) seem clearly irrational.

MANUFACTURING HIT BY RELATIVE PRICE MOVEMENTS

Let us look at the relative prices between the manufactured products and agricultural products since 2005–06 (Table 2.3).

Manufacturing as an activity and population in urban areas depends on vital inputs from agriculture. The reliance is heavy in industries such as plywood industry, processed foods, vanaspati, sugar, jaggery and paper. Over the last 6 years alone, the terms have so drastically altered in favour of agriculture vis-à-vis manufacture that in relative terms manufacturing prices have fallen steeply by 26 per cent. Against a 77 per cent increase in agri-based input prices, the manufacturing sector has been able to recover only about 30 per cent through its end product prices.

[3] See Appendix Table 1.17 (page A22) of Economic Survey 2011–12.

Table 2.3 Terms of Trade (Base Year 2004–05 = 100)

Year	Price Index of Mfg Products	Price Index of Agricultural Products	Mfg Price Index as % of Agricultural Price Index
2005–06	102.4	103.4	99.03
2006–07	108.2	112.5	96.18
2007–08	113.4	121.5	93.33
2008–09	120.4	133.5	90.19
2009–10	123.1	151.0	81.52
2010–11	130.1	176.6	73.67

Source: Economic Survey 2011–12, Appendix Table 5.4.

It should be no surprise that several industries are doing badly in the last 3–4 years pulling down the overall growth rates. Farmers will shift out of low-yielding crops to MSP benchmarked higher-yielding crops and the table of prices for such crops is bound rise in sympathy. Even if an industry is not directly affected, the general rise in the price table affects them and their cost of inputs has gone up steeply.

NEED TO STOP POLITICS OF MSPs

Much of the agricultural product price inflation is engineered by steep hikes in MSPs. There is definite and pressing need to stop politicising MSPs and build market mechanisms gradually so that demand supply and costs determine what is produced. The government can always enter the market and buy during harvest seasons and release during non-harvest season which will stabilise prices. If the production is seen as more than domestic requirements, it can facilitate exports.

There should be more graduated approach to fixing MSPs. It should be indexed to rural cost of living, indexed cost of inputs and should be periodically revised and not used as a political tool with long spells of inertia followed by sudden spurts.

The need and ways to achieve efficiencies through privatisation of PDS are discussed in Chapter 6.

2.3 Cash Transfers and Coupons for Subsidies: What Makes Sense?

Subsidies are a kind of market intervention by government when the market by itself finds equilibrium at a much lower consumption level than socially or economically desirable. The attempt mostly is to intervene and make the goods or services available at a lower price so that the desired consumption level is reached.

India is not alone in indulging in subsidies—it is ubiquitous across the world; nor is it the only country to think of cash transfers as the delivery channel.

The government's think tank seems optimistic about unique identities (UIDs), cash transfers and coupons (direct transfers) to deliver subsidies to deserving target. Direct transfers are being talked of as the panacea in major areas involving subsidies—food, education, fertiliser, kerosene, etc. It sure will overcome the leakages involved in physical distribution and ensure that a greater percentage gets delivered to the target beneficiaries. Controls in modern communication and money transfer methods are far more effective than traditional methods and hence should have a beneficial impact.

POSSIBLE ADVANTAGES AND LIMITATIONS OF DIRECT TRANSFERS

Firstly, since equilibrium is an interplay between demand and supply, the intervention can also be from either side. The choice of side to intervene from is therefore important. Direct transfers work most effectively from the demand side where the recipient uses the coupon or cash to buy the goods and services in question and increases his consumption. Not all goods and services are amenable to intervention from the demand side. Supply side interventions try to work by altering the cost structure (mostly marginal cost) of the various players. The government can bring down the cost structure by supplying some inputs at cheaper prices (like coal for electricity producers), reducing taxes or handing out subsidies for specified inputs. If the variable costs come down for all suppliers, and government ensures competitive conditions, markets will drive down market prices. Fertilisers and fuels are examples where supply side intervention will be far more effective than cash transfers and coupons.

Imagine the complexities if one were to attempt distribution of coupons to consumers to subsidise fertiliser. Apart from problems of 'how much to whom' which will itself open the flood gates for corruption, massive increase in the number of people to be dealt with will require creation and administration of a massive system. If the transfer size is same for all irrespective of land holdings, then there will be enormous spillage due to mismatch; if based on land holdings, falsification of size will be natural besides it being unequal and regressive. The government think tanks' hopes on proper information systems and UID system to effectively tackle these issues look naïve. For similar reasons, fuel subsidies (petrol and diesel) work much better through supply side, rather than issuing subsidy coupons to millions of truck owners, auto drivers, 2- and 4-wheelers.

Secondly, a good subsidy system should also consider the 'hierarchy of wants' of the target segment. If the consumption good/service being targeted for subsidy is way above the current consumption profile of the recipient, he is more likely to sell his coupons or direct transfer than necessarily consume the desired goods for which he was subsidised. Physical transfers like subsidised rice score far better here even if on relative terms.

Here is where politicians like Tamil Nadu's late Chief Ministers K. Kamaraj and M.G. Ramachandran (MGR) made far more practical economists. They exchanged 'what the target segment wanted' (physically distributing food by mid-day meal scheme) in exchange for 'what the state wanted them to consume' (education) and delivered education. Education was way above the target's immediate consumption hierarchy 30–40 years back. A coupon or cash transfer system here would have mostly failed, since the target population would have preferred to work the fields to earn their bread and use the cash for other immediate (according to their individual preferences) needs including filling their belly: intellectual pursuits could wait.

Thirdly, the argument of cash transfers reduces corruption. Any transfers involve giving out entitlements by some 'authority' without the recipient paying commensurate value. Unless the system of policing is highly effective, it makes for an ideal ground for the giver to demand bribes and the receiver to pay it. One already sees it in NREGA and old age pensions—the per cent to be paid to original certifiers (read local politician) and the monthly dispensers (read the postman) seems well established. Every touch-point provides opportunities for 'extracting' bribes.

Even between cash and coupons each may have its merits in a given situation. Areas like higher education where prior qualification determines eligibility and thus restricts spillage, coupons may be better. Even the choice of goods to be subsidised needs careful selection. It requires careful analysis of recipient, nature of goods in question, and several other factors that may not be addressed by a single–size-fits-all approach. Unfortunately, mistakes in designing economic systems take unduly long to discover.

2.4 Threats from Foreign Direct Investment (FDI) in Retail: Is It Real?

One of the most widely debated reform measures in the recent times has been FDI in multi-brand retail as if India's very existence depended on it. Let us see the validity of arguments of both the protagonists and their opponents.

The opposition to allow FDI in multi-brand retailing is strident—ranging from 'road to slavery' to threats of blow up specific symbols of organised retail, to political divorces by some parties from the ruling coalition, and political posturing including threat to reverse the policy in case they come to power, the last of which is potentially the most dangerous.

RELATIVE VALUE CREATION

The subject should have been approached by a clear understanding of the value creation process of the small retailers and *kirana* shops. If they are adding value which are not capable of being replicated (or to the extent it is not replicable) by large retailers they will be relatively safe. Their value addition can come from small size delivery fit for day-to-day consumption, door delivery, personal touch, quick turnaround, non-standard size, etc. If the organised retailers are capable of competing value creation or their process is capable of over shadowing small retailer value creation, then the small retailers will mostly lose their jobs. This will obviously vary depending on products, market size, income of customers, region, concentration of population, etc. There cannot be a blanket answer to this without understanding the way and quantum of value creation. Unfortunately, very little research or debate seems to have been done on these lines.

Those opposed to FDI in retail should realise that if the existing retailers keep doing the same job in the same way using the same technology, they will only continue to get the same income, at least in a relative sense. There is a need to cut the current high levels of wastes, enable better processing and improve several existing practices along the chain. While retailing is not just about farm produce alone, the distribution trade engages several sections who are otherwise vulnerable and their job loss anxieties need to be adequately addressed. We need a more informed debate—based more on reliable data and empirical evidence—and build safeguards to mitigate the impact on those affected and provide more secure alternative means of livelihood to them.

EMPLOYMENT ARGUMENT

Let us first see the merit of government's argument—will create 1 crore jobs, consumers will get cheaper goods and the farmers will get better prices. How can it simultaneously give better values at both ends even as it adds so much employment which can only add to costs? Is it the government's argument that the entire additional value to consumers, producers and salaries on the additional jobs will be squeezed out of the reduction in wastes? Sounds farfetched!

It is difficult to see how organised retail will create additional jobs on net basis. It will surely add some jobs in food processing and packaging, labelling, grading and sorting which are scarcely done under the current dispensation. Actual employment per unit of sales value at the final point is, however, much lower in organised retail. The net additional employment creation may not be as rosy as made out. Retailing is the second largest employer today in India after agriculture and one should be particularly careful in tampering with it. Particularly since it employs people with various degrees of skills who might, on displacement find it difficult to get re-employed and hence be readymade recruits for the growing army of reform displaced.

REAL THREATS

Two threats which seem to have missed the eyes of many discerning are the kind of potentially dysfunctional market structure that organised retail can lead to and the net negative effect on certain sections in rural areas.

1. *Increasing imperfection in markets:* Perhaps the biggest threat from the proposed measures is the likely market structure that could evolve. Organised retailers have deep pockets and can achieve considerable backward integration. As of now right along the retail chain, it is 'many buyers verses many sellers' kind of 'perfect competition'

situation which does not allow anyone to dictate prices and garner disproportionate profits. However, once 'deep pocket retailers' grow roots, they will be 'few against many retail consumers' at one end and 'few buyers versus many farmers' at the sourcing end giving them disproportionate market power at both ends.

Modern retailers will contract directly with fast moving consumer goods (FMCG) and consumer durables companies and eliminate many distributors, stockists, sub-stockists, C and F agents, and wholesalers who abound in the current scenario in addition to the ultimate retailers. This is a move away from the ideal structure that economists recommend—'perfect competition', a situation that prevails now with many buyers and many sellers at each stage of distribution—to a relatively more monopolistic structure.

It is not necessary for the modern retailers to establish control on all links in the chain to usher in restricted competition or create monopolistic structures to take a disproportionate share of the economic value gap that exists between the producers and the end consumer. It is enough for them to control just one vital link (does not Intel just have near monopolistic control over just chips and corners much of the profits from laptops and computers?) and the link can garner much higher than its due share. This should be the worst fear and economic side effect that we should be focusing our attention on.

2. *Possible net negative effect on non-farm rural sector and landless labourers:* The next is the net effect on the non-farming rural sector. Retail may create some higher-profile jobs and fetch higher prices for farmers who have a net surplus to sell. Contracting may also take away pricing risks and help cultivators plan their cropping patterns. But the biggest concern should be the impact on marginal farmers and landless labourers and those engaged in non-farm employment in the rural

areas who are all net buyers of food. For them the impact may be net negative considering the employment effect, price effect and wage effect.

Firstly, the impact of price increase of food crops at farm gate (loosely cited as a possible benefit by the protagonists and government) will push many BPL families who are net buyers of food further below subsistence level. *Secondly*, retail may dictate changes in cropping patterns from food grains and cereals, which are locally required to those suiting the urban markets and those suitable for food processing and will impact their availability for the rural folks. *Thirdly*, higher incomes for 'net surplus' farmers will soon translate into higher mechanisation—farmers with contracts with retail biggies can easily flaunt them to get bank loans—and may further shrink rural employment opportunities.

Will not the higher payments by retailers (when and if it happens and to the extent it happens) translate into higher rural wages? Unlikely. The rural labour market is distinct from the agriculture produce markets and higher prices in one need not automatically transmit into the other. When farm labour is in high surplus and when one can find as many hands as one wants at the current wage levels, why would anyone increase the wages to his labourer?

Transmission of benefit of higher prices for farm produce to higher employment would require that the consumption of the immediate first-level beneficiaries go up. This may result in diversification of consumption pattern and create additional employment opportunities (if others can re-skill themselves to do it). With available labour being absorbed in allied or newly emerging activities, the demand for labour will go up and supply of labour for farm work might shrink pushing up both wages. But this social transformation (if it happens) would require several years, but marginalise the already marginalised in the interregnum: not a welcome proposition.

SPURIOUS ARGUMENTS FROM BOTH SIDES

The feared penetration of FDI into Indian retail markets seems an overblown threat. Modern retail is unlikely to locate their outlets in rural and semi-urban areas where the purchasing power is widely dispersed. In urban areas, India's rentals are perhaps the highest in the world in relative terms to income. This is due to our high population density and for most Indians real estate is the primary investment instrument. Modern retailing requires large space and rentals might prove a constraint. In the West, most large format outlets are located far out of the city (to contain rentals) and people travel great distances (by our standards) to shop once every month or week. The proportion of people willing to do this in Indian cities, given travel constraints and difficulties, is unlikely to be facilitative to modern retail.

Again although double income families are rising, the percentage of families managed by home makers who have prematurely quit or have never worked, or is managed by either parents or by joint families is comparatively large and their preference is towards day-to-day shopping not periodic shopping as in the West. It may take several years for this to evolve to the benefit of modern retailers.

The protagonists argue that organised retail has not created problems in various countries that have allowed it such as Malaysia, Singapore, Thailand and Taiwan. It may be factually true, but we have to appreciate that these countries have never faced the unemployment rates that we face. If we usher in the same technology and mechanisation as in most western countries, it may be possible to carry out most of our agriculture and rural activities with just one-fifth or one-fourth of people that are currently employed, releasing the rest into the unemployment queues and social unrest.

Another argument of the pro modern retail lobby is Indian corporates have already been allowed in multi-brand retail and they have had no side effects, why not foreign firms. But the level and scale of technologies, buying practices and financial muscle of foreign firms are of a significantly different genre. People who have seen a sample set of each of this will vouch for the difference. The cost of funds is also a differentiating factor. We have seen many Indian firms who started struggling even after establishing good customer base and footfalls. For most Indian firms, the start-up cost of each store weighs heavily, losses in the run-up are a burden and any sluggish period is a pain. But most international retailers can easily withstand all these struggles.

There is needless escalation of passions from both sides of the political spectrum and media as well as freelance reform die-hards. Given the lack of conclusive evidence and the nascent stage, it may have been better to soft peddle the issue so that political statements do not fly about thick and fast and inflict collateral damage on investor sentiments and general mood.

PAY-OFFS AND SAFEGUARDS

We need to at least partially modernise our retail if only to serve as a reference base for our age-old retail practices, improve farm practices, better sorting and preservation, higher food processing, etc. Even select penetration of high end retail will adequately serve this purpose. The wastage in the Indian food chain is rather high and needs to be contained. These can also be achieved by training, appropriate legislation and implementation of standards.

Consumers' ability to pay has increased in the last few years. Customers (to varying degrees) are willing to pay much better prices for the goods and services. People who were paying ₹35–40 for shaving creams are willing to pay 2–3 times for shaving gels and 4–5 times for even more convenient foams. Tailor-made shirts are replaced by designer labels 5–6 times the price. This is visible everywhere in India including in rural India, where home-made products are replaced by FMCG goods in small ticket sizes, and home remedies are replaced by over-the-counter medicines. Equally, there is a good scope for adding value between the farm/factory gate to the consumer by better packaging, ensuring quality, better handling and branding, catering to convenience. The scope for adding value has to be harnessed (at least from those who are willing to pay better) and used for increasing employment along the chain and setting future reference quality standards for others to follow. Modern retail might help in this effort.

In order to contain the threat from distorted market structure getting formed due to deep pockets of FDI investors, we need some safeguards. For a starter, we can restrict them to one per city or within defined radius (so as to curb undue concentration at selling end) and *confine them to source primarily through the local wholesale markets*. They can impose all their sanitation standards and packing requirements at this level. If the sellers in wholesale markets see enough pay-offs, they will graduate and it will lead to better remuneration to producers for a visible value addition, unlike in say onions where periodic price spikes benefit only the middlemen who are the sole beneficiaries of all sporadic market distortions.

Economic reforms are all about timing (speed) and sequencing. The measures announced at this stage of development may invite threats of immolation; 10 years later, no one might notice if enough rural jobs are created by then and when say another 10 years later, if there is a shortage of labour, FDI in retail may be a necessity and one would even invite them with incentives.

We need to start somewhere so that we have enough experience for evolving proper policies when it becomes a matter of necessity. FDI can be allowed in select areas, with varying safeguards and shareholding so that we gather the requisite experience for future roll out. If the benefits are also there for all to see, hopefully the strident voices would also lose some of their potency.

2.5 Land Acquisition Bill: A Futile Exercise[4]

THE CRYING NEED FOR EFFICIENT LAND USE

India has the highest population density for any large country. The skill sets of more than 60 per cent of the population especially at the bottom end are land dependent. Growth requires land both for natural resources and setting up factories, developing new cities, and centres of economic growth. Land has hence to be used with utmost caution and careful planning.

However, it is one of the least attended areas. The last legislation on land acquisition took place more than a century ago. It is imperative therefore to come up with a legislation which balances the various interest groups. It should be an innovative yet balancing act which would give faster access for economic and commercial activities even while ensuring sellers a source of sustained livelihood and a sense of psychological security (rather than just a fair price).

The underlying assumption of the proposed Land Acquisition and Rehabilitation and Resettlement Bill seems that the price paid to the farmers is unreasonably low due to dominant power of industrial buyers/government. The draft however seems listless and may neither accelerate the pace of land acquisition for industry nor overcome the psychological barriers of the landowners which impede land transfers. First, let us consider the psychological barriers, which limit supply.

FEARS AND PHOBIAS OF LOW-INCOME LAND OWNERS

One of the main reasons for the farmers' (and land dependents) reluctance in selling their land is the *agonizing fear of*

[4] At the time of going to the press, this legislation was awaiting approval. It is quite likely some of the measures discussed here may have been taken care of by amendments.

not having an alternative means of livelihood—a fear of the unknown. This fear can only be overcome when the problem is brought to a rational level. It requires development of alternative skills which gives them the confidence of securing their livelihood in the long term. Rehabilitation efforts should have largely focussed on this.

Fears and phobias do not bear a linear relationship with price. For example, can someone with deep fear of public speaking overcome the same just because his fee is hiked multi-fold? Highly doubtful. How effective (even if desirable) the higher compensation proposed by the bill in overcoming the farmers' fear and induces them to sell is debatable.

The second psychological barrier to overcome is the *phobia of switching from one asset class to another*. People in tribal and rural area are only comfortable with land: it gives regular income, is inflation proof and guarantees capital appreciation. The only alternative asset class he is comfortable with is gold. The penetration of even primary level banking is very poor in our rural areas. It would require a much greater degree of financial inclusion to make them comfortable with financial assets as a means of sustaining livelihood or alternative investment vehicle. Even after decades of tax incentives, information bombardment and marketing, the percentage of people[5] investing in equities is hardly 2 per cent. Even in urban areas familiar with banking and financial assets, people have strong inertia for switching from other assets such as gold, real estate and bank deposits into equities. To expect that rural folks will switch from land to financial assets (accept cash compensation, put them in banks to earn interest to sustain livelihood) is highly preposterous.

Unless farmers psychologically feel secure with an alternative source of livelihood and alternative ways to hold wealth, the battle of land acquisition will be a continuing saga.

[5] See 'Inclusion Will Drive Markets' by Joseph Massey, *Business Today*, March 2011.

INDUSTRY PERSPECTIVE: SLOWING ACQUISITION PROCESS

Next, let us consider the buyers' travails. The minimum compensation prescribed (4 times in rural areas) together with the cost of rehabilitation and resettlement (R and R) pushes up the cost to the acquirer from (say) ₹5 lakhs (per acre) to well over ₹30 lakhs (under given assumptions of two affected families per acre). If the land cost was 3 per cent of project cost before, the proposed bill can increase the total project cost by about 15 per cent—a hefty increase indeed which can alter the viability of many projects from 'accept' to 'reject'.

Moreover, the price multiple to be paid is benchmarked on the average of previous 3 years. Once it is known there is an impending acquisition, prices will spiral upwards even further and perhaps creating speculative bubbles (like in stock markets) in select areas. This can only become a fertile ground for touts and middlemen.

In return the industry would have hoped to get faster, smoother and secure process. The minimum time to complete the process which may be upwards of 3 years and the multiple doors (forget the single window) to knock on—Collector, Gram Sabha, Chief Secretary Committee, Administrator for R and R, oversight members, etc.—can sap the energy out of the most enthusiastic entrepreneur. Besides, the R and R requires creation of several infrastructural facilities from creation of places of worship to post offices to health centres to burial grounds. If higher price to be paid for land dilutes competitiveness, the physical impositions can serve a knock-out punch.

In countries like Vietnam, government does most of these, establishes roads, power and water connectivity and offers land almost off the shelf for 50 years and above at nil annual rentals. The one-time upfront cost (starts variously from ₹10 lakhs per acre) is used largely in developing the site infrastructure and resettlement. China does it even better. How can Indian manufacturing—not so competitive already—compete with such countries?

The bill's approach is fundamentally flawed: that of fixing the price arbitrarily high and hoping demand–supply will adjust to fit such prescribed price levels. Achieving social justice in a private economic transaction can be ineffectual. It simply does not work. We have seen it in agriculture credit.

Agriculture and rural areas require industry to absorb the excess labour as well as growth. There should be a free play without any artificial barriers so that land changes hands faster to facilitate industrialisation of rural areas and jobs get created.

The proposed actions seem to usher in more structural rigidities which might over time not just be a constraint but mean 'curtains down' on non-agricultural pursuits of meaningful scale in rural areas. Economic policy mistakes take several years to discover. We lost 40 years with our socialistic pursuits. We may lose another 40 with this bill.

NEED TO INCREASE 'SUPPLY' OF LAND

We tend to view land as two-dimensional. There is a need to look at creative solutions including the three-dimensional use of space over land for easing the pressure and increasing 'supply' of land. Some examples are as follows:

1. Most of the railway stations in prime locations in metros and busy areas have nothing over their roof. Most of these could be developed in and multi-storied usable space can be created over them. Even the railway tracks are in multiple layers in some cities overseas. Delhi Metro has also proved its viability in our cities. Maybe a crowded city like Mumbai can duplicate its tracks over the existing ones. Courts, police stations and administrative offices—all areas where we are far short of requirements, can all be built on top of tracks without in any way affecting operations of railways.
2. Most public parks have nothing under them. Instead of parked cars obstructing free flow of traffic one can always create car parks below them.

3. Most slums are in single story. Imagine the value of land in Dharavi of even 100 sq ft in single story. If only many such units can be aggregated and developed, we can deliver better houses to these slums besides easing urban land pressure.
4. Most open defecation takes place somewhere at ground level not in terraces or upper stories. In most cities, these lands if developed properly could perhaps pay for development of proper facilities even while helping solve one of the vexatious problems dogging us.
5. Maybe the government should legislate a minimum number of floors for buildings—like say 20–25 stories in crowded business districts, 10–12 stories in relatively less crowded areas and a minimum of 6–8 stories in other areas.
6. The government should perhaps bring more and more newly developing areas on lease from government rather than on freehold basis at least in cities or identified areas so that the government retains the flexibility.

2.6 Inflation Control: RBI's Inappropriate Response to MSP Genie

SIGNIFICANCE OF INFLATION CONTROL IN INDIA

The way inflation is controlled has a special significance in India. We have a large section below the poverty line and plenty more on the fringes. These can so easily slip back BPL. Our manufacturing sector is rather shallow and gets affected when the need of the hour is fast expansion to absorb the ever growing population. The levels of monetisation are low and the reach of monetary policies somewhat restricted. All these impose very many constraints and limitations on the kind of measures that the government can exercise to control inflation. It calls for a delicate balance.

SOURCE OF INFLATION SINCE JANUARY 2010

Beginning January 2010 inflation has been close to or in double digits consistently after being benign before that for some time. In January 2010, it reached 8.53 per cent from an average of 1.65 per cent for the previous 9 months of fiscal 2010. From that time, it has been hovering at around 8–10 per cent levels consistently. High inflation can hurt various sections depending on its origin and source.

Nowhere is the disconnect between the ground realities and policy response and the assumptions or theories behind them and even independent analysis so gaping and inadequate as in this case. The official response to sustained spell of inflation is like 'treat patient A for tuberculosis, to cure B of cholera' even if A has no illness, since A is the only patient under its control and tuberculosis medicine is the only one in stock.

Between 2008–09 (average) and December 2010, the food articles price index shot up from 135 to 189, a 40 per cent increase, food grains and processed foods by 19 per cent each, whereas fuel and manufactured products grew by a much lower 11 per cent and 9 per cent, respectively. The share of manufactured products in inflation was about 35 per cent—far less than its weight in index of 64.97 per cent (Table 2.4).

It is conclusive that food inflation was the main source of trouble although its relative contribution had come down in 2011–12. The full impact of our monetary measures however falls on manufacturing sector due to its close linkage and dependence on formal credit systems.

INAPPROPRIATE POLICY CHOICE

The government has a variety of responses at its disposal to combat inflation and soften the market prices including monetary and fiscal policies apart from physical actions of

Table 2.4 Index Numbers of Wholesale Prices

	Weightage	Average of Monthly Numbers		% Incr		% Incr
Items	**in Index (%)**	**2007–08**	**2008–09**	**8/9 Over 7/8**	**Dec 2010**	**Dec 2010 Over 8/9**
Food articles	14.34	124	135	9%	187	39%
Within which food grains		131	145	11%	173	19%
Fuel	14.91	121	135	12%	150	11%
Manufactured products	64.97	113	120	6%	129	8%
Within which processed foods		110	120	9%	143	19%

Source: Economic Survey 2010–11: Appendix Table 5.1 (page A62).
Note: % increases annualised. Weights do not add up to 100 due to exclusion of minerals and non-food articles.

increasing imports, restricting exports reducing the duty structure or subsidies or concessions on movement of such goods. It can also subsidise the prices at the consumer end so as to soften the impact on consumers especially where they are vulnerable. To be fair, the government had initiated several of these especially in the latter part, although the cumulative impact from all those measures pale into insignificance when placed against the single most potent weapon deployed—monetary policy by the RBI.

MONETARY POLICIES CAN BE INEFFECTIVE AGAINST AGRI-INFLATION

Monetary policies can have effect in well-functioning markets where the investment decisions by businesses and personal financial decisions are impacted by the cost and availability of credit from banks.

In our agri-rural space, price of fertiliser, a key input, is controlled by the government. MSP, the price the farmers get and which may decide the cropping pattern, is decided largely by the government. PDS's (prices in fair price shops) prices are once again determined by the government and are hardly a function of market, cost of credit or its availability. Under these conditions where neither the major input, nor production nor consumption decisions are subject to interest rates set by RBI, what impact or control our monetary policies can have?

Again the official credit for food grains at about ₹78K crore (November 2011) is less than 2 per cent of gross bank credit, whereas monetary policy measures affect the balance 98 per cent as well. Total direct agricultural credit at ₹300K crore (March 2011) is less than 8 per cent of total commercial banks credit. Agriculture relies heavily on informal credit, moneylenders and self-financing, all of which are beyond the RBI's *dictat*. Monetary tightening on the other sectors which have hardly contributed to the inflation is sure to be growth-anaesthetic, as has been seen by the sluggish growth in IIP numbers. Growth rates have slowly crept back to 5–6 per cent range during 2011–12 and 12–13 from 8 to 9 per cent earlier.

The increase in MSPs as presented in Table 2.1 presented earlier in this chapter clearly indicates that the main reason for sustained spell of food inflation is the political action of hiking them indiscriminately. The annual increases which were in single digits (maximum of 7 per cent) from 1990–91 to 2007–08 went up steeply to 30–70 per cent in just 1 year (2008–09)—an action which has been repeated in 2012–13 which will prolong the food inflation spell.

Add to this the money injected by the NREGA programme in the rural areas. When such large-scale injections take place over such a short time in insulated rural and agri-markets, inflation gets created as an inevitable end result. This is not the handiwork of market forces where either demand grows faster leading to supply shortfalls or cost inflation in key inputs create price spirals: it is solely the by-product of politically motivated actions *a la* Thailand's rice pledge programme.

MONETARY POLICY AXE HAS FALLEN ON THE MANUFACTURING SECTOR

While the problem has its roots in agriculture, the axe of monetary tightening has fallen heavily on the manufacturing sector which relies most on official bank credit but has contributed the least to inflation. Prices in fuel sector cannot be controlled by monetary policies as they are governed more by international ruling prices. The government can at best soften the blow by absorbing it or cutting down a plethora of taxes on these or absorb the short recoveries by raising other taxes and reducing the fiscal burden so created. Ironically, food sector (price increase of which have contributed the maximum to inflation and where the flow of credit should have been moderated or curtailed) has shown the highest growth in bank credit between March 2010 and November 2011. From ₹48,562 crore, it has grown to ₹77,890 crore—an increase of over 60.3 per cent as against an increase of 27.9 per cent in overall credit.

A similar suicidal approach had been earlier experimented in mid-1990s with dreadful consequences. In order to control inflation in the run-up to the elections in 1996 the then government resorted to monetary tightening and the interest rates went up steeply to high teens. The resultant effect on the manufacturing industry was so constraining that it took the next 7–8 years before it could regain its growth instincts.

INFLATION CONTROL

Effectiveness of monetary policies depends upon how much the consumption decisions at the individual level and production and investment decisions at the corporate or investor level are influenced by the cost and availability of credit. The level of monetisation and financial inclusion, level of indebtedness and debt servicing levels at business or individual levels, etc. will all have their bearing on its potency.

The various situations under which monetary policy has to operate may be tabulated on the twin dimensions: (i) whether the expenditure is discretionary or not and (ii) the degree of linkage and control that the banking system has over the sector/decision (Figure 2.1).

An item of expenditure may be discretionary at the individual level in which case it can be postponed or advanced depending on the availability of funds or cost (interest) thereof. If it is not discretionary but essential, the individual may find it difficult to adjust the timing of expenditure. In items like food, the best one can do is to shift from one grain to another. However if prices of all food items increase, they may be left with no option but to re-allocate money from other items and spend a greater portion of income on food. It is unlikely that credit tightening will significantly impact consumption and rein in prices of such items. The government

Figure 2.1 Monetary Policy: Where Best Applied/Likelihood of Success

Where capital or consumption expenditure is	Linkage to banking system	
	Weak	Good
Discretionary	Education (for poor), personal travel, purchase of consumer durables and appliances in rural areas. 1	Business investments, auto loans, house loans (investment units), speculative working capital, margins on futures 2
Essential	Food, marriage, housing (end-user), although its linkage to banking is growing 3	Corporate core working capital 4

may have to resort to reducing other taxes on such items, import and thus increase availability, curb speculative activity like leveraged trading (futures) or hoarding, etc. to soften the impact on consumers.

Monetary actions on a given sector cannot be effective if that sector does not depend on banking systems for its credit needs. In much of rural areas, the monetisation is low, credit is largely from informal sector and a sizable number of transactions are still on barter. Wages of agricultural labour are still made in kind at the time of harvest in several villages and rural areas. Reach of our formal systems is rather poor and so is financial inclusion. The credit needs in the rural areas are largely met by moneylenders and self-savings which have no linkage with banking systems.

Reach of our formal banking systems is good in urban areas, where bulk of credit is for financing business and manufacturing and the transaction size is large. Where these sectors are the chief villains due to emerging credit induced demand runs ahead of supply expansion, monetary policy can have a potent effect.

It is difficult to see how monetary policy will be effective with matters in boxes 1 and 3 in Figure 2.1. In box 4, it may prove suicidal unless price spiral is from hoarding. Monetary interventions are likely to be highly effective in box 2. Even here it is essential to direct actions in select sectors responsible. Unfortunately, monetary policy strains like selective credit control which were capable of precise application for localised effect have more or less gone out of fashion of late globally. The general purpose in-fashion tools such as bank rate variations, open market operations and reserve requirements–based policies have a general effect and many innocent bystander sectors suffer collateral damage. It is difficult to direct these at the exact source of trouble.

In any case, it is difficult to justify the monetary policy stances of 2010–12. It is easier to reason how it was the chief villain in sharp deceleration in manufacturing.

POSSIBLE ALTERNATIVE APPROACHES

The government seems guilty of not exploring the full breadth of alternatives at its command. Some effective alternatives could be as follows:

Firstly, there is a need for a more reasoned and graduated approach to fix MSPs and need to stop the politics of MSPs as seen earlier.

Secondly and more immediate need of the hour is to facilitate industrial sector to set up supply chains into rural sector to soak up the excess liquidity created by MSPs and NREGA. This requires an expansionary policy—expansionary for industrial and service sectors—rather than a contractionary monetary policy. In any case, the squeeze on industry and urban sector was hardly the right recipe for the recent inflation fever.

Thirdly, the incremental MSPs (over and above what is required for off-setting costs) mandated by political compulsions should, at least in part, be distributed in deferred payments—say through long-term time deposits through organised sector banks. This would reduce the immediate liquidity overhang in rural areas and may increase the reach of formal systems and help increase financial inclusion over a period of time. In the absence of alternative spending avenues, the excess liquidity is invading gold, the only investment vehicle rural India knows of, increasing India's imports year after year thus needlessly promoting non-productive savings/investments.

2.7 Agricultural Productivity Gains Might Marginalise More into Poverty

There is a need to increase our agricultural productivity. This will increase the margin of safety available to us in times of drought when government can initiate 'food for work' welfare programmes by moving surplus grains to deficit areas. Higher output can give India an export surplus and partially cover the perpetual deficit created by oil. Higher farm incomes can increase consumption there which will facilitate manufacturing sector. If higher productivity can release some areas from agriculture, it will make available land for industrialisation or urbanisation.

There have been strident demands for increasing India's agricultural productivity as a solution to poorer growth in rural areas. Economic survey 2010–11 calls for incremental productivity growth and technology diffusion as a pre-requisite for inclusive growth. There are calls for farm mechanisation, corporate farming, use of man-made or modified seeds, introduction of futures, besides of course better irrigation, research, agricultural labour skill upgradation, etc.

Given the current state of things, this is not without risks. Any sharp or sustained productivity gains might prove socially problematic. Let us see some of the risks and possible mitigation measures.

RISKS OF HIGHER AGRICULTURAL PRODUCTIVITY

Firstly, let us discuss the likely shrinkage of income. As articulated by the well-known International Trade theorist Jagdish Bhagwati as the 'Theory of Immiserising Growth',[6] total incomes of suppliers tend to fall beyond a point in response to increases in supply. This is more likely in closed markets like India. This is both due to rigidities on demand side and perishable nature of most commodities. Perishability

[6] Jagdish Bhagwati. 1958. 'Immiserizing Growth: A Geometrical Note', *Review of Economic Studies* 25 (June). Although the theory was proposed in the context of export-dependent economies, it stands to reason that it can have validity even within an economy for a particular sector if terms of trade move against it due to increased supply.

(vegetables and fruits), high storage and carrying costs (rice and wheat) and threat of price erosions due to fresh arrivals from next crop (tea and coffee) all have a dampening influence on prices.

Price slumps benefit the urban poor. But income shrinkage can seriously affect the land owners and landless agri-labour. Landless rural labour is mostly paid in kind and hence, at first glance, may not suffer from any price reductions. But they will definitely suffer due to the likely shrinkage in crop area, as discussed below.

Secondly, let us see the threat of likely increase in unemployment. India currently wastes nearly 10–13 per cent of its food grains as variously estimated. Hopefully this will be plugged first. If further we have significant productivity jumps (Indian productivity for various crops is only between 30 per cent and 60 per cent of the best achieved in the world), it will lead to a rapid shrinkage of area under cultivation, unless accompanied by increased offtake. Even with the modest 10–15 per cent increased productivity and similar cuts in wastes, it will potentially release nearly 20 per cent of the land and 10–11 per cent of population engaged in agriculture. These people have no marketable alternative skills and suffer occupational rigidities. With no (or declining) incomes and no jobs, there is a huge risk of malnutrition and hunger besides frustration becoming a readymade hunting ground for naxalism.

Thirdly, productivity gains will no doubt increase the value of high-yielding land. But the lesser productive lands will mostly become surplus and vacant. If even 10–15 per cent of our agricultural land becomes surplus, it will lead to a steep fall in their prices, since our industry and infrastructure just cannot absorb such vast amounts of land. Owners of such land will have no (or declining) income besides seeing rapid decline in their land values. It may increase the inequalities in rural areas much deeper. All these have adverse side effects.

POSSIBLE CURES AND CARE

Firstly, it is as important to manage the demand side of agricultural produce as the supply and productivity. Changes in consumption patterns are not easy to achieve in a short time. To build the demand side, it may be necessary to encourage food processing so that 'those who eat an orange can instead drink the equivalent of three oranges'. Increased meat consumption will utilise about 5 times equivalent grains for a given level of human protein consumption. Demand build up has to lead supply and productivity increases, than lag it if social tensions have to be minimised.

Secondly, the adverse effects (income declines and land price deflation) are a lot more in closed system than when we can build export linkages. India should strategically choose those crops where the increased yields can make us globally a cost competitive player. This would require careful and consistent policies than the ones we had seen in cotton in early 2012—impose ban and remove them within a week—which will make any international trader wary of Indian supplies.

Thirdly, we need to carefully assess those land areas which are most likely to be rendered surplus and incentivise their alternative use or for growing alternative commercial/industrial crops. Singur or Nandigram may not be the best examples of identifying or transferring land for alternative uses. We need to put in place a more credible mechanism—one which is more voluntary as well as socially cohesive. A significant change in our laws governing land use, acquisition and transfer is necessary.

Fourthly and most important is to prepare the landless labour with skills required in alternative occupations. Besides re-skilling, actual deployment in alternatives is a must for a smooth transition. Blind mechanisation and its indiscriminate incentivisation may suddenly release too much labour into other sectors which may not absorb them at the desired rate.

In fact, most of the current drawbacks in agriculture—low yields, high wastes, low labour productivity, low mechanisation, etc.—may all be a blessing in disguise. This delicate balance of things needs to be carefully sequenced if we are to avoid catastrophic social consequences.

2.8 The Relevance of Right to Education (RTE)

IS EDUCATION RELEVANT TO ALL?

The government has been placing a lot of emphasis on education through several programmes like the Sarva Shiksha Abhiyaan, and its follow on Rashtriya Madhyamik Shiksha Abhiyaan, Mid-day meals scheme in schools, Model Schools Scheme, Saakshar Bharat, Adult education besides other focussed programmes. The central and state governments spent about ₹250,000 crore or about 3.25 per cent gross domestic product (GDP) on education which is about 11.1 per cent of their total expenditure in 2010–11. Education garners nearly 45 per cent of the social services expenditure of the government. The RTE Act has given it a fundamental rights status indicating the seriousness of the government. No one can critique its noble objectives or the pressing need to achieve higher levels of literacy so that government's social and economic interventions prove much more effective and perhaps lead to eradication of illiteracy's close cousin—hunger.

RTE and its various clones ignore one major factor working on the mind of key decision makers and why many children do not enrol themselves (or their parents do not feel responsible to do it) or having done so, drop out at stages not considered socially desirable.

POOR PERCEIVED RETURNS

The social or socio-economic rate of discounting for most of the target group of poor families (rural or urban) in India is very high. People from the target beneficiary groups borrow at 80–100 per cent per annum and in some cases of social (and thus financial) emergencies such as marriages, religious rituals, meeting cost of terminal illness and cremation commit themselves at even higher rates for longer periods; even 200–300 per cent per annum implied rates are not uncommon.

For the parents, putting their children in schools involves two kinds of costs—paid out costs (fee, cost of books, transport, etc.) and the foregone earnings of not having them work the fields or run petty errands to earn. These constitute their 'investments' in education. Unless target beneficiaries feel (based on what they see and observe) their 'investments' will earn commensurate returns, it will be irrational for them to send their children to schools. Currently, the demonstrated returns from being a successful secondary student, if discounted for 12 years at the high rate of discounting confronting them, would be infinitesimally tiny and the net present value (NPV)[7]—perceived or actual—may be a huge negative.

The poor may not be mathematical geniuses working out NPVs and internal rates of returns (IRRs).[8] But faced with ordinal choices between two alternatives, they can decide what serves their interest better and the preference given the high rate of discounts is for immediate benefit. We see this working in voting patterns as well. The fruits of development and good administration are distant dreams compared to few wads of notes (or other such short-term gratifications).

It is far too optimistic to expect the children themselves to see far ahead and feel captivated to attend school especially where peer pressure is weak.

WHY DROPOUTS

Why dropouts at various stages? The rate of discounting is different for different families depending on income level, assets owned and savings. It lies along a spectrum. In some

[7] Net present value is the value today of a series of inflows and outflows in the future at the given rate of interest.

[8] Internal rate of return is the method of calculating the implied rate of interest when multiple payments and receipts are involved.

families, there may be other family members to take care of household work or running petty errands for daily earnings. The opportunity cost increases with age due to physical maturity and reduce the relative attractiveness of academic education. Surrounding literacy levels may also limit mental abilities. When any of these emerge, children drop out of school.

Given the social expectation of females' roles which is rather limited in such groups, there is no incremental revenue to be gained from incremental knowledge base (since most of them are socially conditioned to take up only house work or farm work) and hence the dropout happens sooner than for male children.

Peer pressure is also very poor in such groups. In pockets where illiteracy exists, the proportion of illiteracy is far greater than the national average of 30–40 per cent. It is no social stigma to be illiterate in these groups when several previous generations of theirs have remained illiterate. Whatever peer pressure exists, it is more at younger age, less at secondary and least at graduate levels, explaining dropouts at stages.

MAKING RTE WORK BETTER

It is difficult to reduce the socio-economic rate of discounting of poor and rural areas fast unless we bring about financial inclusion and bring down interest rates sharply. Till then we have to work on reducing the 'investment' or immediate costs required in education.

Firstly, to reduce the cost of foregone incomes, the schools will have to adjust their timing so as not to clash with the timing of their alternative work or errands. For example, education vacations should ideally be synchronised in rural areas with harvest, transplanting or sowing seasons and there should be no classes during these times.

Secondly, mid-day meals will reduce the burden on parents and provide an immediate return on their 'investment'.

If children get better food they may themselves feel tempted. Out of pocket costs in books and transport may be covered by the government. The government expenditure on mid-day meals in 2011–12 was ₹9,440 crore which appears the most likely to succeed.

Thirdly, the target group should at each stage feel that every additional year in education is worthwhile by increasing revenue-yielding potential. After children attain basic physical maturity when the families get tempted with alternative employment, the focus should shift to skill development[9] where incremental skills promise returns commensurate with 'investments' of time. This broad approach would serve us well till at least average income in rural areas reach ₹100,000 ($1,500) per annum levels.

The present scheme 'everyone should do secondary level' is rather naïve. One is not sure if any studies have been done by the protagonists of RTE regarding the economic returns to education for the target beneficiaries at various stages. Such studies can lead to better designs.

As of now, it appears that the government's keenness in imparting education far exceeds the enthusiasm of the beneficiaries—a situation very closely resembling population control measures. Poor affordability as a factor may not fully account for this apathy for in many cases opportunities are passed up despite availability of government facilities and funds. The demonstration of economic benefit is one of the pillars why our green revolution was so successful. When the peasants witnessed the enhanced yields after the initial years, most of them adopted the changed practices voluntarily abandoning age-old systems, beliefs and seeds.

MOTHER'S INFLUENCE

The role of mother and her altruistic disposition (let not my children suffer the same fate as mine) has been responsible, to

[9] This is further explored in Chapter 4.

a large extent, in sending children to school and pushing up India's literacy rate from about 18 per cent in 1950–51 to 74 per cent by 2011—a significant[10] achievement indeed. This beneficial social circumstance has to be utilised to the maximum by the government in its efforts in spreading literacy.

To conclude, if education is so important as to be made a fundamental right, it should be made a fundamental duty or obligation as well and a punishable offence for parents not to send children to schools and children not to attend school. This might have some impacts at least in urban or metropolitan areas.

2.9 Fuzzy Divestment Logic

Government has to be clear on its investment policy for its corollary (disinvestment logic) to be appropriate. As India goes through various phases of growth, priorities change. Sectors which call for investment will be vastly different. Since the government does not have an endless source of funds, the only way is to re-cycle—to move out from areas where the objective has been achieved and invest in newer priorities.

The policy and approach carried in the website of the Department of Disinvestment are rather fuzzy. Even the more clearly enunciated policy of 2004 through the Common Minimum Programme of the United Progressive Alliance (UPA) 2004 induces no better hope. The key cornerstones as enunciated in the 2004 policy are as follows:

1. The UPA is pledged to devolve full managerial and commercial autonomy to successful, profit-making companies operating in a competitive environment. Generally, profit-making companies will not be privatised.
2. All privatisations will be considered on a transparent and consultative case-by-case basis. The UPA will retain

[10] Even if India's definition of literacy seems euphemistic or dubious, the uniformity of the scale still makes it significant.

> existing *navaratna* companies in the public sector while these companies raise resources from the capital market. While every effort will be made to modernise and restructure sick public sector companies and revive sick industry, chronically loss-making companies will either be sold-off, or closed, after all workers have got their legitimate dues and compensation.

The thrust of the policy seems to be to retain profit-making enterprises with the government and divest loss-making ones.

Over the years, our policy seems to be pushed more and more by political expediency into submission (as reflected by the meek language in which it is couched now) to become innocuous. The total cumulative proceeds from disinvestment so far under reforms from 1990–91 to 2012–13 at ₹1.19 lakh crore[11] is a poor commentary when compared to the annual capital expenditure of public sector in just 1 year (2011–12) of about ₹7 lakh crore.

PROFITABILITY CRITERIA—IS IT MEANINGFUL?

Why should profitability be the driving criteria for determining retention or divestment? Any new investor (retail or wholesale) would hardly be enthused with loss-making units. Hopefully, the new investor/owner would be interested in running the enterprise as a going concern. Conventionally in such cases, the valuation is determined by discounted cash flow rather than the breakup value. In loss-making units which have bleak or negative cash flows, the discounted values will be negative or negligible. Is realising such low values the objective of our disinvestment exercise or raising moneys for newer investment? Profit-making units with good and sustainable cash flows with high price earnings multiples are

[11] *Source:* Website of Department of Disinvestment, Ministry of Finance, GOI.

the best indication of economic viability and represent the best chances for realising good amounts for the government.

Supporting the general budget deficit which seems the unstated purpose of our disinvestment exercise can hardly be supported by our approach of divesting only loss-making ones. In the least, we should at least completely turn around loss-making units before off-loading and then divest like the Thatcher Government did in the UK two to three decades ago.

Unfortunately, the government has not anywhere clearly stated its policy or priorities for further investment. In this sense, the policies during the Nehruvian era were a lot clearer. When public investments were initiated in the 1950s, the objectives were (i) employment promotion, (ii) conserving scarce foreign exchange, (iii) balanced regional development, (iv) affordable prices for essential products like drugs, pharmaceuticals, etc., (v) self-reliance and (vi) prevention of monopolies and concentration of economic power in private entities. There were also areas where the private sector was shy due to the scale of investment (e.g. Bokaro Steel[12] where despite being offered, a well-known big business group declined citing size of risk involved being too big for them).

Some of these objectives have been fulfilled or are contrary to the current run of reforms or can be taken care of by other methods more effectively.

If the vote bank represented by public sector undertaking (PSU) employees is the attraction of parties with leftist orientation, they should keep the following in mind: (i) the employment intensity in public sector enterprises is less than one-third of private organised sector (i.e. the capital deployed per employee is more than 3 times) and (ii) the average per capita emoluments of a PSU employee are about 12.5 times[13] that of an average Indian as of 2010–11. This is in sharp contrast to the average differential even in Europe and

[12] See *Indian Economy* by Ruddar Dutt and K.P.M. Sundaram, 24th edition, p. 154.

[13] See Tables 1.1 and 3.2 of Economic Survey 2011–12.

advanced countries where the ratio is about 1.2 to 1.4[14] the average citizen's. The capital intensity of PSU commercial enterprises is such that it will take centuries to create jobs to absorb even the existing unemployed workforce—even on proportionate basis.

It is far better for the government to re-cycle investments and keep creating new employment avenues and handing over the already created employment avenues to private sector, rather than locking up capital and just protecting the already employed.

It is difficult to see how the current policy of 'retain profit makers and off-load loss makers' will protect employees. If at all it is the employees in loss-making units who would need protection more than those in profit-making units and hence should be with the government.

A SUSTAINABLE ALTERNATIVE APPROACH

At early stages of development, there are several social goods such as education, health care and hygiene goods while desirable are not within the reach of people whose preoccupation is meeting even more basic needs such as food, clothing and basic shelter. It requires government intervention and investments in such social sectors and 'missing link' economic sectors which have a lot of forward and backward linkages.

As the economy grows and per capita income expands, people's affordability for social goods increases. Increased demand and affordability make them more and more economically viable even for private commercial ventures (e.g. hotels, hospitals, air travel)—first in pockets and as we grow further for the sector as a whole. Likewise, the demand for

[14] See Table 4 Evaluating Government Employment and Compensation by Benedict Clements, Sanjeev Gupta, Izabela Karpowicz and Shamsuddin Tareq; IMF Fiscal Affairs Department; Technical Notes and Manuals TNM/10/15; 21 September 2010.

some economic goods which were poor and low to begin with expands making them a viable proposition.

At this stage (which will vary from sector to sector), it will be possible to hand over the further growth and expansion to private sector and the government to exit.

Government should ideally stay only up to this stage and plan its exit. This is what a typical venture capitalist or an angel investor would do—incubate ideas and enterprises which are in their primitive stage, grow demand and when it is about to take off plan their exit. The government should largely follow this model. While the venture capitalists may have a horizon of 3–5 years, government can afford a much longer time frame. It may be better for it to exit and invest in emerging social sectors or economic initiatives which exhibit poor demand due to its nascent stage, incubate it and grow it and exit when the sector is about to take off. The valuations are most attractive for such maturing industries in growth phase.

This approach continuously re-cycles government investments and aids development and employment creation and enables government to concentrate on newer frontier areas—social or economic—and private sector to specialise in mature sector or areas where demand supply dynamics attracts enough private capital for future growth.

It is quite possible that the government exits from a sector in one geographical area and invests in the same sector in another backward area which is in a more primitive stage of development. If an investment is loss making even after a specified period of say 10 years or so, maybe it signifies that there is no or insufficient demand for such a service or goods which calls for exit on breakup-value basis.

For India's current economic state, the following areas may be appropriate for further investment: research and development, essential infrastructure in tourism, training, seeds development, high end medicine (which is still to reach much part of India), pharmaceutical development, nuclear energy, solar energy, waterways development, water treatment, etc. These are some areas where currently private sector may not have reached the required level of maturity. Investments in such areas will help build capabilities for the future, create meaningful employment opportunities and provide cash at a later date for more emerging areas.

2.10 Goods and Services Tax (GST): Needs Some Fine-tuning

The changes sought to be introduced in indirect taxes through GST might lead to overall reduction in compliance travails and costs, and increase tax collection and collection efficiency, but it is doubtful whether it will lead to greater public good, especially to those who need help. Let us see how.

EQUITY ISSUES BYPASSED

Firstly, a single rate structure of GST, one where the rich and the poor pay the same tax, is iniquitous given the disparities in income in India, which have only grown during the reform years. Even at equal rates of taxation, the burden on net consumption is more on the poor.

A GST of 16 per cent translates to 16 per cent of the total income and consumption for the poor, whereas the same rate may be 8 per cent for someone who is consuming only half his income. The excise regime (before CENVAT[15] with all its drawbacks) and even CENVAT was much more sympathetic to this and aided the poor by fixing lower rates for wage goods or articles consumed by the poor. The 2–3 slab structures currently under consideration may have to wait till most of the population is well beyond 'poverty line'.[16]

[15] Central Value Added Tax (CENVAT)—a tax on production of goods levied by the Centre instead of the Excise duties previously collected.

[16] At the time of going to print, the government is reportedly working on these lines.

Secondly, India needs the full breadth of tax policies for delivering on or correcting so many social and economic disparities. Most advanced countries are through with solving these basic problems and need only largely concentrate on economic stabilisation as the main objective of fiscal or monetary policy. The monetary authorities have chosen to depend heavily on monetary policy to do this, as seen recently during the financial meltdown.

GST will virtually remove fiscal policy as a tool for achieving any of the social and economic objectives and leave the entire task to monetary policy, which is largely ineffective in India, given the low levels of monetisation. More than half the population would actually need government help through tax policies on a sustained basis or during a crisis.

Tax equity need not be the only objective of taxation. In India, we need it for achieving social, regional and economic equity as well. It is important that we retain this within the states' domain.

Thirdly, the argument that GST is an effective plug on tax leakage and does away with administrative interference is less than convincing. At the retail end, an evasion of 16 per cent GST on their gross margins of 10 per cent is 1.6 per cent of sales out of a net margin of 3–4 per cent—a substantial inducement. There will be a definite temptation to show just as much sales as to absorb the input taxes paid.

This will result in the tax authorities asking for physical stock reconciliation for cross verification—first for internal consistency and next with third party suppliers and buyers. And soon enough, more rules and regulations will follow which negate the spirit of simplification.

Fourthly, GST makes it tricky to target and deliver benefits and incentives to select segments. GST will make it easy to trace the tax impact but the 2–3 slab structures will almost make it impossible to use it as an effective instrument of fiscal policy. The proposed GST has mostly abolished the tax rebates and incentives from its ambit.

The main weapon left for the States is to refund taxes or resort to cash pay-outs if they are serious about providing incentives to any select segment. Incentive administration through tax rate adjustments is far more efficient. A section embedded in the law is less discriminatory than hand-outs, which are discretionary. If all incentives have to be delivered through only cash transfers and subventions, it can only lead to corruption and timing uncertainties. There will simply be a substitution of the retail corruption with wholesale corruption.

Government could have gone for GST for all intermediate goods and for final goods alone it should have retained flexibility of multiple tax rates.

2.11 Needless Worship of False Gods

There are some areas where India seems to be laying blind faith in some fashionable concepts whose relevance may not be as much as made out to be. In any case, these needed to be tailored to our circumstances which seem to have not been attempted seriously. Some of these areas are discussed below.

A. TAX CUTS: THE CHIEF NEMESIS OF REFORMS AND GOVERNANCE

India has perhaps paid a heavy price for its needless dalliance with this rather narrow and simplistic concept named as Laffer's curve,[17] which suggests that as tax rates are cut tax collections increase.

It started in 1997–98 Union Budget when corporate tax rates were cut from 45 per cent to 35 per cent (a reduction

[17] Laffer's curve is a relationship between the tax rates and tax collection of the government. According to the theory, in certain circumstances, reducing tax rates might increase tax revenues by better tax compliance.

of 22.22 per cent) and maximum marginal personal tax rates were reduced from 40 per cent to 30 per cent (a reduction of 25 per cent) and the budget documents assumed an increase in direct tax collections of 15 per cent. The theory has some sound basis but it works only within limits. It is therefore necessary to establish the limits within which it will work for us.

Lesser tax rates can induce better compliance. Since the pay-offs for evasion is lower, maybe people would prefer paying taxes. However, when one is used to evasion and gotten away with it for several years, why would anyone change his habits all of a sudden? The government should simultaneously tighten its enforcement and impose far heavier fines for the theory to work efficiently; but most of our fines have lost their financial relevance since they are not periodically revised in line with inflation or personal income.

Need to Know the 'Break Even' Tax Rate

At the individual level, the alternative to paying taxes is not earning income (leisure) which is a 100 per cent tax in a way or evasion. But leisure itself has a positive psychic or physiological pay-off or return, which goes to reduce this. The net implied tax rate of leisure will settle lower at say 60 per cent or 70 per cent. Where this will settle, beyond which individual will prefer leisure or below which an individual will prefer to work (or comply with laws) and pay taxes is highly individualistic.

For the late technical genius GD Naidu (of Coimbatore known as India's Edison), the neutral rate was 0 per cent (for his refusal to pay any taxes on production) due to which the country lost the fruits of his genius. There were others who were still working and paying taxes when the maximum marginal levels were as high as 92 per cent. Maybe for them there was a prestige value attached to being in that tax bracket, which compensated them enough to ignore the high efforts involved. The society's break even rate then has to be well established and periodically revised for it is unlikely to be static. There is no evidence whatsoever that this is being done.

Is Our Tax Rate Too High?

India's tax GDP ratio is not high by any stretch of imagination. At around 18 per cent for central and state taxes together for direct and indirect taxes (after adjusting transfer from centre to states), it is way below most other advanced countries (as seen in Table 2.5) which have a far greater degree of privatisation. For a country like India which wants to provide food to shelter, fertiliser to petrol, to provide highly subsidised education to most of its citizens, provide employment, buy farmers goods at remunerative prices and indulge in so many social intervention programmes besides provide even economic goods at subsidised rates our tax rates are far less than optimal.

Table 2.5 Gross Tax Revenues as Percentage of GDP

Singapore	14.2	Russia	36.9
Malaysia	15.5	UK	39
India	17.7	Netherlands	39.8
Korea, south	26.8	Germany	40.6
South Africa	26.9	Austria	43.4
USA (All levels)	26.9	Finland	43.6
Japan	28.3	Norway	43.6
Switzerland	29.4	France	44.6
Australia	30.8	Sweden	45.8
Brazil	34.4	Belgium	46.8
New Zealand	34.5	Denmark	49
OECD (unweighted average)	34.8		

Source: Heritage Foundation 2012. As quoted in Wikipedia.

Needless Aggression by Tax Authorities

Steep cuts in taxes along with higher tax collection targets to officials only result in needless aggression by tax officials in pursuit of honest tax payers more vigorously. The end result is indulging in frivolous cases, needless witch hunts, and unjustified demands from time to time for making payments to meet targets. The amendments in direct taxes in the last 4–5 years, new interpretations given to VAT, CENVAT and the increasing aggressive litigation have more or less nullified the benefit of reduction of tax slabs. The slew of new legislations such as DTC, GST and Companies Act will only result in a flood of disputes further diluting the benefit.

While there has been no study in increased compliance due to lower taxes, what has been achieved or (planned to be) through Laffer's curve principle could perhaps have been achieved through (i) simpler rules properly propagated, (ii) stricter enforcement, (iii) higher and deterrent punishment duly carried out and publicised and (iv) better governance standards within the government's various arms including reduction of corruption.

India should have aimed at 'governance optimality' instead of seeking 'tax optimality'. It should have looked to increase its tax rates to 20–22 per cent of GDP and simultaneously expand government services such as police, administration and justice in line with growing population. The target tax collection should have been worked out based on revenues needed to support the infrastructure and tax rates based on such requirements. Needless pursuit of Laffer's curve has only resulted in massive deficit of governance, increased unemployment and budget deficits.

B. BANKING REFORMS AND BASEL NORMS: WILL IT ENSURE FINANCIAL STABILITY OR INCLUSION?

For a country like India, the main goals of monetary systems are to (i) achieve financial inclusion, (ii) promote wider reach of formal systems so that the monetary policies have greater transmission efficiency and (iii) ensure that the systems channel society's savings into productive investments in the most effective way. Ensuring financial stability as the bank for international settlement, the author of Basel norms[18] assumes is just one of them.

While India has taken several measures to faithfully implement Basel II and now taking steps to graduate to Basel III, events of 2008 clearly indicate that India was perhaps its most faithful worshipper. Caution and risk management were at abysmal levels throughout the western world and the complicated financial structures that were found to be constructed by banks had not an iota of respect or concern either for the customers or the economy. Some vital questions about Basel norms in the Indian context are discussed below.

Stability Prescriptions versus Structural Problems

In the last few years, if one were to add up the profitability of investment banks and reckon the relative share of savers, investors and the intermediaries, it would be clear that the intermediaries and the banks are getting fatter at a faster rate than either savers or investors in the real sector.

In conventional economics, savings and investments are supply and demand curves of the same savings market, with the price being interest rates. But, increasingly, this market is being split into two distinctive markets—one between the savers and the intermediary banks, and, two, between the intermediaries and the investors. This gives them an upper hand at both ends and leads to lower rates to savers (and usurious charges as witnessed in credit cards) and maybe higher interest rates to corporate (especially smaller ones).

[18] A set of recommended rules and regulation issued by the Basel Committee on Banking Supervision meant to protect banking systems against failures by providing adequate capital for taking care of risks they are exposed to.

Any regulation such as Basel norms, however well-meaning, acts as an entry or continuation barrier. Consolidation becomes a necessity. Some central banks have spliced Basel norms further with their own 'size ensures safety' minimum capital requirements in value terms, which further shrink the number of players. Thus, it pits the large number of retail savers against a few banks, and the savers are denied the benefits of 'perfect' competition and higher price (interest) for their savings. Banks in several countries merrily indulge in various kinds of monopolistic practices an offshoot of disproportionate market power, besides of course the ever increasing spreads between their borrowing and lending. This means investors pay more and savers receive less and the resultant lower savings and investments can reduce the economy's growth rates.

Does It Do Enough on Stability Issues?

Firstly, commercial banks, whose primary source of funds is the personal financial savings (savings and current deposits from retail customers), are increasingly investing in the stock market, risky instruments and derivatives on a proprietary basis. Or they fund clients who do.

While the profits on this belong to the shareholders and the management and traders manning the various desks in the form of bonuses, losses are offloaded onto the unwary savings and current account holders in case of bank failures. It is unethical to pile such losses on those who have neither contractually nor implicitly authorised the banks to undertake such financial trapeze-jumping.

Since Basel's primary concern is risks, it had an obligation to create a fool-proof firewall between these two activities. It has not dealt with this question.

Secondly, as things stand today, profits on notional valuation gains on investments and statutory liquidity ratios (due to interest rate variations) can be distributed as dividends on ordinary stock in most countries, leaving the coffers empty when valuations suffer with increasing interest rates. Again, there is no reasonable ruling here.

There was a lot that needed to be done on the credit rating and assessment procedures of the banks in most countries. These are found wanting, time and again, in most countries and as events in 2008–09 proved, the biggest culprits are the banks in advanced economies. They come under fleeting scrutiny immediately after every crisis but fade from memory immediately thereafter.

Lastly, several of the prescriptions have no proven basis to ensure that the loss will be limited at a given level. How can a single set of weights ensure same results right across the globe? A corporate guarantee may be exercised in one country in 1 month, but when one is talking of a Dabhol (of Enron) in India, even a sovereign guarantee can take a generation to exercise. Standardised norms fail to capture the idiosyncrasies of individual markets.

Does It Ensure Effective Financial Systems?

In most emerging economies (and particularly India), the reach of the formal systems has to substantially improve for the central bank's own good so that its monetary policy changes will have more depth and potency as well as enable its developmental initiatives impact faster.

Most informal markets have their own logic, their credit practices are safe by convention even if they are not exactly Basel-compliant, fragile by structure but excellent in track record in meeting social objectives (e.g. micro credit institutions in Bangladesh).

Basel norms may make our domestic banks shrink slowly from serving our peculiar social objectives and some others which are within the formal fold now—not exactly what a developmental economist would have ordered.

Perhaps Basel has to re-define its purpose to 'evolving/developing effective financial systems' rather than just 'financial stability'.

Perhaps we would need to evolve our own Bombay norms which take the right lessons from Basel in actual operation in line with our objectives and concerns.

C. EQUITY MARKETS: HOW PURPOSEFUL?

Indian stock market systems—trading platforms, settlement systems, regulations—are perhaps amongst the best in the world today. The government has also been continuously giving various incentives—80cc, incentives for Equity Linked Savings Scheme, very low tax rates for capital gains on stocks, etc. Equity markets are for mobilising savings for funding the risk capital requirements of enterprises.

Table 2.6 presents the amount raised through primary equity issues as a per cent of gross domestic savings (GDS).

Table 2.6 Amount Raised in Primary Market (Equity)

	Amount Raised		**GDS**	**Equity/GDS**
Year	**No.**	**₹ Cr**	**₹ Cr**	**%**
2000–01	138	3,226	515,545	0.6
2001–02	15	1,272	585,374	0.2
2002–03	17	1,457	656,230	0.2
2003–04	51	18,949	823,775	2.3
2004–05	55	24,388	1,050,703	2.3
2005–06	138	27,372	1,235,151	2.2
2006–07	121	32,901	1,485,909	2.2
2007–08	120	79,739	1,836,332	4.3
2008–09	45	14,272	1,802,620	0.8
2009–10	72	54,875	2,182,970	2.5
2010–11	80	57,667	2,481,931	2.3
Total	852	316,118	14,656,540	2.2

Source: SEBI Website for primary issues of equity. Economic Survey, 2011–12 for GDS (Appendix Table 1.5).

Despite the several initiatives, incentives and publicity and making the best of platforms available, the performance has been rather lukewarm. In the last 10 years, primary markets issuances of equity have accounted for just 2.2 per cent of GDS; retail subscription will be even less. Is it worth the effort if its performance even after 30–40 years is so abysmal? Or have we built systems and infrastructure far ahead of time?

Indians for reasons explained elsewhere seem to prefer gold and real estate as preferred form of real savings and bank deposits as financial savings. They seem to be uncomfortable with equity as a savings instrument. Apart from the business-cycle risks, there are also the huge counterparty risks (risk of fly by night operators) and whenever the going is good, there are slew of issues from companies who sell their stories for a quick money mop up only to vanish without a trace thereafter. The response of the system to trace and punish these and thus act as a deterrent in the future is rather poor.

Need for a Viable Alternative

Our regulators have done wonderful work on introduction of several instruments in the Indian markets—including mutual funds, derivatives like stock-specific futures, index futures, options, etc. Some of these are the first in world variety and in any case the products available match comparable standards in the world.

The role and efficacy of derivative instruments in mobilising primary money for growth is suspect. It is more about re-cycling. Heightened interest in trading does not necessarily mean higher volumes in initial or secondary public offers, which is what should count.

There is a serious need to design an equity instrument (or hybrids) which reflects the characteristics that gold or real estate exhibit. India has to construct an equity instrument which ensures capital preservation even if it offers low current yields. It should also have ready liquidity and marketability (like gold) in rural and semi-urban areas. Voting rights (in equities) hardly seems to matter in our context as much as safety of 'real' (adjusted for inflation) value of capital.

Equity the way it has evolved in the West simply does not seem to fit our buyer/investor psyche or requirements. There seems to be no point in insisting on this dead horse to deliver.

While there is apathy form the savers towards equity, the ever increasing rules, regulations and compliance requirements on the issuers of equity have made more companies question the wisdom of staying listed. Of late, one is seeing increasing urge to de-list from the exchanges. If the momentum picks up what we will be left with is sophisticated systems but neither savers nor issuers—a kind of world class orchestra playing to a deaf audience.

D. FUTURES AND OPTIONS: DOES IT HELP OUR CAUSE?

There are debates on whether futures and options should be banned and these are held to be contributory to farmer suicides and price spirals which take place from time to time.

World oil prices have been on hovering above $100 per barrel for almost a decade even though the cost of production of costlier marginal wells are supposedly less than half of this. Even 30 years of organisation of petroleum exporting countries cartelisation prior to this spell did not cause this kind of spiral or maintain it at that level. The excessive element of speculation that has crept into oil trades seems to be the chief reason for holding up prices.

How does the futures and options or indeed any derivatives affect the market and offer protection to buyers or sellers. It is necessary to understand this for anyone to conclude whether it is beneficial or otherwise and to whom.

Speculators Tend to Gain More Than Actual Players

Speculators in derivatives are basically price predictors and make their profits from price differential. Quite often their volumes far outweigh the actual physical transactions (in the global forex markets, the speculative transactions not involving delivery are widely estimated to be 98 per cent of all trades; the actual transaction is only 2 per cent). Their influence in price movement is therefore far more than what the actual players exercise.

But traders are also analysers of data, and they analyse the weather, cropping pattern, demand by industry or end consumers, etc. It is possible to come to similar conclusions by most of them if not all. This makes for uni-directional movement even if there are contrarians and it will only slow down the pace of movement than influence the direction itself.

In this herd mentality situation those who are inside the ring are the first to move in or out. The actual buyers and sellers usually sense the trends much later due to their preoccupation with real activity. If the actual buyers or sellers are large corporate customers, it is possible that they will track the movements and the underlying forces far more diligently than individuals. Our farmers, however big (the maximum permissible land holding size for agriculture in most states is 50 acres per person and the average in most states is only about 2 acres) lack the training, wherewithal and time to do these analyses and time their action ahead of or at least along with traders.

Constraints on Use by Actual Players

Even if they do their analysis, being producers quite often they have no choice—they cannot burn their growing crop, or start new ones mid-season or switch from one crop to another just because the price trends in futures markets suggest so. What use are the price signals emanating from futures and options mid-way through the crop cycle?

Thus, the profits from price movements will largely accrue to people who analyse data and predict prices and executes trades accordingly than the physical producers or users. Even if they get a share of it, they still have to part with a good share of it with traders who have no part in production or consumption. This surely eats away from the total kitty and may in the longer run dilute the incentives to the actual users and affect cropping patterns.

There is a Jataka tale where a do-gooder Bodhisatva living in Varanasi who had for ever done charity one day asks for all the grass in the city's vicinity to be delivered to him. Although puzzled the residents feel so morally bound to him that they readily oblige. The following day a large trader of Arabian horses arrives in the city to sell his horses in what is an annual exercise. But to his surprise he finds there are no feeds for his horses anywhere in the vicinity of Varanasi. When he realises he has been cornered, in an act of desperation he sells half his herd for the blades of grass with the Bodhisatva. Thus, much of the profit accrues to the hoarder than to the horse breeder or the users of horse. It is possible that a disproportionate (to economic value addition) share of the profits accrues to traders than the actual users diminishing their incentive.

It should be remembered that futures prices (or premiums) are not static like MSPs. They move from day to day. It is not that all trades are put through at the same time and price and that the actual producers will all get a sort of price protection. The prices in the subsequent round may not be same as the first round and may not be economical enough in the successive rounds to offer the seller the required protection. What may be the point to the seller if the futures price settle at ₹10/kg of sugar or to the buyer if it settles at ₹100/kg—just the same way oil has settled at $100/barrel now putting most of net buyers in deep distress. Even producers who have benefitted may be scared to open new oil wells or open wells which were closed when oil prices were below $50–60 due to fear that once they open the prices may move sharply enough and make it a unviable decision in retrospect.

The arguments presented both for and against in the media and before the Sen Committee appointed to study this subject seems to largely miss this vital point. It might be far more helpful if the government gives a minimum price protection (or promises to buy a minimum quantity from the market). Futures may not be the only way or the most equitable or cost-effective way.

Meaningful Information Dissemination

The farmers should be able to plan their crop pattern for the ensuing season so that they do not end up producing something that faces a glut when it arrives in the market. Instead of exploring ways to make this happen, both sides of argument seem to exclusively concentrate on whether futures cause volatilities or price inflation and related arguments.

The farmers ideally require price signals at the local market level within which his produce is likely to find use, whatever the number of intermediaries it passes through. This would require demand supply analysis at the local (district or even lower) level and information on cropping patterns, sown area and weather conditions at the micro level. It is doubtful whether the futures traders will have this information with them or if they do would be inclined to part with it free of cost to actual end-users and serve the farmers interests. The economic value of information will be fully harvested by the futures traders by way of futures premiums and movements therein.

If the farming community's interest is central to the government's efforts, it should develop and disseminate information about cropping patterns, cost movements, demand supply aggregates, market by market at the state, district and, if need be, even lower levels and announce MSPs for all products well ahead of the cropping season (rather than guided by electoral timings) so that farmers can plan their cropping pattern properly in time rather than feel cheated in retrospect. This would perhaps help even futures traders analyse and give out meaningful price signals to the agricultural community.

2.12 The Myth of Delivery Losses

In recent years, politicians have made a great deal of noise about the inefficiencies in public service delivery. It was our late Prime Minister Rajiv Gandhi who first revealed that for every rupee the government spent only 15 paise (an 85:15 ratio) reached the intended beneficiary. This may be as true today as then.

As a fact, it may be correct; as an exhortation to his civil servants to control inefficiencies, essential, but if we are hoping for a dramatic improvement in delivery efficiencies it is probably hoping too much. Let us see why.

DISTRIBUTION IS A COSTLY EXERCISE

Let us look at the reasons for the emergence of low-cost airlines. The main reason as first articulated or publicised by the European low-cost airlines was the travel agents commission. The total distribution cost of tickets for the airlines in the pre-internet days, including the agents' commission at 9–12 per cent, charges paid to GDS,[19] credit card company's charges of up to 3 per cent, was 23–28 per cent presumably including periodic freebies, slab discounts, the system set-up, etc. No wonder eliminating some of these by Internet booking has led a whole new industry—the low-cost airlines, which make more money and more consistently than the full service airlines where making reasonable return on capital employed (ROCE) is more an exception than the rule.

Now, let us consider the delivery costs of FMCG products. Let us say the final price of a cream, bar of soap, soft drink or shampoo is ₹100. Knock off 10 per cent for retail margins; 1–2 per cent for last mile movement of goods and delivery to these points; 12–16 per cent CENVAT; 6 per cent for the town stockists or wholesalers; 2 per cent for the transport cost of reaching it to them from the state nodal point; 6–12 per cent state sales tax; 6 per cent for the state distributor; 3–4 per cent for insurance, transport, handling from factory to state distributors; and so on. In addition, there are

[19] Global distribution systems such as Amedeus, Apollo, Sabre, Galileo and Worldspan.

periodic price-offs, write-offs, two-for-one type schemes, product promotions, volume discounts and personnel costs along the channel. For the best in the business, these can be an additional 15–20 per cent.

These percentages are telescoping (that is, calculated on the cost up to the previous stage) and the FMCG company would not get even ₹40 for every ₹100 you pay. It could be much less. Deduct the advertising costs (which may be substantial for FMCG), sales overheads, interest and packaging costs (which are often 40 per cent of the core product costs).

The core product—the powder, paste or water—will not cost any more than 15–20 per cent of what you pay. Anyone involved in distribution function will testify to this. The 'Rajiv Gandhi ratio' will be 80:20.

If this is the case for private enterprise, are not we being rather hopeful in presuming that the government will do better? With the best of efforts, the 85:15 might become 80:20 or 75:25—good, but not enough to make deep inroads into poverty.

INDIA IS NOT ALONE

The World Bank's World Development Report (WDR) 2004 is full of lament after lament (they call it diagnosis) about how systems have failed and not delivered to expectations on every conceivable public service across countries such as Cameroon to Cambodia and Brazil to Bangladesh.

There is an essential difficulty in delivering services to people located in uneconomical numbers over a vast area and little buying power. How do you establish a postal system to deliver two letters a week to a village of 300 people living 4–5 km from the nearest mud road? How do you deliver affordable health care to the people sitting in a remote jungle, who are not literate, who blame fate and evil spirits for their illnesses and have not heard of medicine. Even the WDR does not seem to have a credible workable proposal capable of general application.

SMALL DELIVERY SIZE: A MAJOR CAUSE

One may argue that service is not goods and that costs in distribution of goods, such as interest, storage, insurance and transport, are not applicable to services. But laying electricity lines, building schools and primary health centres, so essential to deliver services, are even more capital- and interest-intensive than physical distribution. In addition, there are other hurdles and peculiarities—like the consumer marketing companies created ₹1 or 2 sachets for soaps and shampoos when the ₹20–30 packets were beyond the reach of the low-income groups. But we cannot create 'sachet' packets for many of the government services.

Breaking bulk in most of the government and social services had their practical limitations. While mobile libraries, mobile health care units, have been experimented, not all services are amenable to such encapsulation. One cannot encapsulate primary education in 2 weeks; one cannot construct toilets (even community level) at 1/24th the cost just because it is effectively used only for an hour a day.

In addition, many of the social services that the government wants to give are not still in the radar of hierarchy of wants of the recipients. For a man starving for the last few days, literacy, health care and sanitation are distant priorities.

Even commercial marketing involves sustained efforts over a long period even if the goods yield instant and visible gratification. The 'sustained efforts over a period of time but benefits years later' syndrome in education, literacy, family planning and so on adds to the lack of 'pull' factor and apathy. Overcoming these involves a lot of money. No doubt we should work on corruption levels and delivery efficiencies. But to rely exclusively would only deliver disappointment.

2.13 Regulation: Control by a New Name

MICRO CONTROLLING IN THE NAME OF REGULATION

In 2012, the Director General of Civil Aviation put restrictions on some low-cost airlines selling their first row seats (which have more leg-room) at a premium—a directive that can neither be justified as a measure of safety in the skies nor necessary for promoting orderly development of aviation industry.

Recently, the Competition Commission of India (the equivalent of Commissioner under the erstwhile Monopolies and Restrictive Trade Practices Act) slapped a hefty fine on India's leading real estate developer for defective contracting with its customers—a job that should have been left between the two contracting parties and civil courts.

Perhaps a more significant action of Competition Commission was a hefty fine for cartelisation on cement companies. Such huge fines have the effect of substantially re-writing the balance sheets and profit and loss accounts of affected companies, if implemented. What would be the compensation payable to several bankers, financiers and other stakeholders who deal with those companies in the meanwhile?

The itch to assert their authority in individual transactions, generally play the super 'saviour' and indulge in micro controlling is evident all too often.

These are not isolated instances betraying a lack of sense of reforms or the way to work it. There are several more examples in insurance, education, banking, stock markets, etc. Regulations should have largely focussed on developing appropriate market mechanisms and establishing rules for their orderly growth and effective functioning. Reforms required a different mindset and it would have served to accept lateral infusion of perspectives and experience.

What we have instead is the very same bureaucracy driving largely the same command and control structure in new names—regulators instead of being controllers. Probably instead of regulators we should have 'market development facilitators' with mindset, role and roster backing it appropriately.

Queerly most of the regulations on monopolies tend to define dominance and control based on size, market share, etc. These do not give due credence to whether the balance between buyers and sellers gets unduly distorted and dictated by one of the parties who is able to impose his will on the counterparty. If the concern is really that economic decisions should not be thus distorted by dominance, then we should be hearing as much about dominant buyers as well, which is not the case.

B2C TRANSACTION MORE PRONE TO MONOPOLISTIC EXPLOITATION THAN B2B

The biggest source of worry (where the counterparty enjoys dominant power) is the business-to-consumer (B2C) transaction where retail consumers and their decisions are unduly influenced to the advantage of business. A doctor who prescribes unwanted medical tests, a school which makes students take tests at its will and sells sundry services which the parent would not be able to refuse for fear of backlash, sellers indulging in clubbed sales, airlines and credit card companies indulging in usurious practices, are far more widespread and market distorting. In business-to-business (B2B) transaction, at least both may have the means to negotiate based on expert knowledge and if the deal is not fair, import the material in question (since most of them are freely importable now). But such an option is quite often not available to the end consumers. In B2C transactions, consumer courts address only a fraction of issues of undue influencing and their track record is not any different from our other courts.

CARTELISATION POTENTIALLY NOT AS HARMFUL AS MONOPOLIES

Pure monopolies are detrimental in that they can restrict output, since the volumes which maximise profits always are lower than volumes which match average cost with average prices, since average price tends to fall after a point.[20] This requires that the monopolist is able and willing in his self-interest to cut his volumes as needed. For successful cartelisation, it would require the group to imitate this behaviour and hence requires that they cut their production proportionately or one of them acts as a balancer and restricts his output for the whole group (as Saudi Arabia does in oil). Without such output restriction, no cartelisation will work to reduce its output.

In a situation (like cement industry) where there are several players, it is impossible to conceive that there are some good Samaritans who are foregoing their volumes for the greater good of the others. Each would be looking for the others to cut their volumes while surreptitiously trying to maximise its own. Given our cooperative instincts (this would be true anywhere else in the corporate world), it is almost impossible to find a Saudi Arabia kind of balancer in Indian business. In any case, most of the cement companies are operating at very high capacity, hardly an indication that output is being curtailed to drive up prices.

The price that is supposedly cartel induced can easily be discovered by the market players (where there are multiple players) by trial and error anyway.[21] In any case the market demand curve is independently determined (without the influence of cartel). Given a price there is only a given quantity that can be sold and the buyers would not be buying more than that volume anyway unless the cartels use coercive measures, which in B2B transaction is very difficult. Even in B2C transactions like in cement sales, the companies cannot force the end consumers to undertake construction against their will. They do not share the same relation as patients to greedy doctors, litigants to lawyers or priests to devotees.

[20] See *Economics of Imperfect Competition* (2nd edition) by Joan Robinson, page 144.

[21] Especially when the industry is operating near practical full capacity.

A MORE SOCIALLY PRODUCTIVE ROLE FOR COMPETITION COMMISSION

The role of competition commission should depend on the stage of development of a country. Instead of a fashionable purpose, given our state of markets it should have assumed a developmental role instead of a 'policing' or controlling role.

There are two areas which call for urgent development of a viable and functioning market—both areas where both demand and supply exist but the market is non-functional. First is food where there is plenty which coexists with persistent long-term hunger of a mass scale. The commission should work on models which will match these and remove this scourge. Sure there are models elsewhere which work. Myanmar and Vietnam—both supposedly non-market economies—manage their food markets far more efficiently. There are not many who face the situation of 'problems of plenty' and 'persistence of deprivation' together.

Next is power. Most areas in India have come to suffer from long hours of power cuts. Power is a basic infrastructure. There are plenty of capacities which have come but not used anywhere close to their optimal levels. The commission should work on ways and structures to put the two together and make use of what we have.

Development of working models in these two areas would serve much more social purpose than catching some over-pricing or orders on how airlines should sell their preferred seats.

2.14 Four Factors of Production: Whither Indian Reforms?

Is India more liberal and reformed than before reforms began in 1991? Out of the four factors of production, *entrepreneurship* definitely has taken firmer roots than ever before. More and more people are venturing out on their own at all stages of their career and the number of people who are calling it quits mid-way to try out something on their own is increasing.

Capital definitely has become easier to access from domestic markets as well as abroad. Domestic companies are no longer afraid of taking over foreign companies bigger than themselves and making a success of it—which reflects both the enhanced risk taking ability and availability of capital.

But the bigger issues are on the other factors—one which India is supposed to be abundant in, i.e. labour and one which India is extremely short of, i.e. land.

While India has surplus *labour*, it is largely unskilled. There were sure signs of easing of tensions due to labour cartelisation and strikes before reforms to a period of tranquillity during reforms despite some pronouncements by leftist leaning parties. But events of late such as the strikes in Maruti seem to signify return of the hard lined ways. But the more harmful phenomenon is the steep increase in the labour price due to employment intervention programmes which have greatly diluted the work discipline. It is a sorry state that the productivity adjusted wage levels instead of adjusting downwards to absorb excess labour has increased steeply thus making it difficult to absorb them in alternative employment. The equilibrium level of *real wages* has gone and stabilised itself so high that industry will find it uneconomical to employ more of them and hence be indirectly forced to seek ways to mechanise more and more—exactly the opposite of what India needed.

Lastly *land*. We needed some meaningful reforms on urgent basis on this front. India has been having permanent problems with matters concerning land and real estate. Urban land ceiling and rent control acts created whole lot of disgruntled landlords and criminal elements who took care of their grievances in an extra judicial way. Growth of industry and urbanisation required supply of land at reasonable prices and it required imaginative policies to ease natural constraints of supply. What we have instead are legislative measures which add artificial barriers on top of natural constraints and increase price of land sharply in most areas.

Thus, while we have done away with some existing constraints, we have created some new ones. The transition from controls to regulation seems more of 'everything is same except the name' than a meaningful graduation to rule-based markets working efficiently.

No wonder it is showing in our relative laggardness in performance during reforms compared to East Asian neighbours. When the world (EU excepted) was seeing green shoots of growth by 2010–11 after the 2008–09 meltdown, India is besotted with problems such as high food inflation, interest rates high enough to de-energise investments, burgeoning subsidies resulting in high budget deficits, currency which has sharply depreciated during 2011–12 and 2012–13, infrastructure which refuses to either attract investments or grow. The growth rates have started drifting downwards dangerously towards pre-reform rates.

Besides the above, India's economic decision making has been a hostage to a flawed democracy where an absolute political majority has been elusive of late. Moreover, corruption distorted economic incentives and operated as a surrogate licensing system. But at least it provided a way of getting things done. But the judgement in early 2012, however correct, cancelling telecom licences earlier issued, based on which billions of dollars had been invested into the country, has put paid to this and created an air of uncertainty in the investors' minds. Action through corruption and justifiable reversal thereof by judiciary is not the best recipe for a stable, sustainable or attractive investment climate.

Chapter 3

GETTING SOME BASICS RIGHT

Injustice, poverty, slavery, ignorance—these may be cured by reform or revolution. But men do not live only by fighting evils. They live by positive goals, individual and collective, a vast variety of them, seldom predictable, at times incompatible.

—Isaiah Berlin in *Political Ideas in the Twentieth Century* (1969)

Chapter 2 looked at some areas where the reform measures have been designed on false logic, in defiance of basic economic tenets, divorced from social ground level realities and hence are prone more to deliver diluted results. This chapter looks at some issues in our economic sphere where we need to get our actions right and properly focused in order to make reforms more effective.

This chapter also looks at ways of achieving better financial and social inclusion, need and ways of recovering appropriate prices and ways to tone down corruption. We need to build a more productive attitudinal infrastructure (even ahead of physical infrastructure) in order to squeeze better value out of our systems. These require some innovative thinking, and often counter intuitive programmes. All these are a vital necessity not only for better budget management but also for achieving higher growth and employment—the surest way to remove poverty.

3.1 Achieving Financial Inclusion

We have argued in the last chapter how the high discounting rates (or interest rates) that the poor and rural people have to pay blunt the effectiveness of intervention programmes in education, subsidies, etc. The interest rates for industry and urban consumers and home buyers are far below the rates that the rural poor have to pay. This is primarily due to lack of seamless integration in our financial markets.

If only credit expands and is made available at the same rates (after due adjustments for size and risk) as for industry to people in rural areas and to the poor, many of the problems afflicting our poor and disadvantaged can be solved very effectively within a reasonably short time frame. Poverty and credit default–induced farmer suicides can thus be well addressed. Social emergencies need not push families permanently into poverty. Asset creation in rural areas will be faster and it is possible that more children will spend more time in schools with less family pressures.

FINANCIAL INCLUSION DEFINED

Financial inclusion[1] (a term not so properly defined till date) should enable a single homogenous discounting rate for all social or economic decisions at the collective or individual level. The savings of the society should freely move from savers to investors and those who need them (even for consumption needs) in a seamless manner without any structural, legal or systemic rigidity. People should get credit at around the same rate whether they are at Kalanhandi District or Kanpur, and a Mumbaikar should be able to invest and benefit from the interest rates prevailing in Meghalaya, Munger or Madurai. The system should provide for seamless movement of money.

[1] The word itself is delusional. Financial integration may have been a better terminology to use. India has enough savings rate. It is just how to make it available across the organised sector and the un-organised, between the urban and rural, between those who have security and those without.

Such a situation would equalise the interest rates for everyone across the country whether savers looking for earning interest or borrowers looking for funds. It will greatly enhance effectiveness of monetary policy and achieve interest rates in the band of say 10–30 per cent across the country. The rate should be different only for reasons of differing credit risk perceptions, high per unit transaction costs due to low ticket size and repayment risks. Two ideas even if largely counter intuitive are examined below for accelerating financial inclusion with a greater certainty.

A. Free Up Interest Rates—Let the Banks Lend at 72 Per Cent or Whatever Rate

Controlling Both Price and Volume—An Impossibility

For years, our policy planners have been getting it wrong on the agriculture and rural credit and credit for the disadvantaged.

Elementary economics tells us that market interventions work best when we try to control either price or quantity. Attempting both simultaneously is a sure recipe for failure. This is precisely what our monetary credit experts have been attempting to do all along. The main approach down the ages has been to mandate interest rate and prescribe certain targets to be achieved. At other times, it is interest subvention or waiver of 2–3 per cent (ridiculous considering the prevailing rates) in the 'informal' markets in rural areas.

The interest rates mandated have just not interested the banks, which is why the achievements vis-à-vis the targets for such lending are pitiful. This has been going on for years. Given that deterrent individual punishments or cancellation of licences are not the RBI's methods of coercion, we need a fundamentally different approach.

Each moneylender is a monopolist within his village market, where there are only one or two moneylenders per village. The villagers are generally unlikely to go to other villages to borrow. If the supply of credit to the rural sector can be increased and competition created for the moneylenders' monopoly, interest rates will come down due to supply pressures.

The only way—perverse though it appears—is to let the banks lend at 28 per cent, 36 per cent, 72 per cent or whatever rate they seem comfortable with, even if it seems usurious. This will provide banks with adequate compensation for the high unit transaction costs given the geographical dispersion that such lending entails. When the intended beneficiaries are currently paying 36 per cent, 50 per cent and 3,650 per cent (if one considers the kind of schemes that involve returning ₹11 in the evening for ₹10 lent in the morning), 28 per cent and 36 per cent are hardly radical. At least, there would be an alternative channel to the moneylender whose recovery practices are dreadful and the only bankruptcy laws that the farmer is faced with is suicide.

Once the supply of funds expands, the borrower beneficiaries get comfortable and the banks achieve critical mass, the rates will drop by themselves. At the very least, after two or three cycles, we will have a 'working system' within the organised banking fold.

Need to Change Our Notion of 'Bankable' Credit

The other error of the officialdom is trying to change or reshape the market to suit our notions of what is good credit rather than accept the rural credit market as it is with all its idiosyncrasies steeped in social traditions and seemingly unviable practices in the eyes of copybook credit analysts.

When farmers go to the extent of taking their lives, voluntary credit default will be the last thing in their mind. (Whatever slackness in credit history has crept in is largely to be blamed on government actions announcing waivers and pardons from time to time destroying the discipline.) Social shame in a closed village or small town circuit works as a far better deterrent than the combined potency of all our bankruptcy laws, debt recovery tribunals and corporate debt restructuring panels.

We have to get rid of our notions of what is 'bankable'. The farmers' consumption needs as much as those related to his agriculture or other ventures dictate the rural credit requirements. It is a composite credit where there is not much distinction between the farmers consumption needs and his agricultural (or other ventures) expenses. The strength and USP of the village moneylender is that he is willing to finance marriage expenses, funeral expenses, small ticket loans for medical emergencies, cattle purchase, house repair and so on. He can lend ₹20 or ₹20,000 at 8 p.m. or 6 a.m. All it takes is perhaps a couple of hours. No elaborate documentation, policy guidelines and head office approvals for him. He only has to be satisfied that the money will come back or can be made to come back. Personal knowledge of the borrower or his 'surety' is good enough reason for him to lend.

Our banks can fret about lending for non-production purposes, security not being tight, and that the loans not being self-liquidating. But that is what the market is. Changing it is a social effort that might take generations.

If the government is seriously concerned with farmers' welfare, it may be easier for the banks to change their ways to suit the prevalent market rather than waste efforts reshaping it. The banks and the Reserve Bank would need to reshape their existing notions of what constitutes security, surety, purpose, default and appropriate rates of interest. These need to be tuned to the Indian rural market realities rather than the distant Basel norms.

Perhaps the concept of non-performing assets (NPAs) for agri-loans would need to be scrapped altogether in favour of a small loans guarantee or insurance to our banks. The aim must be to get a firm foothold in the rural credit market and provide competition to the moneylenders rather than trying to change a 'market' in which it is not even a serious player. To illustrate, the Reserve Bank has debarred self-help groups from taking deposits even before they have made their market presence felt, when taking deposits would have made the rural folk develop a strong stake in them.

Patchwork tampering of the definition of NPAs as is being attempted now and then and policies like not insisting on 'security' (as bankers understand it currently) for less than ₹10,000 may not bring about earthshaking changes to the degree of financial inclusion.

Once the interest rates are completely freed for rural sector, more banks will be interested in setting up networks there and once the supply increases and experience builds up, interest costs will automatically drift downwards.

Freeing Up Deposit Rates in Rural Areas

The government should perhaps free up interest rates for the deposits as well in the rural areas. It could allow the banks to pay 36 per cent or 72 per cent in rural areas so long as the total quantum on which such interest is paid is not more than the lending in such areas—maybe district wise. This can also come with a ceiling of deposits say up to ₹2 lakhs, only one such deposit being allowed per public distribution system card. This will make more and more of them come to banking system rather than rely on chit funds and shady schemes which go burst from time to time.

B. Co-opt Moneylenders as Part of Formal System and Provide Them a Safety Net

The farmer suicide is perhaps the most discussed but least understood issue. Is the moneylender, who is blamed for much of rural suicides, guilty as charged?

If blood or the blood vessels are poisoned or afflicted with cancer, the physician does not create a parallel blood circulation system to administer medicine. He uses the same circulatory system to inject curative drugs. Likewise, the monetary experts should learn to use the existing network of moneylenders in the informal sector. Extending credit guarantees to rural moneylenders (rather than treating them as adversaries) may soften interest rates, reduce recovery pressure and bring down farmer suicides.

Money Lending—An Essential Service

Moneylenders perform an essential service. Commercial banks can never supplant them. By taking the moneylender out of the rural areas, the rate of suicides and the degree of despair will only raise, not abate. The structure of their pricing (interest rates) is the irritant.

The 'usurious' pricing is due to two sets of factors. The first is the poor quality of security, lack of proper registration records and poor enforceability due to legal delays, besides the low ticket size and the high unit transaction cost.

The second factor is the embedded (in interest rates) 'premiums' charged for credit default risks. Given the highly uncertain nature of the borrowers' cash flows and not much back-up of 'quick assets', it would be foolish not to factor it in the price (the interest rate).

Moneylender's Perspective

By diversifying risks, insurers bring down the credit default premiums substantially. Credit risk diversification is achieved normally by spreading the risks geographically or over time periods. For the rural moneylender, there are practical constraints in both.

Let us look at it from the moneylender's perspective. The entire money he has invested in his money lending business is his personal money as prone to risk as 'equity'. If there is a crop failure in the village due to poor monsoon, floods or any other reason, his money is most definitely at risk, even if he is not the one who is in agriculture. Risks of loss by the borrower almost directly transmit to him. Since most moneylenders operate in one village or at best two-three adjacent villages, the scope for geographically spreading the risks is non-existent or limited. For commercial banks (or a general insurer), a credit failure in one zone is made up by normal/better performance elsewhere. Loss of crop in one area is made good by satisfactory performance in others. Not so for the village moneylender. So his interest rate builds in the likelihood of a drought/flood, loss due to crop failure, fire, etc.

Often, organised insurers charge higher premiums to take care of high perceived risks at the start but refund a portion of the premium by way of no- or low-claim discounts at renewal. A moneylender cannot initially charge a low interest and recover higher from only defaulters *post-facto*. So the moneylender charges higher interest upfront but does not feel obliged to return anything by way of bonus or discounts as organised insurers do.

The other way the organised insurers bring down credit risk costs is by using the reserves generated by the superior performance of business in one-time period to compensate for the adverse performance in other periods. But if a moneylender lends ₹100 at 50 per cent in one-time period and recovers the whole ₹150 at the end, the additional ₹50 is not a kind of 'reserve' or buffer for future failures. Rather the entire ₹150 becomes his new base equity or wealth to be as zealously protected as the original ₹100 and hence he continues to charge his 'normal' usurious interest rates on his new base.

Difficult to Diversify Risks

Any crop failure is as much a danger to the moneylender's wealth and survival as it is to his borrowers. Hence, in any adverse situation the follow-up by moneylenders is at its most vigorous. One way this chain can be broken is to take the village moneylender into the formal credit insurance fold. For a low premium of, say, 2–3 per cent (all-India recovery rates for rural loans are stated to be 98 per cent), it may be feasible to bring down their fear-induced default premiums built into the interest rates quite steeply.

Geographical diversification (and to a degree even inter-temporal diversification) can be done by the insurer. No doubt the moneylender will pressurise his borrowers to recover his 10–20 per cent (the minimum the insurers deduct from the claims) but that may not be as much as when his entire portfolio is in peril. This release from personal pressure will most definitely bring down the interest rate, money-lender pressure and the suicides.

Credit Guarantee

The government should extend the scheme of credit guarantee (of the deposit insurance and credit guarantee variety) to the rural moneylender. For a premium of 2–3 per cent, it can reimburse 80–85 per cent of loan failures. Maybe even with a cap per borrower of ₹2–3 lakhs.

If the government intends to give rural credit subsidy, it can route it through lower premiums or higher claim settlement ratios rather than through region- and crop-specific interventions which are highly politicised and not entirely justifiable. Credit insurance for moneylenders will more sharply bring down the interest rates than the combined efforts of formal system.

Co-opting the moneylenders or whatever existing credit systems prevailing in rural areas and assimilating them into the formal credit system, by providing them re-finance and credit insurance may be a much faster way of achieving financial integration.

3.2 Achieving Socio-economic Inclusion

While mobility of money across the country is essential for financial inclusion, mobility of labour and skills is essential for socio-economic inclusion. Modern economic growth is based on specialisation and each one or each community has to find his/its comparative advantage and specialise in areas where they can be the least cost producer or provider.

The policies of the government duly supplemented by the patronising arguments of NGOs have only prevented seamless integration and led to creation of ghettos. In Myanmar whose per capita income is about $600 and Vietnam (about $1,200), there is no begging on the streets even in remote interior areas, unlike India whose per capita income is over $1,400. Nor is there open defecation something that is witnessed even in the heart of Mumbai, the business capital of India.

There are pockets for tribals, urban slums, and pockets of oppressive wealth across which mobility of economic activities and labour seem rather constrained. If integrated, a person can sell his skills where it is most beneficial and economic activities can move to where they are cost-effective and this will gradually equalise income, wealth and welfare across geographic areas and various communities and lead to faster and better economic equality.

This would require skill development, removal of restrictions or impediments on movement of economic activity and needless patronisation of poor and tribals. An illustration of possible route to integrating tribal areas is examined below. The need for skill development and how it can contribute to socio-economic integration are covered in Chapter 4.

REASONS FOR POVERTY IN TRIBAL AREAS

Tribals are economically poor largely due to (i) poor skill levels, (ii) their low mobility—geographic and between skills/jobs and (iii) and in most cases, (not all) poor productivity of land. These factors make for an ideal combination of existence and perpetuation of poverty. Most objections of the government and NGOs against external intervention in tribal matters are about the alienation of land and displacement of tribals from their geography to unfamiliar territories. The argument in itself seems largely real and their concern valid, but fails to present an alternative workable solution for their upliftment.

Upgrading their skill sets is a difficult task. Skills which are imparted should be vocational, useful and take into account the local or regional constraints and needs and should generate income in a short time. The current system of mainstream education system into which the government is trying to integrate them is almost guaranteed to fail. A curriculum with which they have no immediate connect neither inspires them nor are they capable of getting through the system.

BARRIERS TO MOBILITY AMONGST LOW-SKILLED PEOPLE

Brazil embarked on a programme[2] in the late 1960s and 1970s for resettling Amazon tribals into fertile plains under a programme titled 'Land without men for men without land'. It resulted in a massive failure with hardly about 7000 families (out of a target of more than 100,000 families), finally re-settled after a decade of efforts and US$3.9 billion of expenditure. Ironically, the most significant impact of the programme was to make Brazil the largest debtor nation in the world then.

Geographic and job mobility are deeply psychological and hereditary and not too easy to overcome. Addressing the psychological barriers behind their attachments to land is crucial in finding a solution to tribal welfare. The fear of tribals, NGOs and government is very justified where it concerns acquisition for mineral exploitation and mining, where displacement becomes inevitable. But extending this fear to other activities which does not necessarily displace the tribals seems more disposed towards perpetuating their misery than solving it.

[2]*Source:* Burns (1970), as quoted by Barbara J. Cummings, 1990. *Dam the Rivers, Damn the People.* London: Earthscan Publications.

Much of tribal land is mostly dry, not adequately irrigated or fertile enough to sustain agriculture or of unfriendly terrain and yields from crops are rather low. However, since the skill sets of tribals are rather poor, whatever little income is generated now comes largely from fertility of land and hence the fear of the consequences of alienation from their land. But continued reliance on this land and restrictions on change of use and legal transfers can only perpetuate the low yields and low incomes.

NEED TO MOVE ECONOMIC ACTIVITY TO POORER AREAS

If it is unwise to move the tribals to other centres of economic activity, it is essential to move some economic activities to their area. Land use pattern has to so change that the economic value of land comes not from its fertility and productivity but being used for its 'load bearing' capacity to house other activities. This has to be done without uprooting the tribals even while transferring a meaningful part of the incremental benefits to them in return.

The government should work on incentivising shift of some low skill manufacture and services where land costs in urban areas may be a dampener. Sure the existing skill sets will not allow the tribals to assemble mobile phones and laptops, but there is no reason why biscuits and beedies and, papads and several articles of daily consumption have only to be made in urban areas. Some of these activities can be done only with minimal training and may be done within their own households assuaging displacement fears.

Likewise, many services such as training retreats, seeds and clone development in areas suitable for it, old age homes, education, tourism where possible, may also be shifted to these areas. Road connectivity and tele-connectivity might help here. These economic activities may not require large tracts of land like mining. Any diseconomies (such as increased transportation costs and connectivity issues) can be made good by the government by way of remission of duties and taxes.

While some tribals may participate directly in the production process, the others can start being employed as domestic helps, gardeners, baby sitters and so on, before graduating to higher skill jobs (and perhaps gain confidence about geographical mobility).

To make these feasible, it is essential to allow economic activities in tribal areas, appropriate changes in land use, provide for acquisition of land (by lease, right to use or purchase) at least in small parcels for commercial activities. The government may impose restrictions on proportion to total land that can be so transferred/changed within each area and impose development obligations including share in employment. To continue with the existing rules and increasing the cost of acquisition (like the Land Acquisition Bill) will only preserve their misery.

As a part of balanced regional development during our socialist days, the government encouraged private industrial groups to acquire land in rural and tribal areas to set up their units. The acquiring business groups—Birlas, Tatas, Singhanias, Dalmias, many public sector undertaking (PSU) steel companies and refineries, Lalbhais, Bangurs, ITCs, BHEL, SAIL, IOC, TVS and Murugappas have all developed the surrounding areas very well besides growing their business and industrial activity.

Besides providing employment, they have created schools, public parks, old age homes, undertake several social activities in the nearby areas, provide for free medical care besides help in adult education and skill development. These townships are so well contained and balanced that most of them look like small self-contained republics. Many of them have given free space to police stations, excise and tax authorities to facilitate better governance. When they have such a strong track record, for the government to have turned suspicious of their intent and place so many unproductive restrictions seems misplaced.

3.3 Let Us Stop the Excuse of 'Protecting the Poor' and Start Recovering Proper Prices

The low level of monetisation achieved so far is a telling barometer of the reach of our formal systems. The reach and penetration of our democracy (as indicated by our voting percentages) are far wider and effective than its cousins—judiciary, policing, economic activities, education, civic amenities, banking, etc. The effective reach of most economic activities like railways or banking is such that they can at best serve the richest 30 per cent of population. The reach of our education, policing and subsidies may be better at 50–60 per cent. Economic growth may be the preserve of the top half and the other segments may have largely to fend for themselves.

In most areas as seen in Chapter 2, the poor simply may have no way to access the benefits meant for them due to existing rigidities or systems. Hence using their name and arguing that the interest of the poor will be affected can only be bogus effort born out of ignorance. A couple of illustrations are presented below.

FLAWED LOGIC BEHIND NON-REVISION OF PETROL PRICES[3]

Crude oil has been on the boil and its price seems rooted at $90–100 plus per barrel for a fairly long time. The international prices seem more related to speculative forces and less to the cost structure. There are no visible signs of it coming down in the near future.

Even if the international prices are unjustifiable, keeping prices low for local consumers but continuing to pay higher market prices indirectly transfers government resources to

[3] The various data quoted in this section refer to different time periods from 2005 to 2011 and from various sources from the Internet and hence may not strictly add up.

people who consume more of fuel oils. Given our consumption pattern, those at the higher end are more likely to be benefitted far more than at the poorer end.

Other than making a few noises here and there, the successive governments have been clueless on their action plan to liberalise and letting the market find its own price. As usual, protecting the poor is the prime argument for inaction. The more the dithering the more steep the hike required to correct the imbalance. As usual, the nation seems set to reap 'democratic dividends' of indecision.

As with many cases, the argument of protecting the rural and urban poor is hopelessly hollow in this case too even as it causes huge deficits for the oil companies which will soon get reflected in the Union Budget deficit. The fiscal responsibility and budget management (FRBM) claims of having controlled the deficits (till about 2008) and claims, efforts and noises on controlling it thereafter will be meaningless without taking into account the oil deficits of the PSU oil companies.

Let us analyse how the poor are benefitted or impacted by examining the impact of petrol price increases on the urban and rural segments.

Impact in Rural Areas[4]

The rural poor can get affected (i) due to direct incidence of price hike on their consumption of fossil oil for its various uses such as lighting, heating, cooking and as energy for running various appliances, (ii) if price of any of their purchased inputs or consumption articles raise sharply due to freight increases or (iii) if their output prices suffer due to higher freight in transfer of output to the markets. Similar arguments

[4] The various percentage consumption shares in rural and urban areas quoted in this section and the next have been sourced from *Parisara* (December 2005), a newsletter of ENVIS (a project of Ministry of Environment and Forests, GOI).

will hold for urban poor as well. Let us see the impact from each of these.

The percentage of people using baser forms of fuel like wood, crop residues and cow-dung in rural areas touches 80–90 per cent in most parts of our country. These people are at the bottom-most pile in income and are unlikely to derive any benefit from government not increasing the prices. It is difficult to imagine that this segment which cannot afford kerosene and LPG for cooking will use them for running appliances or running tractors in their farms. The 6–7 per cent (but growing) using kerosene and LPG are the richest in the rural areas and it is questionable if they deserve protection.

Nearly half of rural population uses kerosene for lighting; but lighting and cooking fuels together account for less than 7 per cent of their consumption. Even if lighting is half of this, even a 20 per cent kerosene price hike will result in less than 0.7 per cent impact on their total consumption. There may be alternative ways to subsidise this impact.

Higher diesel and petrol prices may affect prices of farm inputs like fertilisers and prices of manufactured articles may go up due to higher freight. There is a separate subsidy mechanism for fertiliser which can be re-worked to cover the impact.

The price increases of manufactured articles from urban centres are unlikely to affect those below the poverty line and landless labourers since their only or main consumption will be food which is locally grown and consumed.

For those with marketable surplus (which is what is exchanged for manufactured products), the period from 2008 has been one of the best patches, through very steep increases in MSPs, which far overshadow the impact from fuel price increases. Prices of farm output transported from the rural to urban centres may increase but is unlikely to affect the rural population since it is at the originating end of traffic. It is more likely to impact the urban poor.

Impact on Urban Poor

Since 90 per cent of urban lighting is electricity based, the impact of higher prices of petro-products will be derived from coal price hikes and is unlikely to be as severe as for those using kerosene for lighting in rural areas. The percentages of households using firewood, kerosene and LPG for cooking in urban areas are 28 per cent, 21 per cent and 46 per cent, respectively.

Those using LPG are at the top end and may not deserve protection. Firewood prices may rise due to freight increase. For those using kerosene, the impact is direct. Ways have to be devised to reduce the impact on them.

The urban poor could be hurt by food price increases resulting from a hike in cost of transportation of food articles. If the hikes on public transport are contained hopefully the impact due to the latter can be contained. Bulk of petroleum energy is accounted for by transport, industry and power generation and household consumption accounts only for one-tenth of total consumption. While mass transportation may merit protection, it is difficult to see how and why individual transportation should be insulated; as people having private transport belong to the highest income bracket.

Undeserved Subsidies

Dithering on price hike is only overcrowding our roads and aiding pollution. While transportation cost of goods is likely to be impacted heavily, food grains transport (which merits the most protection) accounts for less than 10 per cent of total goods movement, it is difficult to see how transportation of mineral ores, manufactured goods like refrigerators and TVs and the raw materials for them, chemicals and computers, etc. which account for major portion of physical transport needs protection.

On close examination, it appears that the petroleum intensity in the consumption basket of the bottom 70 per cent of the population may not be much. Its intensity increases as one's income level increases. By adopting a common approach, the government is only doling out needless subsidies to those who least merit it and who may have to pay for it at a later date, when the government is forced to adjust the prices. The logic of protecting the poor sounds too hollow in this case.

HOW SOCIALISTIC AVERSION TO CHARGE PROPER PRICES HAS DERAILED RAILWAYS

Indian railways are a marvel. If any commercial organisation had been thwarted from raising its end product prices for 7–10 years on the trot, it would most likely have ended up in bankruptcy. Yet railways have not only survived but have maintained its service levels as good as any thriving public sector unit can.

Railways' Potential

At the time of independence, railways had a very good network which connected most parts of the country. It was in a unique position where its development could have delivered employment and growth across the country. It had good systems, a separate ministry and budget and civil services cadre.

Incidentally, railways were the first government arm (way back in 1850s under Lord Dalhousie)[5] to experiment with public–private partnership where railways guaranteed a specified return. At the end of the agreed period, railways retained the option to purchase the concessions and merge it with itself.

With such proven potential and history of pioneering efforts, it could have done a great deal more for reforms and

[5] *Source: India under the British—Lord Dalhousie—Holistic Thought.* edu.holisticthought.com.

contributed to its success. Railways today perhaps serve as a lesson in general how an aversion to raise prices guided by misplaced socialism can derail an organisation with great history and potential and how not to approach growth and development issues.

Misplaced Socialism

The socialist fever seems to afflict our railway ministers like none other. Over much of the reform years, they have all been loath to increase fares—passengers or freight rates, with the possible exception of Mr L.P. Yadav who increased the freight rates using more of economic logic than emotional arguments. But even he stopped short of increasing the passenger fares. 'Railways are social service' and 'poor need protection' are the common excuses given by successive railway ministers for their refusal to recover cost-inflation. A closer look at the facts reveals how untenable these excuses are; in fact, the railways subsidise the rich much more than they subsidise the poor. Let us see who benefits from the reluctance of railways to recover proper prices.

First, the freight concessions. Ninety per cent of the freight comes from nine items, with just coal, cement and iron ore alone accounting for about 70 per cent of freight movements.[6] It is difficult to see how concessions given for such items benefit the bottom (income wise) 70 per cent of the people whose primary (two-thirds) expenditure is on food; these benefit the industry more.

The per capita consumption of cement is far less in the rural areas compared to the urban, and richer areas. Food grains move more from the rural (production end) to the urban areas and freight concessions on these hardly benefit or affect the rural people who are at the originating end of traffic. India's food grains production in 2010–11 was 241.6 million

[6] See pages 167–69 of Indian Railways Annual Statistical Statements 2010–11.

metric tonnes. Railways moved 43.45 million metric tonnes of food grains.[7] This is just about 18 per cent of total production. Its role is mainly confined to interstate movement for Food Corporation of India (FCI).[8] It is hardly involved in intrastate movement and interior locations. Movement for FCI could be specifically subsidised.

Inverted Passenger Tariffs

Next, let us consider the rationale for non-revision of passenger fares, the reason for which varies from helping the poor to fighting price competition from airlines.

Fares for AC classes are not being raised for years on end, sometimes stretching to a decade. In 2010–11, AC first class passengers numbered 26 million (just about 0.2 per cent of the population). Since a person starting from base is likely to return, a maximum of 13 lakh people are likely users, even if we assume that nobody travels twice within a year. Many of these may be corporate users, railway officials on duty or travelling on privilege passes, or members of legislatures, etc.

In reality, if the number of unique fare-paying upper class passengers are counted, it may number no more than 2–3 lakhs. These surely are not from below poverty level (BPL) families. Many of these commuters can afford air travel, but choose rail transport for other reasons such as health, fear of air travel, and travel to destinations not served by air besides of course those who may prefer rail travel for reasons of economy.

The argument, sometimes advanced by the ministers, is that the railways have to compete against air travel. But if passengers have a better alternative and can afford it, why should they not be welcome to use it? Is wooing the rich with

[7] *Source:* Economic Survey 2011–12 and Year Book 2011–12 of Indian Railways.

[8] Railways account for almost 98 per cent of food grains movement of Food Corporation of India.

cheap fares, where alternatives already exist, our definition of social service?

Similarly, it is possible to show that upper class and AC coaches (II, III and chair car) serve, at best, the top 1–2 per cent of the population. And the non-AC sleeper coaches serve at best the top 20–25 per cent. Irony of ironies, the recovery per coach for the first AC is even less than for the II AC and III AC coaches (Table 3.1).

Daily travellers and season ticket holders (in EMUs, locals and as local commuters in express trains) comprise about 75 per cent of passenger traffic, four-fifth of which are residents in one of the four metros. For them existence of facilities in itself is the biggest subsidy. What is the alternative for, say, a person living in the suburbs with the office in city centres such as Nariman Point, Connaught Place, Park Circus or Parrys Corner? He has to either relocate and pay a higher rent, or to take up a job nearer home maybe for a lesser salary or perhaps even remain jobless. A 5 per cent concession (by not increasing the fare) on a monthly season ticket of ₹165 (which itself is a huge discounted fare) means ₹8 per month to him. (For the real poor who earn

Table 3.1 Yield Per Coach for Rajdhani between Delhi and Mumbai

		1st AC	2nd AC	3rd AC
Date	**No. of Berths**	**18**	**44**	**66**
Jun 2001	Fares (₹)	4,180	2,405	1,485
	Yield per coach	75,240	105,820	98,010
Feb 2005	Fares (₹)	4,135	2,210	1,485
	Yield per coach	74,430	97,240	98,010
Jul 2012	Fares (₹)	3,730	2,185	1,495
	Yield per coach	67,140	96,140	98,670

Source: Fare tables of Indian railways.
Notes: The new coaches have more berths in each class. However, for the sake of proper comparison, they have been kept at earlier levels. Yield per coach is rupees per trip for full distance at full capacity.

less than ₹400 per month—the real deserving—there have been specific concessions.)

Our railway system perhaps serves the top about 30 per cent of population. In freight considering the nature of goods carried, urban population is the prime beneficiary, except perhaps in the case of fertiliser, and to a much less degree cement and food, which can all be specifically targeted. As far as passenger traffic goes, 60 per cent of the express traffic is between lines connecting the four metros. More than four-fifths of its local commuters live in these metros. The railways' presence and reach in the interior rural and tribal areas where the majority of our poor live are negligible.

Consequences of Failure

Railways aversion to recover proper prices in line with inflation of costs has led to the following consequences:

1. If railways had recovered their costs at the same rate as WPI between 1990–91 and 2010–11, it would have been better off by almost ₹31,000 crore per annum which is over 30 per cent of its current gross revenues. An amount of this magnitude would have given it the ability to create new networks. Its actual expansion has been an abysmal 0.3 per cent per annum since Independence and 0.175 per cent since reforms. This has prevented expansion of services in under-served interior areas.
2. It has had to shed employment (this is discussed in Chapter 5).
3. It has compromised passenger safety and makes its customers travel in filthy surroundings with so many encroachers. The encroachers are disadvantaged since a systematic expansion would have eased their difficulty.

The government has shown a similar phobia for recovering commensurate prices for electricity, airport user charges, government libraries, national parks, road use, etc.

NEED TO RECOVER PROPER PRICES AND SAFEGUARDS

In the heart of Yangon, the erstwhile capital of Myanmar is the Kandawgyi Palace lake a public park with an entrance fees equivalent to ₹110 and is used largely by the morning walkers and day time sight seers. And the zoo not so far has an equivalent fee. Both places retain their natural beauty, provide clean environs and are litter free. It looks like the entry which is almost commercially priced is helping matters a great deal by providing funds for the proper upkeep of the facilities. A paying entrant is also more likely to value it better and hence less prone to damage it or litter around.

In contrast, Kolkata's Alipore Agri-Horticultural Society in one of the richest localities in India charges just ₹10 for casual walkers.

In most places around the world, most of such services are either handled by private commercial enterprises or where government is involved, pricing is not necessarily less than commercial. This should be helping in better upkeep,

Gurgaon Toll: Creating Value and Killing It

There was a recent court intervention on collection of tolls on the Delhi–Gurgaon road. The episode demonstrates the need for proper understanding of how value gets created for the customers. It also illustrates the need for designing efficient ways to recover the value created without destroying it in the process of collecting tolls.

If the main benefit of faster travel is negated by time wasted in 2-mile long queues, how can one feel that the contractor has understood the game? In that sense, the Court ruling is a fitting response, even if it sends wrong signals to potential investors in roads. After all several systems have been designed elsewhere, which do not cause any delay or hold-up. The toll collectors charge should have been linked to wait time (thus charging only for the net benefit to users) which would have made them come up with better systems of collection long back.

A discount should have been mandated for people who present exact change instead of oversized notes. The tolls prescribed (₹11 and ₹17 and so on) do not reflect alert minds which have understood the process. Maybe the contractor should also have a free-from-charge way for non-willing users to use and see for themselves the benefit of using toll roads in comparison.

maintenance, continuous upgradation of services, warding away non-serious users, besides being able to attract interested staff.

A proper understanding of the value creation process by the government is essential for proper pricing (see box). This would itself wean away our politicians from socialistic instincts.

Safeguards

Safeguards can of course be provided within limits, provided the rationale and target group are both clearly established. We need to have very clear rules of recovery, which may be on the following lines:

1. Goods and services which the poorest 40 per cent need and can access and is relevant to them (or which the government wants them to consume) and which is in their hierarchy of wants—subsidise so as to reach a desired consumption levels within a specified time.
2. Goods and services focussed on the next 30 per cent—at least recover costs.
3. For the top 30 per cent—what the market can bear and the government should continuously seek to discover prices. It should employ modern price harvest methods (*a la* low-cost airlines which have taken this to the level of science). Every differentiation needs to be charged and recovered and this should be used for improvement of services or serving the others.

Currently, there is hardly a differentiated approach to recovery of prices. We, Indians in general, are great bargainers and demand Virgin Atlantic first class levels of services in everything at low-cost airline prices and the government seems ever ready to oblige us. It compromises customers' interests in many ways such as increased safety hazards, diluted levels of availability, cleanliness, besides deteriorating service quality.

Charging Proper Prices—Best Way to Tame Corruption

As we have seen in Chapter 1, failure to recover appropriate prices is the main cause for corruption. Proper pricing will help in better demand management and facilitate gradual expansion of services in line with economy's growth without burning holes in the central budget.

3.4 Need to Build Attitudinal Infrastructure First

The Tokyo railway station has 20 platforms and handles about 3,000 trains per day—on an average one train per platform every 9 minutes (perhaps more frequently during peak hours). This includes the high speed bullet trains, long distance regional trains and locals. Our very own New Delhi station operates 300 trains from its 16 stations.

Imagine Tokyo train drivers become lethargic, people who prepare the trains develop a lax attitude, signal failures are not attended to punctually, irresponsible passengers pull chains for self-serving reasons and hence 5–10 minute delays become the order of the day. Passengers would not know which trains to board, there will be long chain of trains along the track, people will miss their connecting trains leading to chaos, and the throughput will drop down dramatically, maybe to the levels we are witnessing in New Delhi.

It seems only logical to attribute the near 10-fold higher capital efficiency of Tokyo systems (compared to Delhi) to training of staff, their pride in punctuality, duty consciousness of support staff and may be fear of punishment, time sense of travelling public, respect for rules and regulations, etc.—their superior 'attitudinal infrastructure', in short.

But this would have required that all those involved acted with a sense of ownership, accountability and proprietary interest, without motivated bureaucratic indecision (to prove ones superiority, get back at other departments or save one's own skin). We should shed the dreadful attitude 'if it does not pinch me personally, I need not feel morally responsible or accountable for any time, cost or other consequences'—even if it is an open trench in the middle of road, compromised passenger safety, wasting work in progress, etc.

BENEFITS

Our incremental capital output ratio (ICOR) of over 5 is shameful for our development stage. If the Tokyo train system, and Mumbai Dabbawalas, and the efficient way our Mumbai suburban railways operates are any guide, we should be able to increase our capital productivity by 15–20 per cent. We would be able to earn commercially viable returns on our infrastructure projects instead of shamefully screaming for concessions and capital subsidies.

With better civic sense, we will have cleaner and litter-free roads. Better empathy towards the victims and fair play would get us speedier justice instead of insensitive delays and get our income tax refunds on time. Better sense of ownership and accountability will surely reduce the quantum of food grains wasted in a country where hunger is the chief impediment to equality of opportunities.

Better highway sense will discourage highways being used as race tracks and cause needless deaths. Punctuality and a sense of guilt towards unduly benefitting at the expense of others will dissuade politicians from holding up airplanes and wasting precious time of co-passengers. A corruption-free mindset would give us Commonwealth Games that bring the nation pride, business and tourists and lasting infrastructure instead of shame and stress. Better respect for public property will definitely destroy less buses and trains and glass panes.

Needless horn honking, irritating queue jumping, spitting and littering, customer-insensitive tele-help desks, insensitive police may reduce considerably and enhance welfare.

Is it not then more imperative to develop this soft and invisible yet vital 'infrastructure' first before crying for more and more physical infrastructure?

RETURNS TO BETTER ATTITUDINAL INFRASTRUCTURE—AN ILLUSTRATION

Let us see the potential returns to better attitudinal infrastructure. The first place which captures the spirit of our social character, training, mindset and attitudes are our roads. The blaring sounds which needlessly scare others, zig-zagging our way through, signal jumping, road rage, crossing just about anywhere, using our vehicle to settle arguments or prove superiority are common. Heavy and slow moving trucks driving for miles on the rightmost lane next to divider meant for faster vehicles forcing others to overtake from left are the norms. There are the killers—protruding metal bars hanging out: even large socially responsible corporates indulge in such hazardous practices and rampant corruptions at RTOs which home deliver licences for a fee (without the need to present oneself at the testing centre).

These factors ultimately take their toll in terms of higher fatalities on the road. Our fatality rate due to road accident is one of the highest in the world even amongst countries with comparable population density. Table 3.2 presents some sample countries, the vehicle population and the fatalities from road accidents.

The higher death rates on our roads are the negative returns to our toxic road behaviour. Surely, these could be brought down by proper 'investments' on the vital 'attitudinal infrastructure'. Our population density is not the villain—Singapore's density is far more. It is more the lack of discipline and lack of will of the authorities to frame proper rules and even less to implement them. The number of precious lives that can be saved, the present value of the future earnings of lost lives, the emotional distress that are caused to the surviving families, the value of vehicles lost in accidents whether they are insured or not, the time lost due to traffic hold ups, etc. represent the potential returns from better discipline and behaviour on road.

Table 3.2 Incidence of Fatal Road Accidents

Year	Country	Population Density per sq km	No. of Regd. Vehicles (lakhs)	No. of Deaths	Deaths/ Vehicles (%)
2010	Brazil	23	648	43,869	0.068
2009	United States of America	34	2,590	35,490	0.014
2010	Thailand	130	285	26,312	0.092
2010	Indonesia	133	727	42,434	0.058
2010	China	143	2,071	275,983	0.133
2009	Italy	206	526	4,371	0.008
2010	Pakistan	225	79	30,131	0.384
2010	Viet Nam	280	332	21,651	0.065
2011	El Salvador	300	7	1,358	0.190
2010	Philippines	313	66	8,499	0.128
2010	Sri Lanka	329	40	2,854	0.072
2010	Japan	350	899	6,625	0.007
2009	Israel	352	25	352	0.014
2009	India	405	1,150	231,027	0.201
2010	Rwanda	439	1	2,118	2.264
2010	Bangladesh	1,161	16	17,289	1.064
2010	Singapore	7,252	9	259	0.027

Source: World Health Organisation for number of vehicles and deaths.
World Development Indicators for Population Density.

WAYS TO BUILD ATTITUDINAL INFRASTRUCTURE

Firstly, catch them young: It is imperative to teach our children in primary schools beneficial social habits and values (instead of perhaps history and geography). This should include appropriate civic sense, respect for queuing systems, time, road and public discipline, punctuality, etc. We should teach them not to use public property for release of public anger, consequences and punishments of breaking rules and law, clean sanitation habits, need to keep their surroundings clean, etc. Habits and values (beneficial or negative) formed at young age are difficult to break.

It should be followed through with propagation of work values, ethical professional conduct and need for standards of planning and punctuality, at higher education.

In countries such as Philippines, the schools run Good Manners and Right Conduct (GMRC) as a subject in their primary grades. This covers rules of proper behaviour, conduct in public, respect for rules, personal hygiene and upkeep, how to conduct oneself in public, etc. A similar initiative in India through grades 1 to 8 would help since most of what constitutes acceptable public behaviour is not instinctive but cultivated. Specific training modules should also be developed for road users, use of safety equipment in factories, queuing in public, good manners and decent ways of disposal of wastes, rules of roads for regular users as well as drivers of trucks, autos, etc., proper etiquette at sales counters, government offices, etc. Relevant people should be trained on the spot, workplace, schools and through media.

Secondly, we need to create pockets of excellence within India where the surrounding cleanliness, attitudes and fear of punishment begets proper public behaviour like when Indians visit abroad. Hopefully, it will spill over to other areas. The eastern state of Sikkim serves as an excellent indigenous example of what is possible.

Thirdly, fines and penalties. In India, most fines are a joke, never revised for ages and are hardly relevant or deterrent now. There is a serious need for making automatic revisions for all fines with inflation, benchmarked on the date of original legislation. Our court stamp fees in many states have remained at pre-independence levels. Fines and penalties under most acts and rules are pitifully low and are anything but a deterrent.

No system and rules will work without a system of reward for compliance and strict, swift and exemplary punishments for non-compliance. We need to put in place an infrastructure for enabling the same. Graffiti writers should be made to compensate the wall owners (maybe a market for graffiti will develop as a result), people who hold traffic for demonstration or damage public property charged with clean-up costs, and ill-gotten wealth confiscated.

It is of utmost importance that India addresses this issue forthwith. Our neighbours in East Asia seem to have a done lot better in this respect. With a better attitudinal infrastructure in place, our capital productivity will go up reducing capital requirements for a given target of growth. It is an investment worth making.

Building Social Habits through Legislation: Lessons from East Asia

The fines for over speeding in Vietnam even in highways are about $200 and payable (strictly) by the driver—not the owner. It is mostly impossible to rush up the drivers and make them go faster. The fines for drunken driving have been increased in late 2012 to $750 plus impounding of vehicles and cancellation of driving licence for a specified number of days. These are almost a half-year's average income—a level at which it achieves a good degree of deterrence. With these, they hope to achieve better traffic discipline in about 10–15 years—surely long-sighted action. (*Source:* Decree No. 71/2012/ND-CP dated 19 September 2012 of The Socialist Republic of Vietnam)

Singapore runs periodic nationwide campaigns, such as National Courtesy campaigns, smile campaigns, where everyone trains and practices to acquire new attitudes and behaviour traits. This has achieved nationwide results in short timeframes.

Vietnam has a hand washing day and is considering a book reading day to promote beneficial social habits. While these may be possible in small countries, India can attempt such initiatives city or region wise. (*Source:* 'Special day to encourage reading', *Viet Nam News,* 10 October 2012)

The Ministry of Tourism, China has issued a 'Manual on proper behaviour for Chinese citizens travelling Abroad' in 2006 mentioning amongst other things need for personal hygiene, advising against taking off shoes in public, not to talk loud, to treat people courteously, wait for their turn in line, etc. We need many such interventions to make ourselves contemporary to the world setting today.

Recently, Thailand banned all squat toilets replacing them with sit toilets. The matter was widely resisted and debated but carried due to various hygiene benefits. The subject has also been made a part of the curriculum to teach students how to use the sit toilets. (*Source: Bangkok Post,* 29 May 2013)

If the *Principle of Compensation* in economics justifies conscription of private assets for greater public good, even without compensation, Indian government should be deemed justified in making laws, rules and regulations for modifying private behaviour and building training systems to build better attitudinal infrastructure.

3.5 A Strong Lokpal for Breaking the Political Logjam and Reform Inertia

The earliest wakeup call that elections are not won on administrative capability or performance alone in India was delivered by the Dravidian parties in Tamil Nadu when they defeated one of the finest administrators—Chief Minister Kamaraj in the late 1960s. They sensed that the mood was for social change and simply changed the election plank—to social emancipation from administrative efficiency. To their credit, the social transformation has been mostly peacefully achieved. Some other states also fought the elections on social justice (even as of today), reservations for the underprivileged, etc.

But from there things degenerated into using emotive issues like Ram temple, river water sharing, personality-based politics, and in some cases like Assam and Punjab even cessation agendas for canvassing votes. The next stage of degeneration was the entry of money (and last minute indulgences like liquor, etc.) into politics. Money has a better marketability (for those living in utter misery, notes for votes make a lot of sense) than administrative track record or capability.

FRACTURED MANDATES

The multiplicity of planks leads to fractured mandates; the larger the voting area/population, the greater the factions.

Hence, the problem is more acute at national level than at state level or at municipalities. For the small parties, it made sense (even if they had no chance for forming the government) to win a few seats and bargain with major parties.

With our system of government where majority vote is essential, the 'last mile connectivity' small parties wield power and influence far disproportionate to their share of seats. Every legislative proposal is an opportunity for them. And the pay-offs for their support is primarily to turn a blind eye on their corruption. To counter competitive pressures, even the bigger state or national parties had to recruit 'fund raisers' who are basically corrupt or thrive on government largesse or illegal mining, etc. and tolerate them. These elements are as much prone to bargaining from within as small parties from outside.

HOW A STRONG LOKPAL HELPS MAINLINE POLITICAL PARTIES

A strong Lokpal[9] (and equivalents at state level) with strong implementation will greatly cut off the supply line of those whose only strength is using money for vote gathering. If this influence diminishes, and their chief bargaining power with bigger parties is diluted, a great many non-principled parties will vanish. A strong Lokpal can kick-start this process.

The present level of corruption is not fully explained by the election expenses. Once the corruption conduit is established, the individuals indulge in it freely and keep quite a bit themselves. It is simply not possible for the parent parties to establish accountability by segregating corruption and indulge the fund raisers for only authorised corruption but punish them for what is retained by themselves. Lokpal can deal with both at one go. If hopefully the 'base political corruption' reduces, the 'super structure' corruption at the administrative level also will fold back significantly.

[9] Lokpal is an anticorruption bill drafted by civil society in India. The Parliament has passed a diluted version recently.

Hopefully, the elimination of the corrupt and the unprincipled parties will bring about both consolidation and increased participation by saner elements—irrespective of their caste or economic status.

The other vote-catching device is the use of state exchequer to grant freebees. While some can be justified on socio-economic realities, many more are just competitive election practices. State level FRBMs and pressure to raise commensurate financing and keep their deficits within limits will force them to segregate the socially beneficial from the toxic and dilute the potential for misuse of freebees.

Thus, if the two main planks—money and use of state purse to serve party interests—are de-fanged, it will eliminate a lot of players. This can only be beneficial to national and administratively capable parties (who are as of now at the mercy of very many small or unprincipled parties). Even within these parties, those who align themselves to the party ideology will get prominence—not those who are mere fund raisers.

No doubt, some emotive issues will rear their head from time to time. Issues like reservations will favour some parties. But when the winning or losing margins are just 2–3 per cent in most cases, a consolidation of votes of even 10–12 per cent away from money-influenced to real issues will largely favour the mainstream parties. It will most likely result in a ruling coalition of three to four parties facing an opposition of seven to eight parties than a 15 party ruling coalition facing 30–40 opposition coalition.

Social processes are not entirely predictable; there are bound to be many impediments in reversing the degenerative trends that have formed in the last two decades in our democracy. But it may benefit our larger parties much more and thus the country if there is consolidation. Lokpal might provide the right initial fodder. Even if the corruption level comes down, it can make citizens breathe easier—a reward in itself. It might prove largely beneficial to our mainline parties to give it a try.

3.6 Economic Value of Official Pronouncements and Public Debates

PANICKY VERSUS REASSURING PRONOUNCEMENTS

We were once travelling to Johannesburg (South Africa) from Mumbai in the monsoon time. It was pouring outside. While taxiing for take-off, the captain came on the line to announce, 'Ladies and gentlemen, as you can see we are taking off in monsoon weather in Mumbai. I expect some heavy turbulence between minute number three and minute seven. After that we will be over the clouds. Be careful and keep the seat belts on and do not move about. I will get back to you after I switch off the seat belt signs by minute nine (9). Enjoy the flight.'

We could see many faces relax into smiles after the announcement. From clutching the seat in front of me, I slouched on to my backrest feeling considerably easy reassured by the confident tone of the captain. Just to be aware that he is sensitive to the risks and the passengers' concerns and the feeling that the captain seemed on top of the situation itself made everyone breathe easy.

Imagine a captain with equal concern announcing: 'Ladies and Gentlemen, as you can see we are flying into heavy monsoon weather. Do not worry. I am an experienced captain and I have seen several such take-offs. It is better to be safe than sorry. So please fasten your seat belt and as a matter of abundant precaution, get into a bracing position, rest your head against the seat in front of you and clutch it firmly and pray till we get over the clouds and turbulence stops.'

Would that have made anyone feel safer or assured them? Doubtful. It would have only created panic in the cabin. The former is an appropriate mixture of being aware of the risks, self-assured voice and meaningful information sharing. The latter is not likely to defuse anxiety, is vague in its promise and does not share meaningful information available with the captain to a larger audience to make them comfortable.

Many of our official pronouncements and public debate seem to belong to the latter variety.

NEED TO COMMUNICATE CAUTION IN REASSURING WAYS

By June 2013, India seemed to be emerging from the sustained inflation of the previous 2–3 years. Things seemed to be getting back under control. There were potent signs of interest rates easing, which is so essential for growth. The capital and money markets were beginning to look buoyant and there was an air of expectation that growth was poised upwards.

Then came a couple of sharp announcements from RBI that it does not see things the same way. Despite considerable easing of inflation, it saw more head winds and that it did not see scope of interest rates being reversed anytime soon. But then RBI was not alone. Even the statements by Finance Ministry and the chief economic advisor's office did not do much to convey confidence.

Their 'cautious pronouncements' (communicating risks without an action plan from people and institutions in charge) and the appearance of mutual discordance made the markets (sensex) tank by 7.4 per cent between 30 May and 20 June and market cap of BSE Sensex was wiped off by about ₹123,000 crore. Dollar leapfrogged to ₹60 from 54 to 55 levels.[10] These are hardly the appropriate advertisements for boosting investments, leave alone attracting funds from abroad.

Sure, buildings did not shrink by 8–10 per cent due to RBI's or other's announcements; nor did the assets of business vaporise or people get thrown out of jobs overnight. The losses were notional in nature. Pronouncements alone did

[10] Sensex which was 20,215 on 30 May came down to 18,719 by 20 June 2013. Market capitalisation of sensex stocks came down during the same period from ₹16.61 lakh crore to ₹15.38 lakh crore.

not cause the crash (sudden surge in gold imports and tightening of quantitative easing were perhaps the more dominant reasons), nor is it RBI's job to protect sensex. But it affected the sentiments and would have postponed several investments. In such situations, there are costs involved in reviving the investment friendly atmosphere through fiscal incentives, policy changes and other appeasements. The cost and losses involved should be reckoned as the economic costs of official pronouncements.

The institutions, agencies or people vested with the responsibility should be sensitive to such not so overt losses and where possible made accountable for such social costs and losses.

A more sagacious and responsible approach would have been to share the details and the reasons for expected headwinds and communicate the actions being taken to tackle the same. That would have sounded a lot more welcoming and helped to cool down the heat and perhaps help maintain sentiments. Moral suasion as an important arm of monetary policy is an art altogether forgotten these days. Caution itself should be communicated in a cautious manner so as not to disturb investment sentiments particularly if India believes in investment led growth.

RECKLESS DEBATES AND SHORT-TERM ORIENTATION

In most of our discourses within the legislatures or newsdailies and more starkly in TV, the debates are capable of only leaving negative sentiments. Settling scores in public whether by politicians or public servants causes a lot more damage than between the immediate people involved. The social damage needs to be contained and we need a more responsible approach in these matters. Freedom should extend only to highlighting failures with a view to improve them which can be socially value accretive.

Most of the corporate frauds in the last decade or so in the developed world have occurred due to the pressure of producing short-term results. The stock market players have a time horizon far shorter than what physical projects imply. But the mutual fund managers and analysts driven by their compensation compulsions and investor objectives demand spectacular growth in sales and profit after tax (PAT) every quarter. In order to meet these targets, managers in the real sector resort to mergers and take-overs that defy logic and seem flawed.

It appears that even the governments are not free from this. With global mobility of funds, even the ministers are put to test almost every day and year through a running commentary of every move of theirs. In the long term, such a course will influence them to take measures that do damage to the economy's long-term interest.

Alternative Growth Path

PART II

There is no royal road to anything. One thing at a time and all things in succession. That which grows slowly endures.

—Josiah Holland

AN ALTERNATIVE APPROACH

While Part I was about analysis of the present, Part II is about action plans for the future. It is about incorporating lessons from our broken programmes so that we can accelerate our growth, justify our potential and hopefully solve our societal problems faster and in a more sure footed way.

India is the second most populous country and hence is attractive to most marketers. India's per capita consumption in most products and services compared to the current world averages is comparatively low. Even if one assumes that India will catch up with the current world averages 20 years later, in most product categories it would yield an annual growth rate of 12–15 per cent. However, this is a highly fictitious argument.

In this scenario, it is almost suicidal to start with liberalising imports of goods and services at the pace at which it was actually done. Opening up our markets further through free trade agreements led to increasing the share of machines in production either through imports or through more mechanised and competitive players taking bigger share in production. This marginalises sections of labour who could have otherwise found employment in the production of such goods. Take away IT sector and the secondary income streams it has created, India may have been tottering to maintain the even pre-reform growth rates. Perhaps the misplaced strategy is the main reason for job loss or jobless growth that we have witnessed for most part of reform years.

We have started at the wrong end. We should have started with developing 'fit-for-purpose' skill sets (instead of focussing excessively on education) and supplemented it with some rapid creation of 'low skill, low wage' employment. This would have created some demand for products which would have led to growth in share of industries. Secondary cycles would have absorbed more such labour and when the labour is near total absorption, we should have opened up our markets for imports at the consumption end and higher end technology at the production end. Obviously, the timing in different sector for opening up would have differed from industry to industry.

Such an approach and sequencing was also necessary given the paucity of land and excessive number of people dependent on it and the need to absorb them in industry and service sectors. Our economists have neither got the timing right nor the sequencing: probably no one has applied his mind.

While developing skills and commensurate employment are necessary, it is also vital to keep in mind that markets do not always evolve in ways socially desirable, or at the required speed. It has its own nervousness, risk aversion, lack of foresight, besides several other shortcomings.

The government has a role to play in balancing things and creating market structures or legislations which support employment in socially desirable or economically productive ventures. Even in doing so, it should refrain from setting or dictating prices to the markets, or get into the 'how much' question.

India's track record in 'distributing' growth is dismal. We simply seem to have abandoned the economic engine for achieving this and have started resorting to subsidy culture to deliver incomes to people. Growth has just not ensured inclusion (financial or economic or social). Employment creation (especially low wage kind) is a far better way of achieving inclusion. *The power of growth to create equivalent employment may be far lesser than the certainty of employment leading to commensurate growth*. Between growth and employment for most Indians, the preference at the individual level is likely to be the latter.

This Part is about 'developing skills, creating employment and creating proper market structures' as the alternative growth path and examines ways of giving effect to this approach and implementing it effectively. We look at creating certain new growth engines which complements the above steps to make 12 per cent growth rates achievable in perhaps a more equitable way. It is aimed at delivering results to people who have waited the longest, containing social consequences by working with existing resources and strengths.

Chapter 4

REORIENTING EDUCATION TO DEVELOP SKILLS

Not only is there no God, but try getting a plumber on weekends.
—Woody Allen in *Getting Even* (1971)

SKILLS (NOT LABOUR) AS A FACTOR OF PRODUCTION

Labour is often talked of as one of the four factors of production. Ideally, it should have been 'skill sets'. Only when an individual is trained and prepared to execute any specified job with some proficiency, he can meaningfully participate from the supply side. Truth be told, India today is seriously short of *labour* which is imposing a compelling constraint on growth. Since the basic ingredient is available in plenty, it presents a huge opportunity for quickly easing it and thus harvesting the low hanging fruit for immediate gains.

The main purpose of education should be to put some saleable skills in the hands of the recipient for sustained livelihood. For this, the skill sets and capabilities that people acquire should be in demand so that people can get jobs and earn their livelihood and on the other hand the society gets the skills it requires. Let us see how well our policies through the years before or since reforms have served this twin purposes.

Somehow our education system has not evolved with times and seems stuck to its colonial past. School education by rote and a curriculum oriented mainly towards transfer of knowledge seems to be the main direction of our education.

The current system of education is capable of supplying more clerks, secretarial staff, government servants, office assistants, etc. But it is seriously doubtful if it will at least be contemporary if not future-ready going forward, given the stagnation in our education system and administration.

There have been some talks and actions by the government for skill development. Government has instituted a three-tier structure and as per latest statistics available,[1] about 1,300 modules for training have been formulated. Seven thousand training centres have been approved and over 1.2 million people have been trained or tested by these centres. Viewed against the probable requirements, it is too miniscule an effort as to make a dent yet. The Department of School Education and Literacy, Ministry of Human Resource Development (MHRD), has this to admit in its website overview:

> India is referred to as a "young nation" with 28 million population of youth being added every year. Only about 2.5 million vocational training seats are available in the country, whereas about 12.8 million persons enter the labour market every year. About 90 per cent of employment opportunities require vocational skills, something that is not being imparted on a large scale in schools and colleges.

This chapter looks at the need and socio-economic reasons to reorient our education system from stuffing education to imparting skills and a possible yet effective way of funding skill development.

SIX PER CENT EXPENDITURE ON EDUCATION MAY BE WASTEFUL

The last couple of plans have sought to increase the expenditure on education to 6 per cent of gross domestic product (GDP) from around 3 per cent levels currently. The higher

[1] As per Economic Survey 2011–12.

spends, it is hoped would increase the literacy levels, enhance chances of employment and thus reduce incidence of poverty. While raising the required resources is one impediment, the more essential poser is 'even if the proposed increase in spends is achieved and sustained, what will it actually achieve?'

The public expenditure on education in India has been about 2.75 per cent of GDP since Independence. Granted that it has increased literacy[2] and provided jobs for some, created some world class managers, but it has also created an ever swelling army of educated unemployed. The strength of these is growing relentlessly and so is their frustration besides a sense of lack of hope for those joining their ranks. It appears that the marginal efficacy of educational spends is beyond the optimum level even at 2.75 per cent. The existing programmes seem ill-suited and require drastic course correction as there are several countries including in Asia who have achieved much higher literacy levels with 3–4 per cent levels in a shorter period.

How well people demand education depends largely on the demand and supply conditions in the labour market. For this reason, the 6 per cent rationale beats elementary economic logic for it seeks to tackle the problem from the wrong end. The market for education is an intermediate market; the final market is the labour market. In the labour market, there is already an excess supply of educated youth. Any increase in spends on education will only end up increasing the supply of labour and create further unemployment. While at the higher end like IITs and IIMs, the demand today is far higher than available supply; at lower levels, the current education curriculum seems hardly capable of ensuring employment.

[2] We seem to have a far diluted definition of literacy as compared to even our East Asian neighbours. The level of civic sense, discipline in public places, awareness and respect for road rules and laws, queuing sense, sensitivity to others in public, personal hygiene, cleanliness, ability to understand and execute requests at several customer touch-points which one sees as a tourist to other countries point in that direction.

How Skill Development Helps

The reasons for poor productivity of labour in India may be the low level of capital available per labour. But equally potent are the low level of skills and lack of training, absence of facilities and mechanisms for continuous upgradation of skills. Learning on the job is the primary method of acquiring skills in most trades. There is a lack of prescribed skill levels (and certifying mechanisms) for plying/practicing most trades, including potentially hazardous ones like electrical maintenance, construction, etc. *Firstly*, these need to be tackled at systemic levels if our abundant labour is to be converted to cost-effective labour, with which India can compete in the global markets.

Skill-based training and education will increase availability of skilled manpower and hopefully reduce the effective cost to end-users due to lesser wastage induced by trial and error training while on the job. Just as availability of reliable and quality products makes for better demand, demand for readymade skills will most likely increase from the industry.

Secondly, a trained baker, launderer, plumber, computer mechanic, truck driver, etc. is more likely than an untrained one to start some single hand/micro enterprise, since the essential phobia in pursuing many of these is lack of skill. In a way it boosts the demand for labour since a micro entrepreneur creates his own job and is both the demand and supply of labour.

Thirdly, in the absence of proper skill development and training, much of the benefits of our economic growth in the last decade and a half have gone to automated teller machines, internet, standardised solutions instead of tailored solutions, i.e. to capital in general.

We need a more controlled upgradation of technology either by direct measures or fiscal measures. Most of the technology developed for the retail 'point of contact with customers' level which have become ubiquitous of late are premised on low availability of labour and high labour costs of the

Western hemisphere. The Indian scenario just does not fit that description—not yet.

Economic growth creates demand for a wide variety of skills existing as well as new ones—for baby sitters, truck drivers, welders to more polite and knowledgeable tourist guides, fashion designers to better equipped cine artists, cameramen, carpenters, plumbers, bakers, masons, etc. A growing economy calls for upgradation of skill levels of several existing trades. People would definitely prefer better and more versatile tailors, carpenters, *purohit*s, plumbers, etc. whose education does not come only from trial and error at the customers' expense. Just recount the kind of educational infrastructure we have created all these years to deliver these—far less than what is needed. For example, there are just 29 institutes[3] for training people in hospitality so essential for tourism and the capacity is about one-twentieth the general purpose 'management graduates'.

It looks therefore imperative that even if India wants to double the education spends, there is great and pressing need for a drastic change in focus from education of the current variety to equipping people with 'usable/saleable skills'.

Inadequate Capacities for Skill Creation

Polytechnics and ITIs are more effective in developing usable trade skills than abstract education. But there are fewer diploma level institutes with lesser intake capacity than graduate engineering colleges, private and governments taken together, as per the Department of Education's website. The number of seats at ITI level seems even less—a strange situation where we have higher capacities for higher-order education than those focussed on basic technical skills, which should logically have a wider appeal (Table 4.1).

[3] *Source:* Website of Ministry of Tourism, GOI.

Table 4.1 Number of Seats Offered for Technical Education

	Engg./Tech/ Architecture Colleges	Polytechnics	ITIs and ITCs (Industrial Training Centres)
No. of units (September 2009)	2,894	1,914	2,140 Government ITIs 6,116 Private ITCs
Seats offered (approx and estimated)	20 lakhs	10 lakhs	10 lakhs

Source: Department of Science Education and Technology, MHRD.

Besides inadequate capacity, the breadth of skills for which they offer courses is rather limited at just about 114 of them as on date. It was almost frozen at about 36 trade skills for about 50 years of independence till about a decade back. It leaves out several skills, is slow to respond to emerging needs and characterised by rigidity—every skill had to fit into a 1-year course or 3 years; had to have a standardised input qualification and opportunities for mid-career upgradation of skills are low to non-existent.

It would be more useful if we would have a system which will impart at least these lower-order skills to anyone who seeks it rather than bother too much on qualifying parameters. It would make much more sense than guaranteeing just primary or secondary education through Right to Education (RTE). Our approach should be to integrate education with skill development in a far more seamless manner rather than treat these as two parallel issues.

Top-up Efforts

As seen in Chapter 2, people may drop out of school at various stages. This is perhaps a blessing in disguise. Things would have been very difficult to manage if everyone wanted to study till graduation.

Whatever the stage, the government should promise at its expense (free or subsidised) a top-up skill development or training modules which will make them a productive resource in the end-user market. Such training can address development of trade skills, attitudinal training, work ethics, safety practices, rights and responsibilities, personal hygiene and care. For those likely to be self-employed, negotiation skills, appreciation to fulfil contractual obligations, may be necessary. These may differ in intensity depending on levels and trade but there is a definite need and the promised return on such investments may be large enough to surprise us. Hopefully, the increased expenditure will address these issues rather than take the beaten track and add mass to the frustrated unemployed.

FUNDING AND MAINTAINING TRANSITION

The first 30–40 years after independence, the government devoted itself to filling entrepreneurial deficit. It invested in heavy industries, essential infrastructure and those it considered would create positive externalities through forward and backward linkages. This was supposed to result in conducive conditions for private sector industries to flourish in sectors which make use of infrastructure so created. It also invested in areas where private sector was shy for fear of failure, or size of investment or where it did not see sufficiently large demand even if it were essential.

The private sector now is mature and confident. It is able to access the banking system and capital markets here and abroad for mobilising funds for investments. It is time the government re-focuses its priorities and addresses the skill deficit.

The government should set aside a portion (say 10–15 per cent) of its divestment proceeds for its new focus area. Even if the divestment itself runs slow, a specified portion of the yields from its current investments can be assigned for this purpose. Hopefully, the resistance at least from political quarters will be lower given the end use.

It can make use of existing facilities in other institutions such as schools, colleges and polytechnics for running its courses in non-working hours or run short-term courses when those institutions are closed for vacations.

It can make these courses a part of NREGA where a portion of the wages is adjusted against fees. The corporate sector can be given off-sets against their requirement of CSR spends for fees disbursed to such centres besides perhaps mandating them for sponsoring a specified number of people whether employed with them or not.

Perhaps the time has come when instead of attaining 100 per cent literacy, putting an employable skill or two in every adult's hands in the next 10 years should be prime aim of our manpower development efforts. This will serve both the labour and the employers as it will optimise the effective cost of labour which is supposedly our key comparative advantage.

We need to make our education and skill development efforts more sharply focussed. It should almost border on the government telling the target groups *show me your prospective employer; we will train you for the skills for which he is employing you at a subsidised price.*

Chapter 5

CREATING EMPLOYMENT

Growth for the sake of growth is the ideology of the cancer cell.

—Edward Abbey

Employment has been one of the biggest casualties of our reforms. If the socialist era of the first 40 years of independence was about lack of growth, the reforms era is all about lack of jobs.

Indian socialism till the 1990s was too machine oriented with a heavy dosage of investments in heavy industries, ports, steel plants, auto sector. Despite this however, the rate of growth in organised sector employment exceeded the rate of growth of population between 1971 and 1980. In the next 10 years, the rate of employment creation was lower than population growth but still very healthy. But the reform policies have accelerated promoting mechanised wealth-concentrating growth at the expense of wealth-spreading growth, which after a decade of reforms started causing job losses. Between 1990 and 2000, job creation was 6 per cent against an increase of over 20 per cent in population. And during 2000 to 2010, while the population growth has fallen to 16 per cent from over 20 per cent earlier, the rate of job creation fell sharply to 2.68 per cent—hardly the right recipe for winning over people to reforms (Table 5.1).

The reason for this decelerating growth in employment is not far difficult to see. Reforms have opened the flood gates for technology and capital required for higher degree of mechanisation. Ideally, capital would first flow towards such

Table 5.1 Employment in Organised Sector

	Public	Private	Total	Population
Years	Numbers (million)			
1971	11.10	6.73	17.83	567
1980	15.12	7.24	22.36	700
1990	18.77	7.58	26.35	874
2000	19.31	8.65	27.96	1,054
2010	17.86	10.79	28.65	1,225
	Decennial Growth Rates (%)			
	Public	Private	Total	Population
1971–80	36.22	7.58	25.41	23.5
1980–90	24.14	4.70	17.84	24.9
1990–2000	2.88	14.12	6.11	20.6
2000–2010	-7.51	24.74	2.47	16.2

Source: Compiled from Economic Surveys. Population from World Bank, Development Indicators.

areas and sectors where the strength of demand and profitability has already been proven. Before committing irreversible capital investments, it is but natural to look for such zones to minimise risks of failures. It is difficult to imagine, why anyone would come to an under developed market to design new products and ideas, and commit capital investments and risk capital loss. Hence, increased mechanisation of existing areas is inevitable and job losses become a corollary.

The only area where employment has grown significantly between 1990 and till date has been the software sector. Employment in IT and ITES has grown from about 2.8 lakhs in 1990 to 106 lakhs in 2010 (both direct and indirect employment taken together).[1] But for the fortunes of this sector, there could have been a major social backlash on reforms and perhaps at the society level.

[1] Economic Survey 2010–11, page 252.

INVERTED POLICIES

In a capital-short and labour-surplus economy, tax policies should have incentivised conservation of capital while maximising usage of labour. Instead, successive governments have been providing investment allowances and accelerated depreciation, which encourage use of more capital than less of it; there has hardly been a scheme for maximising use of labour.

Flawed investment policies complemented the misdirected fiscal policies. There has been no effective policy towards diffusion of technology, which would come in handy for the geographical spread of industry and growth of micro industries which serve labour and rural areas much better than the behemoth industrial units. Even less comprehensible is the way 'small-scale industry' is defined by the amount of capital employed. A more result-oriented definition would have been based on the labour-to-output ratio (the higher the labour percentage, the better), labour-to-capital ratio, or the number of man-days of jobs created per sales, output or value-added. These more focussed ratios have never entered the calculations in our governmental policies at any point of time. If Tisco was able to create 7.5 lakh jobs instead of the 75,000, why cannot we ignore the size and accord it 'employment promotion industry' status and give it small-scale industry benefits and thus promote employment?

Most of the public investments from the 1950s have been in industries which were on an average even more capital intensive than private sector's. Refineries typically created one job per ₹75–100 lakhs of sales and ₹60–90 lakh investments (by the late 1970s) when, given the stage of development, there were sectors that created 5–10 times that level of employment for similar level of sales and investments. It is difficult to argue that private initiative was lacking in these sectors, rather the government was busy chasing private sector out of such capital guzzlers (like nationalising Air India, steel sector, oil sector, defence supplies, etc.).

EMPLOYMENT GENERATION OR GROWTH: THE VITAL QUESTION

It appears reasonable to conclude that our strategy of increasing the mechanisation/capitalisation content seems to have run ahead of time. It would work when labour markets are tight and employment near full and further growth is not feasible without increased mechanisation. Our official unemployment is about 10 per cent, number of people in live registers of employment exchanges is about 40 million but with disguised unemployment it could be 30–40 per cent unemployment. A more sensitive and sensible approach to employment creation is the need of the hour.

Figure 5.1[2] presents the yearly growth in organised sector employment and real gross domestic product (GDP) during reforms years. It has seen a continuous decline till 2003–04—which perhaps explains why all governments during this

Figure 5.1 Employment (Organised Sector) and Real GDP Growth Rates during Reform Years

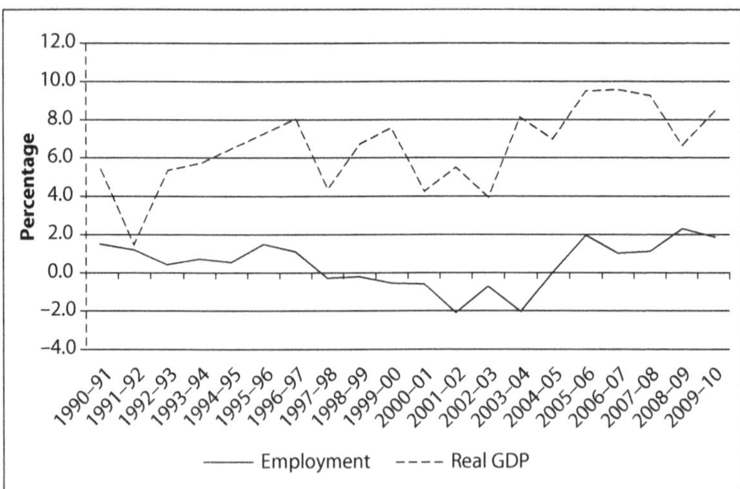

[2] Data for the graph have been sourced from *Handbook of Statistics*, RBI.

period lost their ensuing elections. Reforms are for the people and the primary way they benefit in India is by way of employment.

It is not the argument that employment growth should numerically match the GDP growth rates. But a secular decline over an extended period when the population is growing is a sure recipe for social unrest. Employment should grow at least in line with population and organised sector employment should grow way faster to reduce the unemployment.

A VITAL QUESTION

An 8 per cent per annum GDP growth witnessed in the last few years has not produced 8 per cent employment growth, but will 8 per cent employment growth produce 8 per cent GDP growth?

Suppose the government budgets and achieves 8 per cent employment growth. It should translate, with some lenient assumptions, into a GDP growth of at least 8 per cent if the average income of the newly employed is near the current average per capita income.[3] Even creation of jobs that pay only marginally above subsistence wages in India would still result in about 5–6 per cent growth in GDP. An annual 8 per cent employment growth (in an economy where population is expanding at about 1.5 per cent per annum) even if it means a slower GDP growth of 5–6 per cent per annum can wipe out poverty and the resultant disaffection with the government policies in a more sure-footed way within a decade than the reform strategies pursued in the last 20 years.

Designing sustainable employment models in line with our current strengths and social imperatives is a necessity along with choice of appropriate technology as illustrated in the next section.

[3] It will be lesser as the average income of the newly employed increases.

5.1 Creating Sustainable Employment Models

One of the few well-rounded employment guarantee models the author has seen is the Panchakki water mill of Mughal vintage in Aurangabad. The water mill delivered marketable value that the society needed, which sustained both the asset and the people dependent on it. It was environmentally friendly, based on sustained water flow (naturally occurring), and left no debris.

Employment guarantee schemes should aim at creating assets that provide goods or services which are the priority requirement of the villages or their target markets and are capable of being run economically after the assets are created. Most of the current schemes relate to rural *kutcha* road construction, pond or village tank projects and the like. Such schemes create assets whose ownership is public in nature (and hence nobody cares), and generate value which is not amenable to being priced and hence vanish over a period.

Most of our current employment intervention programmes are 'dig a hole, fill it up' Keynesian variety plans which may provide temporary solutions to get out of recession but are not good enough as a developmental effort.

SOME SCHEMES FOR SUSTAINABLE EMPLOYMENT

Most of our villages lack public transport. With 200 families on an average, it is difficult to sustain round-the-clock bus services. If, instead, one villager is given a mini-van/autorickshaw, it will provide employment to at least one family.

The vehicle would be available to the villagers whenever they want. It is right-sized and can hence be kept going, even with the lower revenues. It can further be used for twin purposes—to transport people or goods. Shorn of all the taxes, advertising and other marketing expenses, it should be possible to price such vehicle at about ₹2 lakhs. The government can finance this under any of its various schemes and recover the capital from the 'owners' depending on the revenue generated, with incentives for accelerated repayments.

One could rope in the private sector in administering the scheme—the vehicle manufacturers would be interested since it gives them access to a large market—six lakh (the number of villages) units every 7 years (assumed economic life of each vehicle) is not a small number. Similar assets can be created in solar power generators, bio-gas plants, large TV sets (surrogate mini-theatres), mobile phone booths, etc.

If it is economically viable, why would the people have not done it themselves already? The current price of some of these assets and the lack of skills and high financing costs are deterrents. But the government could make them viable options by cutting the channel margins, taxes and duties, stocking costs and promotion. The government could finance the auto makers but make them responsible for recoveries from beneficiaries.

A proviso could be that the asset would revert to the government (or the funding agency) if repayments are not commensurate with the revenues generated and the person concerned can be barred from participating in further schemes for a specified period.

There are models[4] operating in Bihar engineered by IITians with assistance from University of Virginia's Darden School of Business where micro power plants at village level generate power from locally available rice husks. Every 1.5 kg of risk husk generates 1 kWh of power to be locally used (and hence no transmission loss). The remains from the power plant are used in making incense sticks by womenfolk. Each power plant which manages to supply enough electricity for 3–4 villages reduces kerosene and diesel consumption by 42,000 litres and 18,000 litres, respectively, besides cutting carbon emissions.

[4] See Usha Rai, 'Bihar's Husk Power' in *The Hindu Business Line*, 20 October 2012.

There are also other earlier experiments of power generation at village levels using biomass, illustrating how for an investment of ₹3–4 lakhs, biomass is converted to 2,000 kWh of electricity of an annual value of say ₹120,000—a sum[5] that can employ two–three people including maybe a woodcutter, the fuel-wood grower and the machine operators.

Two thousand kWh for a village is a sustainable consumption. If one such plant were to be installed in each of the villages in India, it would cost ₹19,000 crore (for six lakh villages)—a sum less than even 1 year's NREGA expenditure. And much of this can come out of the electricity subsidy given to our villages.

Such models have the advantage of private ownership and the associated maintenance care. These assets can be used elsewhere if they do not find enough use in the particular village, unlike ponds, roads, and irrigation systems which cannot be transplanted elsewhere. Recoveries can be continuously re-cycled and the programmes can run over a longer time; pond digging and rural road laying would come to a halt sooner or later.

Agricultural output is not going to fall because 5–10 families out of the 200 get out of their 'disguised employment' status. The people who are taken out will engage themselves in new jobs. Others would pay them for the new services enjoyed. Thus, it creates additional output for the village.

In such close-loop models, the multiplier effect will more likely be played out within the village rather than outside. There may be secondary employment creation.

The need of the hour is to design such employment programmes. Our NREGA is not a sustainable model. It can unintentionally stabilise income at low levels and impede growth beyond a point. Once it is withdrawn, it would lead to collapse of demand in rural areas. It is more important that we create sustainable employment opportunities based on

[5] Perhaps much more if marginal prices to consumers or total costs to society including cost of loss in transmission are duly reckoned.

marketable goods and services rather than ones based on doles and external infusion.

5.2 Inappropriate Choice of Technology

AN ILLUSTRATION FROM GOLDEN QUADRILATERAL: RIGHT ROADS BUT WRONG WAYS TO BUILD THEM

The Golden Quadrilateral (GQ) road scheme must stand out as one of the achievements during the reforms period. Even the most die-hard critic will find it difficult to puncture too many holes in its implementation.

Having lived within 500 yards of a national highway under development, the author has witnessed its various stages of development and has been an immediate beneficiary. The pace is frenetic, something perhaps even the private sector would find hard to match. The roads are good, and where both directions are complete, one can zip through at maximum speed. The vehicle is the limit to speed not the roads any more.

FLAWED BALANCE IN OUR PUBLIC EXPENDITURE PROGRAMMES

But the way these roads are built raises serious questions on the nature, purpose and efficacy of our public investment programmes. And most crucial is the choice of technology: should it be governed by modernity of technology or socio-economic imperatives.

Let us raise a hypothetical question. Suppose God were to grant a magic wand which would give instantly twice as much as all that the society needs, but the wand were to be given to only one person who shall get paid quid *pro quo* by the rest of society. Would any sane economist accept such a proposition? Unlikely. The others would have no productive activity which has economic value and hence may not have the wherewithal to pay the one waving the wand and such a society will soon degenerate into near absolute poverty despite having the means to produce all that it wanted. Public expenditure programmes whose payouts are concentrated in too few hands have very little social impact. Ideally, the payouts should be as broad based as possible.

Public works programmes have several objectives, one of which is asset creation. And the objectives of employment creation, buffering economic cycles, creating positive externalities for other economic activities to become viable, balancing growth and so on cannot and should not be thrown away at the altar of the speed of asset creation. It was one of the mistakes of Nehruvian socialism that they chose, in a relative sense though, airports and aircrafts, BHELs, Nalcos and Balcos and the like. These do not allow too much of substitution of labour for capital. After all, one cannot employ people instead of aircraft to ferry passengers through air, nor use people to generate heat or convert ore into steel.

Projects such as road, dams, waterways qualify very well for public investment for their scalability (or divisibility), shiftability (both across regions and time periods) to meet the objectives of balanced regional development, countering economic cycles and so on. Most important, they are excellent in their higher employment generation potential for a given level of investment as they are non-standardised in nature. But unfortunately, Golden Quadrilateral as well as its equivalents seems condemned to repeat the mistakes of the past.

CREATING LIFETIME EMPLOYMENT OUT OF GOLDEN QUADRILATERAL

For instance, in Mumbai, some 55–60 flyovers were built in 4–5 years between late 1990 and early 2000s. The construction looked more like an assembly line production, what with bulldozers, pneumatic drills, cranes and mixers working round the clock. Surely, these machines found employment and may have created (here or abroad) some employment in the capital goods sector, again a highly mechanised one. But is that the aim of public investments?

Some of the work could have been easily translated into low-skilled manual jobs and, thus, could have employed 3–4 times more people than it actually did. It is ironical to find that when sections of German Autobahns are taken for repair, one finds dozens of people for regulating the traffic from both ends, people for marking detour roads, erecting barricades, safety inspectors, etc. When a small patch of road is repaired in Hong Kong during night times, there are people for alerting or cautioning people about the on-going work, regulating traffic, besides carrying out work. In our cities which could have so easily afforded these and more, even those going down a manhole for repair work in crowded areas do not have anyone to assist them even for basic safety.

It is not that Mumbai could wait for 50 years for the flyovers, but could not bear the wait any longer, or that all of them had created an equal social return. Based on social returns, these could have been graded into three–four phases.

If each such phase had taken 4–5 years, and the work had been carried out serially it could have provided continuous employment for 20 years to the concerned workers. The average life expectancy of people at this strata is far lower (maybe in mid-40s to early 50s), and hence 15–20 years would have been lifetime employment and one that would have permanently pulled these families out of poverty line. If a public investment of ₹20,000 crore is so phased out and the manual job content is enhanced by even 10 per cent, it could provide lifetime employment to about 50,000 families.

Researches have proved that people with stable income outlook are more likely to spend their income on education, housing and in general responsible ways. Those with high seasonal or windfall incomes tend to fritter it away in wasteful ways.

One is not arguing for manual work to the complete exclusion of machines or contending that it was done completely with machines to the exclusion of manpower in Mumbai; it is about the relative proportion.

It is not being argued that GQ or National Highways Development Project (NHDP) road projects are killing employment. But has the government squeezed the best employment potential out of these? The answer seems a resounding no. In a country of chronic unemployment, these projects should have been conceived in such a way as to squeeze the maximum employment.

In the following pages, we see three concrete examples of socially meaningful ways of creating employment which are nearer to the capability profile and skill sets of people who need it the most, and economically viable and relevant to the general public so that it voluntarily pays for it.

5.3 Greening for Employment and Growth

One of the areas where employment generation of the kind that can deliver optimum results with the existing environment is afforestation. India needs to improve its forest cover rapidly for its own good. The tribal and forest dwellers need higher income to get them out of perpetual poverty. Their income levels are low and credit facilities are hard to come by. Due to this, they are not able to wait for 5–7 years (which the commercial plantations take to mature) and attain their optimal economic value. Bulk of the wood is used as fuel[6] which stands as the least remunerative way below saw logs, veneer, use in construction, pulpwood, etc. Given the scarcity of land in India, we need a sensible land use policy which maximises the yield per every acre—of produce as well as employment.

Proper policy intervention can deliver much better incomes to tribal/rural people besides increased yield from land as has been successfully demonstrated by countries like

[6] Wood removed for fuel was about 261 million M^3, whereas wood removed for industrial purposes was 46 million M^3 in India in 2005. *Source:* Forest Area Movement, 2010 by FAO.

Vietnam with land tenures and ownership rights different from ours (communist in flavour) and Brazil (pulp wood), Malaysia (oil palms) and Syria (olives) with land rights similar to ours.

VIABILITY OF VIETNAM MODEL IN INDIA

It is estimated that nearly 40 per cent of India's forest (which is about 69 million ha)[7] in government's control is degraded—i.e. over 28 million ha cultivable wasteland and degraded forest land besides sizable miscellaneous area wrongly classified as forest land (the Nagpur leg of Maharashtra state assembly is supposedly sitting on one such 'forest').

The government can grant specific (tree growth) land use rights to interested commercial establishments in timber,

Greening Programme: The 5 MHRP Vietnam Model[a]

In mid-1980s, a few officials of Vietnam attended a presentation[b] in Malaysia on promotion of growing trees as a plantation activity to create employment even while producing marketable output (like oil palm plantations which had preceded them). Based on the lessons, Vietnam created a model for state sponsored re-forestation programmes with hybrid acacias.

Vietnam's latest greening programme started in 1998 with an aim to re-forest 5 million ha under what is known as 5 MHRP.[c] Under this, land is allotted to individuals, state forest enterprises and corporations and local communes. The programme carries minimal subsidies and concessional credits, and allows flow of overseas development funds. The growers get to market the produce and share royalty with the state. By 2005, 2.8 million ha of forests had been developed under the programme.

The economic outcome of this initiative is to create permanent employment to about 2 million people. Vietnam whose forest product exports were $108 million in 1998 saw it grow to $1,700 million by 2005 and further to over $4.1 billion by 2011— woodchips being one of the major contributor to this phenomenal growth. It became the largest exporter of woodchips in 2012 overtaking Australia.

(Box Continued)

[7] Report of National Forest Commission, 2006.

(Box Continued)

Sure there are problems in Vietnam such as land allocation, coverage, pace, allotment irregularities, etc. as is only to be expected in any social systems. Yet the achievements are impressive—an increase in forest cover by about 3% in 7 years between 1998 and 2005, besides the additional employment to over 2 million people and marketable output mentioned above.

[a] Based on information gathered by the author during field visits.
[b] *Source:* Acacia Hybrids in Vietnam, Impact Assessment Series Report No. 27. Martin Van Bueren, Center for International Economics, Canberra and Sydney, August 2004, p. 11.
[c] Ibid., p. 17.

plywood, paper, bio-fuel and other forest products by appropriate relaxation in land acquisitions laws (have not we done it in tea, coffee and other such plantation industries?). The allotees can have secure right to produce and harvest commercial trees with a share of harvested value going to the state in lieu of land rent. The conditions could include the degree of mechanisation (to ensure maximum employment potential), restrictions of using only local labour and regulations on pattern of land use (including for forest dwelling, fuel wood generation, even if better variety).

The marketable value of harvest in India varies from ₹240 to 260,000 per growth cycle of 5 years assuming 120–130 tonnes of output per ha at ₹2,000 per tonne. The wage component can be half of this—₹120,000 per ha per cycle, given that it is the main input. Indonesia has contractually mandated the land lessees themselves to carry out social developmental activities in lieu of a part of its share of rent which further benefits the local inhabitants.

SYNERGY AND BENEFITS

Our tea industry is spread over 450,000 ha and provides direct and permanent employment to about 1.1 million people, roughly 2.4 people per ha. Wood plantations are much less intensive and may be capable of employing one person per ha or two. Five million ha of otherwise below optimally used land can yield a direct employment to 2–3 million persons. If the maturation time is 5–6 years and one-fifth is harvested each year in a cycle, it will ensure an outstanding incremental green cover of at least 80 per cent of the scheme area at any point of time.

There is a beneficial synergy of positive circumstances in India. We have wasteland/degraded land; we need green cover. Our tropical climate is good for growth of trees. There is commercial demand. The local skill sets can easily be upgraded by minimal training for this purpose (training for any other activity is bound to be longer and is an unfamiliar subject for the tribal/rural inhabitants).

There are sufficient examples outside India to replicate. While for other countries being green may be an ethical goal, for India it is an economic necessity for reduction of poverty and unemployment.

5.4 Railways: Re-railing to Generate Employment

If the powers that be want to find out the real reason for the job loss growth during reform years, they need look no further than the railways. Railways are our largest employer. Sadly its employment numbers have exactly peaked in 1990–91 when reforms were initiated and have been declining ever since relentlessly. When it is an essential service and that is of increasing importance, one of the basic infrastructure requirements, and vital to inclusion and connectivity, continuous reduction of employment is incomprehensible.

EMPLOYMENT POTENTIAL

As argued elsewhere, if the railway had created jobs at the same rate at which its traffic has increased in real terms since reforms, it should ideally have added 17 lakh jobs at the minimum

Table 5.2 Track Record of Indian Railways in Creating Employment

Year	No. of Employees ('000s) Group A and B	C	D	Total	Passenger km Million	Freight Net Tonne km Million
1990–91	14.3	891.4	746.1	1,651.8	295,644	235,785
2000–01	14.8	900.3	630.2	1,545.3	457,022	312,371
2007–08	16.1	907.4	470.9	1,394.4	769,956	521,371
2008–09	16.4	913.3	456.3	1,386.0	838,032	551,448
2009–10	16.7	926.5	418.9	1,362.1	903,465	600,548
2010–11	16.8	1,076.9	234.5	1,328.2	978,508	625,723
Growth over 1990–91	17%	21%	-69%	-20%	231%	165%

Source: Indian Railways Year Book, 2010–11.

instead of shedding 3.23 lakh jobs. This leaves a huge (unemployment) burden of 20 lakh jobs to be created by other sectors. This could have so easily over shadowed the additional employment targeted to be created by NREGA. Recoveries of fares in line with the wholesale price index (WPI) indices since 1990–91 would have left the railways better off with about ₹31,000 crore by 2010–11 (every year). Average salaries in railways by 2010–11 were ₹4.07 lakhs per employee. Even if one assumes that railways created jobs at the average wage rates, it would still have paid for 750,000 jobs. It is an irony that railways have shed jobs by 20 per cent during the reform years and most regrettably at the lowest end (Class D level) where it has shed 69 per cent of jobs (Table 5.2).

SAMPLE AVENUES OF EMPLOYMENT

There are several opportunities to provide employment. Even if the railways employs one cleaner for every two coaches and four shifts, it would create employment for up to 100,000 people, given its coach strength.

When one travels by Swiss rail system or Amtrak in the US, the tickets are checked every time one boards the inter-city or inter region trains. Each coach seems to have a travelling/train ticket examiners (TTE) and the checking is almost immediate and well before the next halt. It is rather surprising that India—a labour surplus economy—has continuously cut down on this vital delivery essential. One is told that even on the premium service trains like the Rajdhani, our TTEs have at times to attend six coaches (these have increased from just one or two) and the examiner is not in sight well into the journey and sometimes after one–two halts. TTEs in every coach can control ticketless travel; if only hand-held devices which communicate with the central computer are given to the TTEs, they can easily recover their costs by selling vacant seats in 'in-between' stations. This can employ another 100,000 to 150,000 people.

It is time perhaps for railways to see its social responsibilities in totality and shoulder its fair share of employment generation.

5.5 Recovery of Freebee Externalities to Create Employment

Our roads are used as parking lots for motor vehicles, road-side vending even if it encroaches the space available for movement of people and vehicle. During festivals, marriages and shopping seasons, we park almost anywhere at will. Even if it is a no-parking zone so long as we find some other vehicle, it gives us the legitimacy to leave our vehicle behind them and go about our business.

This creates a nuisance value for others and a positive benefit to shops, restaurants, hotels, marriage *pandals*, schools, offices, business establishments, hospitals and several such entities that get to benefit from their customers. They think nothing of creating their own space for their customers. This positive benefit they get and the negative cost (be it psychic or economic or physical) should be ideally charged and recovered from the beneficiaries so that the creators of such negative values feel the pinch and modify or moderate their behaviour.

All residential and commercial establishments should be mandated to create their own space for their vehicles and of their visitors. Where our municipal authorities deem it safe to allow parking they should clearly identify and earmark such areas and recover charges based on value created for users. This may depend on the traffic volume, time of day or season, duration, type of vehicle, proximity to where they want to go, etc. Each such space should be auctioned to contractors periodically once in 6 months so that price gets discovered properly at regular intervals.[8]

The other big annoyance is vehicles on rent including rickshaws, autos and taxis. They pick up passengers just about from anywhere and tend to crowd around bus stations, railway stations, crowded markets, public places, etc. The concept of parking or queuing seems alien to us both as users of such vehicles or as people soliciting such custom. Government does not deem it necessary to regulate such bothersome behaviour. We should create and administer proper pick up points and clearly demarcate such areas and administer them with heavy fines for errant conduct. In roads clearly marked as not available for parking we should impose heavy fines.

If properly done and one person is employed for every 10 slots of vehicle parking, we may have employment for maybe 2–3 lakh persons. The moneys raised by auctions may be used for proper administration of such systems,

[8] It must be admitted that some attempt is being made in this direction but it can only be considered a feeble attempt without any effort at proper price discovery which when recovered will start moderating public behaviour. Again if the full value of such negative behaviour is recovered, the 'market size' of such loops will dramatically increase giving us more opportunities to expand employment.

training the attendants in polite yet firm behaviour with their customers, traffic research and maybe construction of parking towers. The government needs to find every such available excuse for creating employment of low-skilled people by making people pay for the inconveniences caused by them and imposed on others.

Inclusive growth cannot happen spontaneously. It needs creative ways of utilising the existing available skills, creating a market, making people pay and using such pay-offs to employ people.

5.6 Expansion of Civic and Government Services

Liberalisation and engagement of private sector in provision of economic services justify the shrinkage of government employment in related sectors. But a growing country will need so many government services and consequently its employment has to grow in line. The government, however, has been shrinking its staffing levels continuously since reforms. As has been discussed in Chapter 2, cutting tax rates seems to have an over-arching priority over provision of services resulting in poor service levels and rapidly failing health of government finances. Our civic services, justice, policing, etc. are woefully short of people to ensure the levels of services even as of 1990–91 leave alone improving the delivery quality or improving service standards to better levels (if not world class), and also meet growing demand. Expansion of civil services will provide meaningful services to the citizens while providing even more meaningful employment to the people.

For instance, the Indian census data get outdated for any sensible marketer (who ideally would be looking for the next 5-year projections) by the time they are published. The justice delivery system is as famous for its delays as for its independence. Civil policing is in disrepair; in some places, it is well-nigh impossible to even register an FIR, even where political interference is not involved because of the sheer volume of workload thrust on a poorly trained staff. In main arterial roads like the ring road in Delhi, there are no policemen for regulation of traffic or catching offenders in a country where traffic violation is ubiquitous and in-built given the lax methods of issuing licences and road sense near absent.

The number of people employed by several social services in India is way below world standards even in thrust areas like education or essential services like justice for which the citizens have nowhere else to go. Table 5.3 shows the extent of shortfall in four such essential services and how catching up with the world averages could add 14 million organised sector jobs in the country. These could be financed by recovering costs, levying user charges or fines and penalties, or through

Table 5.3 Additional Employment Feasible in Public Services in India

	Population of 1,200 Million			
	India Per Million	**World Average Per Million**	**Difference Per Million**	**Additional Employment (Million)**
Policemen	1,300	3,000	1700	2.04
Judges	15	107	92	0.11
Military	4,100	10,750	6,650	7.98
Additional employment				10.13
Education: reaching international level of pupil/teacher ratio				
		Pupil/Teacher Ratio		
Class	**Students (Million)**	**India No.**	**World No.**	**Additional Teachers (Million)**
Primary	135	35	24.6	1.63
Secondary	93	35	18	2.51
Additional employment				4.14

Notes: 1. 107 (in the column World Average) is the number of judges recommended by 127th Law Commission Report, 1988, not the world average. 2. Data in Education table from Statistics of School Education 2007–08.

taxes which could be raised to contemporary and comparable levels with the rest of the world.

5.7 Need to Increase Breadth and Quality of Services in Private Consumption

Besides improving social services, the government should also aid expansion of manpower-based services in private consumption expenditure. There are several services that can get absorbed in the private consumption expenditure, if quality services become available.

For example if trained staff are available, most newly emerging rich- and middle-income groups in India would not mind employing a cook, a driver, personal assistant, caretaker for babysitting, housemaids, gardeners, masseurs, etc. In the cities of Saigon and Hanoi in Vietnam, artist shops are ubiquitous selling at rates that even middle class could afford. It is an irony that in our cities and metros, there is a tremendous shortage of skilled manpower to tend to regular house maintenance such as electrical repairs, plumbing work, carpentry, painting, gas pipe mending and sundry work. Whatever one gets after days of trying is also largely informally trained, with poor execution capabilities and quite often incapable of leaving a good impression for being called for repeat work. Availability of satisfactory services will most certainly create employment in larger numbers than airports and expressways.

It is time the government made employment creation its primary focus of the fiscal policy and budget making, at least for a decade rather than be excessively fixated only on growth. In parts of Jakarta, Indonesia, there are traffic restrictions compelling full occupation of vehicles. There are people who volunteer for making up the minimum numbers required for a fee, by travelling along with the hiring passengers to their destination. This may be un-unproductive but is excellent mechanism to diffuse income and achieve economic inclusion. This kind of 'job' creation may still be better than NREGA or cash subsidies in that it requires commensurate effort and may not breed lethargy in the long term.

Given our poor track record in creating employment—reforms or no reforms—and that patience may not be in limitless supply, it may be worthwhile and necessary for the government to create such opportunities for employment, perhaps in more socially and economically productive ways.

Chapter 6

CREATING APPROPRIATE MARKET STRUCTURES

No port can survive on dredging alone.

—A popular saying

REFORMS AND MARKETS

Reforms are all about letting the markets play their role in allocation of resources, price discovery and achieving a balance between demand and supply.

Markets *may* not be an effective mechanism to determine price and quantity where social goods are involved. It may not be possible for many of the products and services that the society desires to meet the conditions under which markets function effectively. In some cases, the markets may attain a demand–supply balance at a level much less than levels which are socially desirable, like in education, health care, sanitation and even in food consumption. It does require government intervention to correct these by appropriate measures. Power sector in India today perhaps is the best example of a failed market and most aptly illustrates the pressing and compelling need for the government to intervene so that the society gets the optimal returns for its investment.

There are several well-documented reasons for government interventions in markets. Hence no attempt is made in elaborating them here. But from the Indian context some compelling reasons are as follows:

1. The quantum and availability of entrepreneurial skills are comparatively low even if there is depth in some pockets. With low incomes over several generations, there is a general risk aversion. Our high savings itself is the result of high-risk aversion driven by the high degree of uncertainty in agricultural yields, in getting and retaining jobs, social stigma, family background, etc.
2. Markets are not the most efficient when it comes to equitable distribution of income. Government efforts are required for achieving distributive justice and equity.
3. There are several areas where there are developmental debris being dumped on society, which needs to be tackled and probably taken advantage of for creating employment and growth.
4. There is still a need to make some lead investments which facilitate private sector investments of a much larger scale (like airport to aviation).

In this chapter, we see how and why government should get to actively 'design' or evolve market structures to serve to correct distortions and channelise resources into right areas through a few examples.

6.1 Correcting Distortions in Higher Education Markets

There is perhaps no other market in India today that so completely marginalises the consumer and producer interest as much as higher education and the markets for justice and legal remedies. To correct the aberrations in the market, it is necessary to channelise the huge amounts spent by society on intermediary coaching classes and lawyers for financing the actual end-education and justice administration, judges and courts. As an example, let us see ways to develop proper market structure for higher education.

With every placement season of the IIMs, there is a frenzy of competitive announcement of ever higher salaries for the outgoing students: hefty increases in the start-up salaries are bandied about as if they are indices of the quality of the institutions. How much of this is media hype and how much of it is true is difficult to tell, particularly when the data are unverifiable. But the euphoria masquerades a deep problem in the functioning of the market for higher education.

DISTORTED STRUCTURE

One of the requirements for ensuring that the markets function optimally is to keep the intermediation costs to the minimum. For example, if stock brokers garner much of the equity appreciation, it will neither benefit the investors who seek alternative avenues nor the companies that raise funds.

The growth in the supply of quality professional higher education in India has been rather sluggish compared to the demand which is growing at a rapid pace—one need not look beyond the growth in aspirants for seats in IITs and IIMs, NIFTs, NIDs, IIFTs, etc. which is forever running so far ahead of the growth rate in seats. Beyond any doubt, these institutions have created a huge positive 'externality'[1] which should have largely been garnered by these institutions and the aspiring students. While the students passing out take their share, the biggest beneficiaries (of the positive externality in these institutions) seem to be the intermediaries—coaching classes, not the actual institutions creating the value. It is much like sowing seeds and growing trees for someone else to reap.

[1] If the benefits of education are reckoned as 30 years income due to the incremental chances in the job market and the resultant higher salaries, higher education must rank as one of the most lucrative investments. No wonder there is such a mad rush!

An overwhelming majority of the aspiring students goes to at least one coaching class and many to multiple coaching avenues to increase their chances of getting admission. The ratio of aspirants to successful candidates may be 25–50 times. Most of these coaching classes charge fees equal to what the institutions charge as tuition fees during their entire term, although the situation is getting corrected of late as the leading institutions have increased their fees steeply upwards. Even after the correction, the coaching fees collected from the potential aspirants by the universe of coaching classes may be 10–12 times more than the fees collected by the IITs and IIMs—a ridiculous situation where the intermediation market is much larger than the final market due to high aspirant to seats ratio.

The distorted market structure caused by unimaginative government policies is mostly to blame for the sluggish growth in the supply of seats. Since the revenues of these institutions are poor (due to anaemic tuition fees), they are not able to grow on their own. Since the government finances are never healthy, they are unable to fund any quick expansion. Further at the frugal rate at which it pays the faculty, it is lucky to find a few who are still interested in teaching.

CORRECTING THE ABERRATIONS—A POSSIBLE STRUCTURE

It is necessary to channelise the huge amounts spent by society on intermediary coaching classes for financing the actual end-education.

The successful candidates can be financed by the commercial banks at market rates against a lien on the degrees, passports of the borrowing student, which can be released after the full repayment. The annual average starting salaries of the outgoing graduates are about 2–3 times the annual tuition fees of these institutions. The students can be issued provisional certificates with the loan key numbers. There can be a centralised database of all such loans for free information and the borrowers can be given the facility to pay from anywhere, any bank in the networked world. Given the good Indian repayment culture, harsh enforcement mechanism may be hardly needed. Even the institutions themselves can finance the loans based on re-finance from commercial banks. Any non-payment by the students should be verifiable and the track record therein can be the first check on the candidate's integrity and commercial compliance.

The institutions should be allowed to charge the market rate freely, or as an intermediate step at full cost. This would facilitate quick expansion of available seats rather than being constrained by government finances. The faculty salaries should be freed from controls to enable the institutions to attract the best brains in society.

The elitist institutions should be free to expand according to the market dictates at their will. They should be thrown open to foreign direct investment (FDI) from educational institutions abroad. Such free expansion of seats will sort out quite a few current distortions in the markets for higher education.

The 'available seats to aspirant' ratio will go up, bringing down the coaching class fees with it, and more of the fees will accrue to final end-service provider. The tension level of the students is inversely proportional to the number of available seats and, hence, is bound to go down. In fact, they might spend more of their time in updating their subject knowledge rather than 'multiple choice' and 'one word answer' knowledge.

The quality of the IITs and IIMs remains largely untested currently since there is no meaningful competition. If the Harvards, Kellogs, MITs and the Stanfords are freely allowed to set up shop in India, the strength and quality of the institutions may get validated or competition may force them to improve their quality (there may even be an influx of foreign students seeking seats in our institutions when they compare foreign and domestic institutions and find our institutions to be far better), which will help commercial expansion.

GOVERNMENT'S ROLE

The government should not impose constraints on finances and stymie the growth of higher education: it is inexcusable. The government should at best allow the institutions of merit to raise finances for expansion by standing guarantee, and as these institutions graduate in the credit market, the government should re-price its guarantees on commercial basis.

It should use a part of the education cess and the service tax on coaching centres for covering the defaults of the students or providing incentives for socialistic programmes such as reservations, creating facilities in remote centres and so on.

ATTRACTING FACULTY

There is a tremendous shortage of inspired teaching staff of high quality. This will probably get worse as we move ahead given the growth of compensation in industry and anaemic growth at high end academic institutions such as IITs, IIMs, IIFT and AIIMS, which are all pegged to the government pay scales. Slowly, we will find teachers at two extreme ends manning our premier academic institutions—either the most inspired at one end or those who do not find employment elsewhere at the other end. This situation needs correction.

Restrictive compensation diminishes supply of people willing to commit their careers to teaching (this is purely an individual economic reason). But there are several artificial entry barriers such as minimum qualification and requirements of PhD. The institutes should be allowed to commercially price their offerings, a part of which should be shared with the faculty which will overcome the economic constraint.

The other way to increase supply is to draft professionals from industry whose satisfaction from teaching may be high given the general human urge to share experiences and the 'prestige value' in being associated with premier institutions. Such part time faculty may not be versatile or capable of offering a wide variety of subjects but will bring in a wealth of experience in a narrow range. Specialised capsule courses (say 3 months) can be offered to such professionals where they are trained in pedagogy and one or two subjects along with case histories and base required reading to become single subject part time professors. They can take a lot of load off the regulars and leave them to concentrate on pure academic portions and research and development of the subject curriculum.

6.2 Affordable Health Care

As seen elsewhere, it is monopolistic practice to abuse one's fiduciary capacity or trusteeship position. For the service providers, imposing choices that favour them more at the expense of their unsuspecting clients is an economically restrictive practice—perhaps more so than monopolies in goods. There is no area where monopolistic exploitation thrives as much as in medicine and legal services. They are today perhaps the most abused systems where the unsuspecting pay a disproportionate price for the services they receive. Fear of death or illness is something that modern medicine has exploited wickedly to extract as much fees as the patient can bear. While love of life makes most of us voluntary victims, distorted market structure is the main reason for the high cost of the modern day medical diagnostics and drugs. There is a definite need to bring in more competitive structures to rein in the exploitative pricing and the exorbitant 'distribution margins'. In terms of market penetration and affordability, most diagnostics and allopathic drugs are much like air travel in the 1960s and 1970s. It is restricted to a few cities and urban centres at costs which only a few can afford. Considering the huge positive externality from a healthy society, it definitely calls for government intervention. The government has set up AIIMS which while being successful, quality-wise has not had the desired geographical reach. The primary health centres have largely been failures.

Medical costs comprise doctors' fees, rentals and diagnostic charges besides cost of drugs. Some alternative ways of creating a competitive environment in diagnostics and medicines to keep a check on prices and reduce the incidence of malpractices even while its reach expands are explored below. 'Creating' competitive structures is not new. After all, the Indian government has created compulsory auctions for tea at select wholesale centres several decades ago, which are working well. More recently, an active market has been created for carbon credits the world over.

MAKING DIAGNOSTICS AFFORDABLE

The risk associated with high initial capital investment in establishing hospitals is a dampener for private sector expansion. The government facilitated increased use of air travel by setting up airports from 1950s till 1980s when no private airline could have afforded to set them up. A similar approach is called for now in health care. However, the government should ensure that the benefits of its intervention should largely flow to the patients through reduced prices rather than the hospital owners only. Just an example of how this can be done in medical diagnostics.

The equipment costs involved are high due to small installed base and consequent poor economies of scale for the manufacturers of the equipment. The high initial capital costs and the anxiety to recover their capital quickly have made the owners of diagnostic centres price the services way out of reach of most patients, besides indulging in inducements for prescribing tests where they may not strictly be needed.

ALTERNATIVE STRUCTURE FOR INFUSING COMPETITIVENESS

The government can invite bids from the equipment manufacturers where it can pay them the cost of equipment (or a substantial percentage) upfront. The manufacturers (or their trained partner associates) should be eligible for setting up diagnostic centres and the lowest quote for patient user being chosen for contract. This would interest most of the equipment manufacturers themselves since it expands their markets. Since capital costs are paid upfront, the quotes will be based on running and variable costs alone and these are just a fraction of total in most such services. With such prices, the market penetration for diagnostics can expand at a rapid clip like the low-cost airlines have expanded the airline industry. The government can recover its capital costs through a fixed charge, which may be subsidised as deemed appropriate.

By fixing the prices after factoring in the reduction in set up costs upfront, there is a definitive commitment on pass through of benefits to patients. This is unlike the current practice where land is granted at low land lease rentals which does not necessarily ensure that the benefits are passed on to customers; nor puts a cap on pricing based on costs. And the promise of delivering a certain portion of services at subsidised rates to poorer sections remains largely unfulfilled. Competitive bidding process would have hopefully eliminated the 'commissions' to the medical fraternity which only inflates the costs without corresponding value addition.

With an investment of ₹2,000–2,500 crore per annum, the government can help establish a centre or two in each of about 600-odd districts at an average capital cost of say ₹2–3 crore a centre. Over a period of 4–5 years, geographical coverage could be as good as may be required.

TAMING HIGH COST OF MEDICINES

Government has from time to time tried imposing drug price control orders (DPCO) based on costs, with some success.

However, any price to sustain in the long term should factor in both demand and supply factors besides the high cost of research and development involved in bringing these medicines to the market.

Most high end medicines involve years of research and are as of now largely the preserve of overseas MNCs. If India gives them market access, it has the right to dictate the conditions under which such access is granted. The current exploitative pricing and practices are the result of patenting where each drug discoverer enjoys 'monopoly' for the drug in question. There is a need to create 'competition' even if the drug is patented.

The government can mandate that any drug discoverer desirous of market access should invite bids from third party manufactures. Only those with appropriate approved facilities can be qualified to bid for such licences. The third parties can enter into a revenue sharing model (*a la* telecom) or upfront licence fees or any combination with the drug patent holder. It can mandate that there should be at least half-dozen such licensees who will all manufacture the drug under the supervision of the patent holder and in the same brand name and specifications. These outsourced manufacturers should be allowed to market their produce pan India without any restrictions.

The bidding manufacturers will most definitely do their market research to determine the market potential before bidding. This will mostly ensure that the bidders pay the right price while the patent holder gets the 'market determined' compensation. If at the retail counter the same drug from competing manufacturers is available, the hold of doctors (or any other link in the chain) over 'specific' prescriptions will be diluted and the need to give 'margins' to the link may get eliminated. Hopefully without usurious margins and kick backs, the cost of medicines will be lot more affordable. The money 'sponged' by links in the distribution chain which does not add corresponding value may more usefully be split between the drug discoverer and patients.

6.3 Forex Reserves: Ways to Use Them in Infrastructure

NATURE OF INDIA'S FOREX RESERVES

The mounting foreign exchange reserves[2] (US$295 billion in January 2013) even as there is a hue and cry about lack of funds for infrastructure investment has become as much an embarrassment as having large food-stocks while one-third of the population lives below poverty line.

There is an essential difference between China's and India's reserves. China's reserves are earned surpluses from exports being greater than imports which are invested elsewhere, whereas India's reserves are borrowed money pending utilisation. Both occupy the cash till, but in the latter case it is corrosive: if not used judiciously to earn returns greater than the borrowing cost, it soon diminishes.

RESERVE BANK OF INDIA'S CONCERNS

The RBI has the forex reserves but wants to keep this war chest to keep currency raids or volatility at bay. But lending for infrastructure, as the planning commission has been suggesting, entails long payback periods. In any proposed solution, the RBI would prefer to retain an 'option' on its reserves (wherever and however invested) for quick and immediate withdrawal. For which it is prepared to pay a premium (by way of accepting a lesser interest rate than what the actual *post-facto* tenure would have implied[3]). Any solution, for it to

[2] Foreign exchange reserves are the amount of foreign currency available with the central bank of a country (RBI in our case) accumulated either from excess of exports and remittances over imports or from net borrowings.

[3] As indicated by RBI's preference to hold low-yield securities in its portfolio where low yields are partially due to tenure and partially due to better credit risks of the issuing institutions.

become feasible and acceptable to the RBI, should primarily address this legitimate 'quick encashability' concern.

The solution thus is to find that 'intermediary' institution (whose credentials RBI respects) that takes 'liquidity' from the central bank in return for long-term funds to infrastructure projects. The RBI could place, say, \$20–25 billion with such intermediaries—maybe the World Bank/IMF, the International Finance Corporation, or the Asian Development Bank—with an option to 'call' these in one or more lots with a pre-defined 'call notice' period. Since the RBI is unlikely to require the entire amount at one go even in a crisis, it could agree to give a graded notice, say, 2 days for the first 10 per cent, 10 days for a further 25 per cent, 1 month for the next 25 per cent and so on. This would largely address RBI's concerns.

RECIPROCAL FUNDING ARRANGEMENT

The arrangement should entitle the Government of India (or its nominees) to borrow against these deposits—hopefully at a better interest rate than usual as the loans are backed by reciprocal funds. The entire deposit may not come back as loans, but the government can raise 75–80 per cent of the RBI's deposits. (If the intermediary agencies lend more than what the RBI places with them, it is all the better.) The funds should be earmarked for infrastructure investments such as ports, national highways, airports, railways, etc.

If the private sector is involved, it could be subject to independent appraisal of both the government and the funding agencies. In the event of default, the intermediary agencies should have right of set-off for the amount actually in default. Not all the projects would fail simultaneously. Hence, the RBI's deposits would not get wiped out at once. The government should then make good the amounts to the RBI against the funds so forfeited due to defaults.

If there is a crisis-driven withdrawal by the RBI, the loans should automatically be covered by government guarantee[4] to the intermediary agencies and their pricing adjusted till such time the deposits are restored. There will be a differential between the borrowing rate and the rate at which the RBI would be placing the funds; this is only to be expected given the tenure differential and the country risk rating. But the borrowing rate for the projects so funded may still be cheaper as there is back-up funding provided by RBI to the lending institutions.

HOW WOULD IT INTEREST VARIOUS STAKEHOLDERS?

Why would this scheme interest the RBI? Liquidity is preserved (in a crisis, the ability of these agencies to raise resources quickly is far superior to that of the RBI). If the funds are placed with several agencies, chances that all will fail at the same time is remote. Second, money supply and inflation concerns will be much less compared to when fresh forex funds are sourced for domestic infrastructure expenditure; re-cycling existing reserves would be a far better option for the RBI.

Why would multilateral funding agencies bite this? They are highly bullish on India and are keen to raise their exposure given our growth potential. There is a big supply shortfall in infrastructure and it would take another 10–15 years before the situation gets better—an ideal situation for ensuring demand for the product/service which is ideal for the project lender. The multilateral agencies do not have to raise additional funds for this in their traditional markets which become saturated with their paper from time to time resulting in higher rates and sometimes even slippage in their own ratings.

[4] This should be for a standby Guarantee Fee to be collected upfront on these lines.

The government needs the funds for infrastructure but are constrained by the fear of pushing up the fiscal deficit. This mechanism could take it out from the fiscal deficit definition (at least, till an amount actually devolves on the government due to project default).

There is no fantasy in this. Have not we seen our neighbourhood bankers tell us 'if you want a loan please get us some deposits' especially around year ends so as to show growth on both sides of their balance sheet? Is not banking all about intermediation—realigning credit worthiness, liquidity, tenure, lot sizes, etc.—moving these from where they are to where they are most productively used? The above suggested structure is just spiced up to take care of some complications such as cross-border nature, tenure mismatch and within-tenure change of backups.

INVOLVING PRIVATE SECTOR

Reputable private sector players could be allowed to borrow abroad and invest in participatory notes issued by infrastructure companies for which they could get some reciprocal priority in pricing and usage. Or, it could be set off against preference in usage of services so created by investors at some pre-agreed or preferred prices.

If Tirupathi-Tirumala temple is selling its future *puja*s and *prasad*s to its devotees for a lump-sum upfront payment, why would not similar models work for commercially sound and bankable projects such as NHAI? In the case of Tirumala, the devotees' faith and trust act as good enough security. But for infrastructure projects, the related notes could be guaranteed by government (if they could extend it to Enron and DPC, why not local investors) which could hold the security of the assets in return for the guarantee. This could again not be within fiscal deficit till actual default.

To solve the problem of excess reserves, multilateral agencies could be allowed to borrow in Indian markets and their bonds can be given statutory liquidity ratio (SLR) status up to a specified percentage. That will give banks some choice and provide liquidity. This will soak up dollars to the extent of these agencies' net borrowings in the Indian market. This would help the RBI even if it does not do much for infrastructure.

CASE FOR 'FOREX BONDS' TO STERILISE YIELD LOSSES

For the foreign currency borrowers (of ECBs, FCCBs, or even ADR and GDR issuers), it makes sense to borrow abroad at 5 per cent to repay their loans at 7 per cent and 9 per cent and thus make money. But when this money does not get absorbed in imports—project or raw materials—the RBI is forced to deploy it at 2 per cent (or such low yields). The gap of 3 per cent is definitely a loss to the country. Since the benefits of borrowing abroad to repay costlier existing loans accrue exclusively to the foreign currency borrower, the consequential costs should also be loaded on them. It is unfair to let them load others or the system.

Exchange earner's foreign currency (EEFC) account of the exporters removes the temporary export surpluses from the equation but it is not a mandatory requirement. RBI from time to time makes it mandatory to park the funds outside till they are actually required for imports. The RBI can issue special bonds to those who bring foreign money much before they need it, covering the portion that is not immediately needed. On this it should pay the same rate as it earns on its reserve moneys parked abroad, say, 2 per cent.

When the corporate needs the forex, it could surrender these bonds for forex along with any accumulated interest. The full life of bonds can be roughly the number of months of imports cover we have: if not used within this period, the owner should be able to surrender the same at the end of period and claim his interest and principal. Thus, the entire loss (or lower yield) on reserves during the period of mismatch will get loaded on the borrower instead of punishing others such as the RBI, the interest earners, the export earners (who suffer because of currency appreciation).

Even if the government or RBI saves 2 per cent on $50 billion through this mechanism, it is $1 billion per annum (₹6,000 crore)—enough to employ 20 lakh people at a minimum wage of ₹125 per day for 240 days a year—not something to be lost sight of. Maybe accelerated investments in infrastructure will also enhance growth.

6.4 Privatising Public Distribution System (PDS)

Our PDS has been in operation for several decades. Yet, it is one of the most abused systems giving rise to corruption at several levels. It is perhaps time for private enterprise to take over the function.

It is vital to arrest the losses in our food grains (reportedly 7–10 per cent between farm gate and market, additional 4–5 per cent between market and retail store[5] besides another 3 per cent at the consumption end). We need to control this to counter inflation. Almost 40 per cent of the grain in the public system (which distributed 24 million tons of wheat and 32 million tons of rice in 2011–12) does not reach intended recipients and is diverted to open markets.[6]

While no one can blame the PDS exclusively for all the losses, it does contribute a major share. The prime reason for this continuing (and perhaps increasing) losses is the lack of accountability right down the supply chain and the absence of entrepreneurial or private ownership urge to arrest wastes, leaks and maximise efficiencies and continuously upgrade systems and practices to deliver results.

There is a definite need to get the benefits of private ownership even while achieving the laudable public purpose of PDS.

[5] *Source: Food Security in South Asia*, Pradeep Chaturvedi.

[6] Deepak Gopinath, *YaleGlobal*, 27 March 2013.

The incentive structure currently in operation is rather weak or non-existent except at the first point where private ownership of production has responded overwhelmingly to remunerative MSPs and filled up our granaries to embarrassing levels. After this link, ownership instincts are completely absent and there is neither accountability for what rots nor fear of punishment for leakages.

WAYS OF INFUSING ENTREPRENEURIAL EFFICIENCY

It is possible to get private players in consumer products distribution (such as ITC, EID and Levers) who are eyeing the rapidly growing rural markets.

The government can invite competitive bids for each state or region for 'procurement to distribution' with the players bidding the least amount of support required for a given level of procurement prices and final PDS prices being awarded the contract. The buffer stock quantity can be mandated in proportion. The auction systems should allow multiple (say) five–six players per region (like in telecom now) so that there is benefit of competition. The players will procure and disperse the minimum support prices (MSPs) and transport the produce to their allotted markets for local distribution through their network of dealers.

The players can be allowed to brand their PDS packs (we will have multiple brands of PDS products in the market/shops) so that consumers would be able to prefer better ones based on delivery standards, quality, service, etc. Even if the price allowed for PDS is fixed for all, over time, efficient players will achieve scale efficiencies and thus bid better prices in subsequent auctions.

The final outlet selling the PDS goods can account for the dispersed units both in the system and the PDS beneficiary's cards. The PDS allottees should be allowed to go to any of the outlets within their area to collect their quota. This will hopefully curb any monopolistic rash behaviour at the final end.

The disbursements of the 'bid' amount can be half (or some proportion) at the procurement stage and rest based on the final sale to PDS beneficiaries. This will hopefully restrict leakages.[7] The Food Corporation of India (FCI) warehouses can be rented out to private players or part of the concessions can be through reduced rail freights and warehouse rents.

WHY WOULD PRIVATE PLAYERS BE INTERESTED?

Private players are increasingly relying on rural markets for growth. Besides natural growth, substantial quantum of moneys pumped in by both central and state governments, and changing habits are slowly creating demand for packaged goods. For the private players, PDS can provide the basic volumes and scale efficiencies to set up the chains through which they will be able to expand distribution of other manufactured products.

Government and the bureaucracy may be good in policing the private sector but have been a miserable failure in policing themselves. Hopefully, a simple surveillance system would bring down the level of corruption and leakages steeply. This and the presence of 4–5 players in each area will largely check monopolistic practices. At least in retail trade of several consumer goods, there are not too many complaints.

Physical losses in most consumer goods distribution are less than 1 per cent and if similar efficiencies are attained over time, it can have a significant control over prices. This gain itself can take care of the returns to capital employed required by the links in distribution chain. Tamil Nadu used to distribute its PDS grains through a co-operative called Triplicane

[7] At the farm gate, the free market prices are very lower than MSPs as otherwise MSPs would not have any meaning. However, at the consumer end, PDS prices are bound to be lower than the free market prices. The free market prices will cross over the line of MSP–PDS prices somewhere along the chain after which it *may* sometime become more profitable to sell the produce in free markets and starve the PDS. A careful calibration is essential.

Urban Co-operative Society (TUCS) in Chennai in the late 1960s and 1970s, a system which worked wonderfully and was known for its efficiency and clean practices. Maybe it is time to revisit and study and replicate the system on a national scale.

6.5 Beneficial Legislations for Creating Demand and Growth

Most cities around the world from East to West have some landscaping programmes. Road dividers mostly have flower plants. Both sides of roads even in crowded cities are lined with trees. If one is talking of Switzerland whole colonies and neighbourhood co-ordinate their landscaping and greening programmes and the resulting symmetry is so pleasing to the eye. The external roads of cities of Oman, The Hague or Hong Kong seem as carefully designed and maintained as an interior decorator would do a residential house.

There are some social goods and services which citizens may desire to have but individual entrepreneurs may not be able to create a market for them. Many citizens may even pay for it to enjoy the benefits. India has a lot of scope of creating such goods and services both for creating growth and inducing employment.

GREENING OUR TERRACES

Our residential colonies do not normally spend much on decorating their societies, even if they have considerable bank balances. Many of our temples and charitable societies have an enormous wealth but are frugal when it comes to spending a little on them to look better or improve their systems.

Government can legislate (in whatever form) that the roof tops and terraces should be covered with greenery or green nets or mist chambers. Or at least a specified percentage of the open terraces or spaces should be mandated to be covered. A couple of buckets of re-cycled waste water from each household would largely cover the water requirements. A collection of even ₹150–200 per flat/house in a society of 80–100 could pay for two–three gardeners and the related gardening expenses.

Some wealthier ones may go on to create green houses and mist chambers if not butterfly parks. In any case, green-covered rooftops have their aesthetic value, and might induce the residents to decorate their balconies and sit outs.

In national capital region alone this could create 12,000[8] jobs. With a short-term coaching, we could convert street urchins, jobless wanderers and people at fringes of existence into useful gardeners. If all cities join the exercise, it could easily create employment for 120,000–150,000 people who are otherwise under-utilised by society. It would create jobs for the nurseries, landscape designers, decorators, inspectors, etc. and of course a market for goods that these people would spend their income on.

LEGISLATION IS JUSTIFIABLE

The government has recently legislated corporate social responsibility activity rules, which mandates a certain percentage of profits to be necessarily spent on such activities. Similar market making in collection of urban waste has been illustrated in Chapter 8. Our civic maintenance and project execution methods even in private sector are fraught with risks and are highly unhygienic. Upgrading the standards and making them subject to audit can create employment for many. An imposition of 1–2 per cent fines on those who are

[8] Let us assume that only 60 per cent have a roof over their heads and that five people live in each flat and only 50 per cent are organised in housing societies or colonies. For a population of 2 crore in NCR, it would give 12,000 societies of 100 flats each.

short on compliance and an incentive of 1–2 per cent for those in compliance would not only create a market for such services but also fund the scheme for the government. Corporate audits are an example of legislating for welfare creation.

Making it compulsory to have navigation systems in cars or taxis would create demand for GPS systems. Mandatory treatment of municipal waste water would create a huge demand for treatment systems. Commercial night shelters might create employment for many housekeepers besides providing decent shelters to those seeking them. Heavy fines for open defecation could create a commercial demand for related services. Charitable organisations could be mandated to spend a specified percentage of their gross or net income on construction of old age homes, night shelters, toilets, schools, adult education or skill development centres. Legislating visits (say once in 3 years) to the zoo compulsory for urban school children can bring about beneficial attitudes towards animals besides creating demand for zoos.

Tax incentives at individual level for employing domestic servants, personal drivers, cooks, etc. can perhaps add employment. It is an irony that while we have incentives for large-scale industries and investing in machines, there are no tax incentives for creating employment at micro levels.

Chapter 7

TAMING THE TWINS

Save for gold, jewels, works of art, perhaps good agricultural land, ... there ain't no such animal as a permanent investment.

—Bernard M. Baruch

TWO IMPORTANT DETERMINANTS AND ASSUMPTIONS

Two important factors which determine the growth rates that an economy can reach are the proportion of savings to income and how productively they are used. Savings give us the ability to invest in real assets and, thus, create new capacities and the second is about getting the best out of such investments, i.e. productivity of capital. Productivity of capital can be measured by how much additional output we get per unit of investment or how much additional units (or percentage) of capital we need for generating an additional unit (or percentage) of income. Economists have preferred the latter approach (how many units of capital for a given increase in output) and have called it 'incremental capital output ratio' (ICOR). The smaller it is the better since we would be able to get more output for every unit of capital. Higher ICOR numbers indicate inefficient use, less than full capacity utilisation, high capital used up in establishing fresh capacities due to time and cost overruns, ill-trained labour not operating capital assets optimally, bottlenecks, etc.

Our savings rate is about 34–36 per cent of gross domestic product (GDP) and ICOR hovers around 4–4.5 times. It has shown a wide variation between the various plan periods from 1951 and has of late been beyond 5. If we are to believe the economists, growth rates, in general, are determined by savings rates (or investments) divided by ICOR. Hence, a change in ICOR means a change in growth rates. Table 7.1 lays out the growth rates feasible at various alternative savings rates and ICOR. Growth rates are arrived at by dividing savings or investment rates by ICOR. The number in the lower half of the table represents the number of times GDP will be at the end of the decade as compared to the GDP at the beginning for a given level of ICOR and savings rate.

At India's current savings rates of around 36 per cent per annum, an improvement of ICOR from 4 to 3 (lower rates implying better capital productivity), the growth rates improve by almost 3 per cent. Our current ICOR is shamefully high given our low capitalisation levels and low penetration of technology. This shows a fatigue level worthy of an economy at much higher income and capitalisation levels.

India's track record with savings has been impressive given our social habits of frugality. We spend much more (in relation to our incomes) than other nations on family functions such as marriages, festivals, rituals relating to birth and death, and several other occasions marking various stages of life. Most of these expenditures which cannot be classified as

Table 7.1 Growth Rates at Various ICOR and Savings Rates

Savings/Investment Rate (% of GDP)	**ICOR Ratio**				
	4.5	**4**	**3.5**	**3.25**	**3**
30	6.7	7.5	8.6	9.2	10.0
33	7.3	8.3	9.4	10.2	11.0
36	8.0	9.0	10.3	11.1	12.0
Growth in GDP over 10 years at growth rates above (times)					
30	1.9	2.1	2.3	2.4	2.6
33	2.0	2.2	2.5	2.6	2.8
36	2.2	2.4	2.7	2.9	3.1

investments in economic parlance are financed out of lifelong savings. Some people may borrow to spend but make up for it in future periods.

We set aside funds from the current income over a fairly long period of time (and many times even without having a specific target or date in mind and as a matter of routine or habit to cover any unforeseen contingencies) and this by itself promotes and develops in us the habit of thrift and savings. This is one beneficial social habit that we, as indeed all South Asian countries, are blessed with. High savings rate characterises other Asian countries too with China and Macau leading the pack with more than 50 per cent savings rate.

However, we may not be blessed with such beneficial condition when it concerns capital productivity, which is rather low (and its reciprocal capital output ratio rather high). Part of it may be technological, bureaucratic delays, etc., but a large contribution also comes from our social conditioning and habits. Lack of respect for public property, lethargy, lack of time sense, diluted urge to plan and complete in time, lack of accountability, *chalta hai* attitude all have a negative effect on capital productivity.

These traits may be a hangover from the immediate past of a substantial part of our society. In an agricultural rural setting, most of the outcome is dependent on nature—somewhat beyond the control of individual, and crop yields are as much a matter of chance with the weather as deliberate effort. Due to this, people tend to have a fatalistic or resigned view (even if in varying degrees). This is where a significant portion of current middle class and urban dwellers used to be not so long ago.

There is a serious need to examine whether we need a high savings rate or is it dysfunctional and whether it will benefit us to reduce the savings rate and boost current consumption. It is even more necessary to dissect and challenge our high ICOR levels and devise ways to bring it down to lower levels by improving our capital productivity.

7.1 Let Us Save Less to Grow More: Reworking Our Savings Rate[1]

IS OUR HIGH SAVINGS REALLY A VIRTUE?

In this section, we examine savings as whatever is not current consumption—a little different from how conventional economists would define it. Thus, expenditure on gold, speculative portion of real estate, silver or jewellery, etc. are taken as savings. This may not satisfy the purist economist, but is more relevant to the point being made.

Growth, year on year, can come out of better using the existing capacities (if the economy is not in full employment) or creating new ones and using them. High savings facilitate high investment which can add to productive capacity and thus facilitate growth. Savings are a virtue when the economy is operating at full capacity. But this is only one side of the story. Savings necessarily mean postponement of current consumption. Since one person's expenditure is another's income, current savings also mean loss of income for someone else during the current period. Thus, savings hurt by blunting the multiplier effect and dilute current income levels. Savings when the economy is operating at less than full capacity become un-virtuous. We have conditions of high poverty and hunger, high unemployment, bulk of new entrants into job markets going without jobs, all signs of far greater potential and an economy operating at substantially less than full potential.

[1] There are economic theories on optimal savings rate for a society. Every society has to decide how much of its income it needs to consume in the current period and how much to postpone to future periods (savings). The attempt here is to examine in layman's language if it is possible to reduce our savings and achieve whatever we want to achieve with lesser savings. The resulting higher current expenditure can lead to higher incomes and hopefully more employment in the current period.

When an economy is operating at less than capacity, the rates of return on existing standing capacities are less than their true potential which reduces the incentives to additional investments. It is essential then to consume more and exhaust them before embarking on new ones.

There has to be a balance between a society's total entrepreneurial urges and ability (including that of government, business and individuals) and capacity to absorb savings and its actual savings. Our savings do imply that the combined entrepreneurial capabilities are way short. The situation called for the government making up for the deficit in entrepreneurial instincts and risk taking in the private sector. Instead, unfortunately the government has chosen to withdraw into the background. Our private sector has, no doubt, become more risk taking. But it does not appear to have grown sufficiently to fill up the increased requirements due to growth and government's withdrawal from certain economic areas. At the micro level it is perhaps far worse. At the extreme end, even an individual labourer has to be considered an 'entrepreneur' for his services. Unfortunately, he is constrained by lack of skills and our continued inability to upgrade him.

If our savings are productively used for creating additional capacities, it would have been alright. But a large portion of our 'savings' is invested in unproductive (low current yield) assets such as gold and real estate. It is possible to lower our savings in these and thus facilitate higher jobs and employment, without compromising growth rates. We look at some ways of re-working our savings rate downwards before we examine ways to curb our infatuation with gold and real estate.

1. *Broadening the consumption base:* Our age-old consumption habits were shaped by lack of avenues to spend—availability of products and services being low. Individual consumption habits formed during such a phase and carried to the middle years and old age are not amenable

to quick change. Hopefully, the current young generation, of at least the middle- and high-income group, and their children will have higher spending habits. If this happens outside India (foreign travel and imports of luxury cars, etc.), the benefits of such spends will be lost to us. It is therefore necessary to develop products and services of much greater variety than currently available to absorb their consumption expenditure.

Lack of skills is a dampener. Given the income levels, there is a wide variety of services at the personal level that the middle and upper class could spend its money on provided satisfactory service standards which are delivered and maintained. Spas, sports clinics, avenues for entertainment, water sports and tourism and entertainment where feasible, availability of arts and painting are all way behind where current income could be spent. Availability of these services and satisfying experience with their delivery would boost demand and provide employment opportunities. Between goods and services, preference should be for personalised services which have a greater human employment potential.

2. *Recovering proper prices for government services to the upper income segments:* As seen earlier, the pricing of several government services, whether commercial or otherwise, such as justice, railways, airlines, parking services, higher education, escort services for events, fines and penalties for crimes and infringements and petrol does not distinguish between the rich and the poor while recovering costs or prices.

   The government should carefully study and devise methods of tracing the benefits and recovering the same from those who can afford it. This additional revenue will most probably come from incomes which are otherwise being saved as of now and can help the government cover its deficit or promote employment.

3. *Taxation of high income through expenditure taxes:* India has perhaps cut down on its direct tax rates far too soon.

It has increased the share of indirect taxes which perhaps cut into consumption more than direct taxes. It can increase direct taxes and tax expenditure of high-income groups through expenditure taxes which will dilute savings and mobilise funds for promoting consumption and employment.

4. *Alternatives to gold and real estate:* The main 'savings' instruments that the Indians seem comfortable are gold, silver and real estate. These investment avenues share an important return profile that Indian investors look for. Their utility from current consumption is low. Their main aim is to preserve values in an asset which they are bound to need in future—gold for various religious and social needs and housing for dwelling. Due to inherent demand in these assets growing in view of the population increase and limitation in supplies, the real return is bound to be positive outweighing inflation comfortably over long periods of time.

GOLD

India produces 3 tonnes of gold per annum but imports nearly 970 tonnes out of world production of about 2,830 tonnes (in 2011) that is more than one-third of total production.[2] Our familiarity and preference for gold have developed through the ages. Through the Middle Ages, India was a net exporter of goods (spices, silk, carpets, etc.) and the settlement for these exports from the west was mainly through gold which was easy to ship. Hence, gold was accumulated and became a part of our lifestyle and this habit has become a sort of infatuation. Most countries do not have this historic baggage and hence do not show any disproportionate import or consumption of gold.

The infatuation has continued even when India has become a net importer of goods and services. Gold imports

[2] *Source:* World Gold Council.

hurt the economy. When gold is imported (and not received as settlement), the corresponding income goes out of the country and the multiplier effect and employment is played out of the country and to that extent dilutes growth. This is the first loss. If we manufactured the gold ourselves, the story would be different. The income would have been received by other residents and the secondary income-consumption cycle would have helped us in preventing leakage of GDP.[3]

Secondly, the current yields on gold are very low. Most of its gains that accrue on gold are valuation gains which do not add any more physical asset or facility to us and are best not reckoned as GDP.[4] Given India's growth rates and inflation, the nominal yield on assets whose demand grows in line with our GDP should be about 13–15 per cent. Gold hardly yields anything and to the extent results in much lower growth and income.

We need to bring down import of gold but without affecting the effective affinity for gold since savings is a beneficial social habit and without the security of this habit many of the vulnerable sections of society would from time to time fall into financial trouble requiring government intervention. Since official delivery systems are ineffective, such temporary despairs would needlessly result in increased suicides, something we could ill afford.

THE NEED FOR SURROGATE GOLD

The primary demand drivers and user requirements of gold has to be analysed and understood carefully and surrogate financial instruments mirroring its characteristics need to be

[3] Amount spent on import of gold dilutes our national income by multiplier times (nearly 2.7 now) the amount so spent.

[4] At best, the insurance kind of comfort (against inflation and volatility of prices of other assets and against any steep variations in income from agriculture, employment, etc.) that gold gives over time is the only component which should perhaps be included in the services part of GDP.

marketed by the government so that demand for 'physical gold' is converted to demand for 'financial gold'. Firstly, this would overcome the need for importing gold. Hopefully if the banking system channelises the finances mobilised by selling surrogate gold into productive investments, the capital output ratio can improve for the better than when these investments are in gold.

Government should market fully guaranteed gold bonds whose value can be redeemed either with gold or its going market values anytime. A portion of better returns can be shared with the investors even while saving the making charges that gets wasted with gold. Part of the savings so mobilised should be actually invested in gold as reserve (either through mopping up existing gold from the population or importing it) so that the government also insulates itself against price fluctuations in the international markets as well as lend credibility to the scheme.

The government needs to redouble its current efforts[5] and market the scheme more effectively and perhaps rope in private players in this exercise. The Capital Account Convertibility Committee in 1997 recommended that the government should introduce gold futures and derivatives to tackle this issue. The pricing of most financial derivatives such as forward contracts, options, swaps and futures are worked out largely if not solely based on interest rates (following a familiar logic known as covered interest arbitrage). But interest is not the primary motivation for investment in gold: otherwise people would not be investing in gold knowing full well that it does not have any self-generating capability out of which the borrower can service the interest.

The ASSOCHAM study, India's Gold Rush: Its Impact and Sustainability, recommends massive advertising to educate the public on how gold imports is detrimental to

[5] The government machinery is at it already and this section is largely a recapture of logic on a vital component of actions required for accelerating our growth rates.

national finances. This seems rather naïve. Advertising may succeed in creating demand for a new product or benefit more easily, but its potency in making people give up widely held social beliefs and individual habits strongly backed by financial motivation in favour of national economic goals is highly doubtful.

We need to fully understand the primary motives behind consumer in developing a solution. Gold for the individual Indian may be a safe haven; but collectively it imposes a huge burden of foreign exchange outgo. What is ominous is that India's per capita consumption of gold is amongst the lowest in the world leaving plenty of scope of increasing socially unproductive imports.

DIVERTING DEMAND

A significant portion of demand for gold seems to be coming from households saving 1,500–2,500 per month. They can neither buy real estate nor do they invest in equities. One big contributory could be the 'excess' MSPs paid out by the government. In the short-term consumption, habits do not change and most of such 'windfall' moneys invade gold. This could perhaps be solved by paying out most of the excess MSPs into long-term fixed deposits with commercial banks. The commercial banks could be mandated to invest a specified larger proportion of such deposits in government bonds so as to take care of liquidity pressure on government.

Households should also be offered far better interest rates in rural areas as seen in Chapter 3. An interest rate in alignment with the rural interest rates will divert the heat on gold demand.

GOLD RENTING MIGHT ALSO DILUTE ITS GLITTER VALUE

Gold as we have seen is demanded for both its glitter value and as long-term hedge against inflation. While gold bonds can address the hedging need, glitter value will continue. If renting of gold ornaments takes shape and becomes widely spread, it might greatly dilute the 'glitter' need. If gold ornaments are available in plenty for renting, the show off effect will lose its potency and people will not chase it for feeling 'superior' to their peers, friends and neighbours.

REAL ESTATE

The case with real estate which is India's other comfort zone of investment is largely similar. Our population density is high and land will forever gain in value because of demand supply gap when the population keeps increasing.

Demand for real estate comes from (i) actual dwellers, (ii) people investing for future needs (real but deferred demand) and (iii) pure speculative investors who are never likely to want real estate for living or its yearly earnings but only for valuation gains from ever growing demand. The proportion of people investing exclusively for current rental incomes is likely to be minimal, given its returns.

Again as with gold, the current yields in real estate and land are low (2–3 per cent after adjusting depreciation) and real estate has much of the other qualities of gold although in differing degrees. The main disadvantage though are sizing and slicing and the steep costs and procedures involved therein.

The attraction of real estate is all too known. Most of us have much greater comfort with physical assets when compared to invisible assets such as bonds, equity, mutual funds, patents and copyrights even if they exhibit economic characteristics similar to corresponding physical assets. Risk of dispossession is lower, counter party risks and chances of scams are lower, and real estate has by and large delivered capital gains which far outweigh the opportunity or actual loss from low annual yields. This preference for physical asset is not unique to any income class (it is across income class) within India and even other nations are prone to this basic instinct.

REAL ESTATE—THE ECONOMIC WATERLOO

Most of the advanced economies meet their economic Waterloo in real estate. Over a period of time, non-end use demand grows and gets to a point where further appreciation is impossible but by that time market prices have risen so high that the bubble bursts and we have a long-term stagnation in prices. The most recent global meltdown across the world was also founded on this basic instinct and comfort with real estate.[6] Most of them faced unsustainable real estate expansion after reaching high-income or upper-middle-income levels. But India seems set to hit this plateau far sooner and earlier in its economic development than others. This may be due to the high population pressure and highly skewed income distribution where most of the moneys from growth of income have invaded real estate and taken it to economically unproductive levels. Cycles in real estate prices may develop much earlier in our path.

India at the societal level cannot afford to invest its monies in such low current return (2–3 per cent per annum) assets. It is an impediment to our development and detrimental to achieving superior growth rates and results in low ICORs. However, we also need to keep in mind that unlike gold, the money spent on construction is spent mostly within India and facilitates the multiplier effect to play out within India. It has been supporting and sustaining employment of low-skilled labour. Balancing between these is essential.

Some interventions are called for to kill the speculative demand and make it a more stable economic activity. Government may need to introduce and market real estate bonds (like the gold bonds) which mirror the qualities of real estate. To deliver this, it may have to maintain a reserve of real estate (as with most reserves, the proportion can be

[6] Although it must be said that there were several other economic, financial and banking excesses which were built on top of this which magnified the effect.

10–20 per cent) and invest the balance monies in other commercially viable development activities. It has all the powers to influence prices and it should through tax measures, stamp duties, etc. try and moderate the price appreciation. If so required, it should not hesitate using its powers in arbitrary manner (e.g. having the right to acquire non-occupied property at circle rates or at 80–90 per cent of market prices).

REAL ESTATE AS A POLICY INSTRUMENT

Most of the taxes and duties on real estate seem rooted for ages at the same level instead of being floated and used as a policy instrument. Real estate can be potent weapon (perhaps a better instrument in India than monetary and fiscal policies) to moderate economic activity since the expenditure on real estate is mostly discretionary and has a good linkage with employment, both ideal characteristics for an effective intervention instrument.

The government should remove most of the incentives for real estate other than self-occupied and to a less degree the rented ones. There is no need to offer tax incentives for second or third houses and speculative investments (properties that are never occupied or properties bought and sold within a specified number of years, say, 5 years). Capital gains taxes may be at full levels equivalent to regular business incomes. There is a strong case for reworking most of the tax provisions relating to real estate. Most of the poor buy real estate for living needs. Real estate as an investment activity is more the preserve of the rich people or urban sector, neither of which deserves government support.

The argument about India being in deficit (and hence justifying tax incentives) in real estate may be correct to an extent. But then speculative monies are not going to flow into areas (largely rural and semi-urban areas) where there is physical deficit of houses and fulfil them. It is only going to invade rich areas where the land pressure is already high and which is backed by spending power. Areas which are currently deficient in real estate may not attract such investments. If the deficit areas had the spending power, they would create the assets themselves even if in a gradual manner.

Speculative investments in real assets are always premised on appreciation of prices which provides the returns to the speculators. Speculation in real assets only leads to faster appreciation. And such trends of rising prices can hardly help those who are already short of money, the prime source of housing deficit. To argue that speculation will increase real supplies looks very tenuous and difficult of logical construction.

However, if the government sees speculative investments as an aid in solving the shortage, it should restrict incentives to only geographical areas which have a shortage of supply.

EFFECT OF LOWER SAVINGS

It is perhaps better to skim the top layer of savings and channelise the same towards current consumption. If the savings that is mobilised is carefully targeted (like those going to low-yielding assets such as gold and speculative real estate), it may not compromise our growth in a significant way. This would however call for careful prioritising of all investments and devising ways to lop off the low-yielding ones. It may be better to have a savings rate of 27–28 per cent and achieve higher income multipliers[7] and current income and employment even if it means sacrificing an additional percentage point of growth.

The shortfall in savings can always be made good by cheaper funds from abroad. This would call for pragmatic policies and careful development of some sectors such as tourism and promotion of export-oriented industries such as textiles and leather goods to earn foreign exchange to service the same. Our own savings can chase the high-yielding assets in the informal sector and for achieving better financial integration.

[7] A reduction from 33 per cent to 27 per cent will improve the income multiplier from 3.0 to 3.7 (perhaps more if targeted properly) which can make our 'investments' yield better results.

EFFECT OF SHIFT FROM GOLD AND REAL ESTATE TO OTHER HIGH-YIELDING ASSETS

Gold is a low-yielding (current returns) asset and its returns except perhaps for its insurance value, maybe in the range of 1–2 per cent. Current yields from real estate come from rents which are in the range of 3 per cent. The real estate has a large component of speculative demand which may be about 20–25 per cent of total demand. In 2011–12, India spent 3.1 per cent of its GDP on gold imports ($56 billion on GDP of about $1,800 billion). Speculative component of real estate could be about 2–3 per cent of GDP. Together, they are about 5–6 per cent, yielding a recurring income/GDP of say 3 per cent on investment. If these amounts had been invested at sustainable minimum nominal returns of 12 per cent, it would have yielded about 0.45 per cent of additional output. This has the effect of pushing down the ICOR by about 0.1 and growth rates by 0.16 per cent, as illustrated in a simplistic calculation in Table 7.2.

Table 7.2 Differential Growth Rates from Gold and Real Estate

	With 5% in Gold and Real Estate	**In Commercially Feasible Assets**	**Difference**
Investment (₹)	100	100	100
Returns on capital (%)	3	12	9
Proportion in GDP (%) (assumed)			5%
Additional output			0.45
Total output (₹)	22.22	22.67	0.45
ICOR (times)	4.50	4.41	0.09
Gross actual investments in 2009–10 as % of GDP	36.2	36.2	
Potential growth rates (% per annum)	8.04	8.21	0.16

Source: Author's calculations.

We should make all our efforts to diminish the investments in low-yielding assets, by removal of all direct and indirect incentives to such investments. After all India is not short of opportunities for investments and there are several sections wilting under oppressive interest rates.

7.2 Making Our Capital Work Better for Us: Reaping the ICOR Dividend

India is a populous country with a young population in relative terms—making many talk of reaping the 'demographic dividend'. This may prove largely illusory. Their skill sets is low and hence their productivity is poor leading to poor income and spending. With the poor income levels, they are hardly going to create markets for goods or jobs for others. They may not be able to fund their own skill upgradation or education expenses. There is no clear cut plan to get out of this non-virtuous cycle.

It is perhaps easier to work on reaping the ICOR dividend. Results on this may be comparatively easier to achieve, solutions may be more technical and hence more predictable, and examples of methods and solutions may be available elsewhere to learn from and apply.

Our high ICOR (disadvantage) is a function of several factors such as inappropriate choice of projects, needless demands about sub-optimal infrastructure projects, delays in execution, wasting too much capital, choice of inappropriate technology and work methods, and lax attitudes. In the following pages, we examine these reasons and ways to correct them. It is of utmost importance to tame this important economic variable which has received insufficient attention right through—post- or pre-reform years. The four main reasons for poor capital productivity in India are (i) poor project selection due to spurious arguments about our infrastructure deficits and calls for bridging them, (ii) delays in implementation of projects, (iii) poor demand and pricing management and (iv) poor attitudinal infrastructure. We have analysed (iv) in Chapter 3. We will analyse the other three to get them right hereunder.

SPURIOUS INFRASTRUCTURE DEFICITS

Many economists argue that the 'deficit' in infrastructure is the main reason for our slow or sluggish development. The usual arguments for infrastructure are (i) India is woefully short of infrastructure, (ii) infrastructure investments will create 'externalities' and (iii) due to these, the government needs to support them with viability gap funding, investment incentives, tax exemptions, etc. This, it is argued, is required for reaching double-digit growth rates. Let us examine the merits.

Any underdeveloped country will surely be short on many things—literacy, medical services, hotels, schools, even soft infrastructures such as attitudes and discipline, food and sanitation. Economic infrastructures (such as ports, airports and cold chains) for which concessions are being sought are also one of them. Economic returns and not success in wresting concessions should govern the relative share of investments in each economic activity; the rule may be different for social actions. Infrastructure investments should also obey economic logic even if adjusted for externalities. If externalities are recovered from the beneficiaries, it should obey normal commercial principles.

Concessions are sought since the economic returns are far too low. The concessions are sought for long periods—more than 15–20 years and viability gap funding up to 40 per cent (current limit for BOT), both of which imply an economic return of 7–8 per cent. Given India's real growth rates of 7–8 per cent and inflation of 5–6 per cent, the nominal returns required for sustained existence of any venture should be a minimum of 14–15 per cent, which translates to a normal payback period of 5–8 years. The implied ROIs on the infrastructure projects suggest a near zero or negative real returns.

Any product or service in short supply will usually command a premium or higher price. Or if the price is arbitrarily fixed lower, it will result in long queues like we see in railways, airlines, etc. The kind of returns implied by the concession seeking projects is a definite indicator of its poor demand and economic returns.

Some infrastructure can be targeted directly at end consumers such as in telecom, air transport, passenger rail network and life insurance. The additional infrastructure created in some of these sectors has been absorbed very well. However, much of infrastructure (such as ports, industrial zones, data networks and shipping) is an intermediate good whose demand depends on final demand of related goods and services. Creation of intermediate infrastructure should closely track demand for such services. Any attempt to create them at faster rate is bound to result in lower returns and wasted investments.

Some Crucial Questions

Firstly, why should the society fund projects at 7–8 per cent when there are several projects in other sectors waiting at 15–16 per cent? In rural areas and urban unorganised sectors and low tickets borrowing, there are people willing to borrow at 60–80 per cent—which should imply that they hope (sometimes may be foolishly) to get equivalent returns.

Secondly, infra-projects are enormous cash guzzlers and if we fund more of such low return projects, it might unwittingly pull down the overall growth rates in the near to medium term.

Thirdly, the positive 'externalities' generated by infrastructure projects post completion. It is true any infrastructure project facilitates growth in other sectors. Economic infrastructures such as power, ports, airports, national highways, roads, railways, dams, metros and mono rails, intercity corridors, sports infrastructure, railways and roads—are all sectors aimed at serving industrial or business activity or production of goods or services consumed largely by top income quartile. If the project is creating positive externality, why should we not recover the same from these high-income segments? If the beneficiaries are not forthcoming to pay up for benefits enjoyed by them, how do we even know that we are indeed creating positive externalities? Or is it just a case of free loading—if something comes for free why not take it?

Fourthly, infrastructure investments are claimed to be not easily scalable and hence the investments have to be made keeping in mind demand for next several years. Concessions are justified for the 'initially wasting and later productive' investments. Such 'visionary' investments should be governed by the growth rates and inflation rates of the country under reference. For our nominal growth rates of 14–15 per cent, a benefit of ₹100 accruing after 15 years is worth ₹15 in present value. However, for an advanced economy growing at real rates of 2 per cent and inflation of 2 per cent, the same is worth ₹55 today. It makes sense for them to pursue infrastructure with such long-term benefits and payback. But our problems are more immediate in nature, such as basic health care, and primary education and persisting hunger. For us to keep investing scarce resources in pursuing 7–8 per cent, 15–30 year payback infrastructure projects is being irresponsible towards the economically disadvantaged.

DEMAND AND PRICING MANAGEMENT

India is poor at demand management; if we recover full economic prices without subsidies for our airports and trains, the demand may stand perhaps halved and we would not see as much congestions as we do today. It is our compelling national habit to demand everything for free. Holiday travellers travelling abroad spend upwards of ₹50,000 or more for their trip but cringe on paying ₹750/1,000 user development charges at airports and the ever willing government rushes to their rescue. Each time such economically unjustifiable action is defended by the government, we are only creating further mental roadblocks and fear for the future investors.

Need to Make Infrastructure Investments Self-sustaining

We need to make infrastructure investments a sustainable proposition. It just does not pay to create monsters today, short-recover costs and when the time is ripe for modernisation or expansion we stare at decaying services, bankrupt ventures and further cries for concessions. Golden Quadrilateral was supposed to save nearly 30 per cent of costs for the commercial operators in increased billing per day (due to faster movement), reduced fuel and maintenance costs. Road transport accounts for 4.5 per cent of GDP (both passenger and freight included), more than 40 per cent of which is on national highways. The savings accruing to commercial operators alone on these roads should be ₹32,000 crore. If the savings were shared equally, the government could have recovered ₹16,000 crore and doubled the pace of National Highways Development Project (NHDP; annual budget ₹9,100 crore in 2009–10) and made it more self-sustaining.

Concessions for economic infrastructure aimed at the top income quartile are bereft of merit. Within the overall basket, there are several infra-projects potentially capable of earning economically sustainable ROIs of 15 per cent or more. We should start with those and expand them by re-investing and growing with the economy. The time for others will come when they will promise yields in line with the economic costs and interest rates (which may drift downwards in later years of growth) or where our interest rates come down.

There are plenty of funds overseas at rates as low as 1–2 per cent interest rates (without forex cover costs, of course) and they would be keen on investing in India for long periods at low rates. We should access such funds and to the extent such funds are available invest in specific infrastructure projects even if they are low yielding so long as they cover their finance costs—maybe with their technical help. The government can play a facilitating role in such projects. It appears less than commensurate efforts have gone in this direction.

Proper Pricing and Sequencing

The first trans-Atlantic phone call between the US and the UK is reported to have cost as much as £15 for 3 minutes (in 1927 £) through British Telecom.[8] AT&T had a capacity of one call at a time and cost as much as $75 per 3 minutes.[9] If the governments had intervened and controlled the prices, the industry would never have developed and we would not be having limitless capacities which connect instantly at a cost which is one-hundredth of the first calls made. Indian government has been trying to beat the natural logic of progress in most services it provides by fixing unreasonable low prices.

There are some lead sectors which inherently have poor returns; the government is unwilling to recover its price initially from its end-users. Scale economies may dictate certain minimum sizes below which the investment may be unviable to begin with calling for the government to hand-hold the investment for some time. But then the superior returns should be demonstrable clearly at least in the long term before the government invests its monies. The long-term viability can be constructed based on experiences in other countries when they went through a similar phase in their development or from any other projects. It should plan for gradual extension of services by growing in line with expanding demand. It can for example acquire contiguous land but set up only two or four lanes to begin with and as traffic increases develop the adjacent lanes to meet it. It can acquire land or rights initially for a larger project but put up the super-structure only when the demand is proven.

[8] *Source:* www.britishtelephones.com.

[9] *Source:* AT&T website.

DELAYS IN PROJECT IMPLEMENTATION

Delays in project implementation is a major cause of poor capital productivity. As per Ministry of Statistics and Programme Implementation, Annual Report 2011–12, the cost overrun on the public sector projects monitored by it is about ₹84,000 crore or about 24 per cent of original cost. These have a time overrun ranging from 2 to 213 months. While it took a young Japanese team 18 months to complete the trans-Yamuna bridge in Delhi, the Indian engineers could not even complete the approach roads leading to the bridge—a telling commentary on our lackadaisical approach to this very important growth determinant.

In fact, India could have had it much better. We have the benefit of technology which have been developed and perfected already elsewhere and we need not go through the same learning curve as others who have walked the path earlier.

Reasons for Delays

There are many reasons for delays beginning with the decision-making process and execution to attitudes.

There are too many people involved in the approval process from regulators to bureaucracy, judicial systems, administration and in many cases even within the organisation itself—commercial or government—that have low or no stakes in the successful implementation of the project within the time or cost. The more such people are involved in the process the more the cost of delay.

Within the government, its own lack of accountability for results, absence of output and deliverable-based planning, lack of linkage of results with rewards, protection from private sector or foreign competition are the major causes for inordinate delays in projects getting completed. In summary, our approach and attitude towards projects are as indifferent as our approach to hunger and poverty.

Table 7.3 Comparative Ranking: India versus Select Countries

Country	Ease of Doing Business (Rank)	Time to Start Business (Days)	Global Competitiveness Index (Rank)
Year	**2010**	**2010**	**2012–13**
China	89	37	29
India	133	30	59
Japan	15	23	10
Malaysia	23	11	25
Singapore	1	3	2
South Africa	34	22	52
Thailand	12	32	38
United Kingdom	5	13	8
United States	4	6	7

Source: 1. Ease of doing business index and time to start a business are from World Bank, Doing Business Indicators. 2. Global competitiveness index is from www.weforum.org/gcr and © 2012 World Economic Forum.

Poor training, delays in clearances, poor execution systems, poor risk management systems, lax safety systems, endless list of permits and approvals required, lack of follow-up, running into frequent unforeseen and unforeseeable contingencies cropping up, interfering litigation are factors which cause delays.

There are also the delays induced by official procedures. On several parameters such as ease of doing business or starting business and global competitiveness we fare rather poorly as can be seen in Table 7.3. These do result in poor capital productivity and low yields.

Need and Ways to Cut Down on Delays

Between 1990–91 and 2010–11, i.e. since reforms started, the Indian public sector has implemented projects worth approximately ₹4,812,000 crore with an approximate overruns of just over 23 per cent[10] which amounts to ₹1,130,000 without reckoning interest. Just investing this amount at fail-safe government bonds at 8 per cent per annum would have given the government ₹90,000 crore per annum. This amount is good enough to run National Rural Employment Guarantee Act (NREGA) more than twice as big as the current size, or replace the entire rolling stock of the railways every year.

If this is the scale of wastage due to delays, should it not be the first port of call for reforms. Targeting just this aspect with all the might and expertise of the state, it could have taken care of more problems than perhaps the combined effect of many other fiscal and physical measures which have engaged successive governments.

The government has taken some measures for training, follow-up, risk management, periodic review, etc. It may also pay to look at the following measures.

Firstly, there should be appropriate incentive may be perhaps at the organisational level (or supplemented by incentives at the individual level). Organisations performing well may be granted autonomous status as far as it concerns capital decisions. Employees of such organisation (to be reviewed every year) may be entitled to additional pay of 10–15 per cent per annum so long as they retain their status.

Secondly, we need to invite private sector and foreign competition on all projects. Their execution will perhaps put pressure on our departments or contract executors. Maybe over a period of time, learning and implementation technology will percolate to others.

Thirdly, contracts should provide for incentives for early completion and graded penalties for late completion. Maybe we should never start the project until all permits are in place and once in place projects are declared 'open' it should be put beyond litigation.

We should perhaps prepare a dossier of eminent retired persons who should be exclusively entrusted with the task of

[10] RBI, *Handbook of Statistics on Indian Economy*, Table 38.

opening the projects as soon as they are complete without having to wait for incumbent politicians.

Dividends from Curtailing Delays: Additional Growth

For every percentage increase in capital productivity (return on capital employed [ROCE]) of projects, our national growth rate can improve by about 0.12 per cent. The delays in public sector capital projects have been about 23 per cent over the last two decades. One may assume that private sector is not devoid of this problem either, especially when one sees instances such as the Delhi Metro Airport express or Posco. Let us assume a lesser 10 per cent for private sector, due to pressures imposed by individual or corporate accountability. The gross capital formation (which includes the cost overrun component) was 35.8 per cent of GDP in 2010–11, with 2.1 per cent coming from valuables. Segregating the wasted investments from total, the actual investments would be about 31.9 per cent, as shown in Table 7.4.

With output remaining constant, a decrease of 11 per cent in investments would decrease the capital required per unit of output (ICOR) from say 4.5 to about 4.0. With an investment of 35.8 per cent of GDP, this optimisation in ICOR would result in pushing up the potential growth rates from 7.96 per cent to 8.95 per cent—a whole percentage improvement.

Table 7.4 Adjusted Gross Capital Investments

Sector	Gross Capital Investments as % of GDP	Cost Overruns (%)	Investments Sans Cost of Delays (% to GDP)
Public sector	8.8	23	7.2
Private sector	24.9	10	22.6
Valuables	2.1	0	2.1
Total	35.8		31.9
% to Gross capital investments			89%

Effect of ICOR Reduction

There is a needless or bogus clamour for investments in many low-yielding infrastructures which should give way to investments in projects which are commercially viable and where demand and need are proven by willingness to pay. We should divert funds from low-yielding investments to higher-yielding investments in informal sector and rural areas and borrow from abroad where deficits surface. Every percentage improvement in capital returns (ROCEs and internal rate of returns [IRRs]) has the potential effect of improving our GDP by 0.12 per cent, following the logic laid down in Table 7.4. Granted not all our projects are sub-optimal, but scope for improvement is plenty. It will not be impossible to achieve a 1.5 per cent improvement in our growth rate through improvement in our capital productivity (ICOR) alone. It requires persistent efforts, proper training, focussed and serious approach, and an enlightened outlook and approach towards allowing foreign investments and careful selection of sectors to invite such investments, than blind pursuits like FDI in retail which is a poor advertisement for new growth engines.

Feasibility of Significant Change in ICOR: Lessons from Other Countries

Most Western countries reaped a good dividend from rapid advances in technology during the Second World War and dropped their ICORs significantly. In fact, constant research and deployment of technology have helped most nations to fight the usual declining capital productivity.

The capital output ratio of the US[11] improved dramatically between 1930 and mid-1940s post its recession. It improved from just over 4 around 1930 to just less than 2 by

[11] See *Economics* by Samuelson and Nordhaus, 16th Edition, p. 530.

early 1940s, before stabilising around 2.5 for a long time thereafter. Such a dramatic change in total (just to distinguish) capital output ratio implics very low ICOR during the transition period. India's low level of capitalisation, chance of learning from others, ready availability of technology from others can all facilitate reaping quick improvement in ICOR. China's ICOR during the last 20 years is about 0.3 to 0.5 less than India's, despite its much higher income and capital investments. It only signifies their superior evaluation skills, work discipline and execution skills besides of course other facilitating factors which may not be all that democratic.

Chapter 8

CREATING NEW GROWTH ENGINES

The important thing for Government is not to do things which individuals are doing already, and to do them a little better or a little worse; but to do things which at present are not done at all.

—John Maynard Keynes in *The End of Laissez Faire* (1926)

In a way, our Mumbai Taxis (old Fiats still dominating the scene) symbolises India's inertial instincts with growth. If fares had been properly revised from time to time and government had made it mandatory to retire old cars beyond a certain age and devised systems for financing the operators, most of the old cars would have been off the road, ensuring better taxies for the commuters. Without adequate fare increase, retiring these taxis within reasonable time is not financially viable. If the commuters do not pay, they would not get improved services either. Hence, the quality of taxis remains at 'primitive' levels. Thus, even if Mumbai travellers have the capacity to pay, and the city houses some of the richest people in the world, and has gained enormously from reforms, government inaction has ensured a low equilibrium service level at least as far as taxis go in Mumbai. This is perhaps true of other Metros such as Kolkata and Delhi, maybe in different degrees.

Indian economy seems to be willingly stuck at a similar low level economic equilibrium. Low skills leading to low productivity levels and high 'relative wages' (adjusted for productivity) result in low employment. This results in low demand which is further exacerbated in India's case by frugality in spending habits and low aspirations. The inertial economic cycle, in a limited sense, is almost like a chronic recession—not due to temporary lows in consumption and confidence. Consumption habits of future generations of course will be different and conducive to higher demand and growth and India will see a day when consumption will not be scorned or savings necessarily considered virtuous. But this is a slow and evolving process.

NEW GROWTH INITIATIVES ESSENTIAL

Some of the actions required for breaking out of this shell and shoring up sagging confidence were seen in Chapter 7. This needs to be supplemented by creating new avenues of demand, consumption and investment. Even in advanced economies, at times of recession it is the government which pitches in to break the temporary inertia. The government here has a responsibility to break the chronic inertia caused by low entrepreneurial skills, fear of job loss (given the chronic unemployment levels), aspirations and habits which have got frozen at low levels for several decades.

The government has to play a leading role in creating new avenues of growth. The growth has to be (i) meaningful, (ii) economically and commercially viable and (iii) socially productive or welfare additive. There are several areas where the current levels of consumption are low, desired services are absent or in short supply, or the opportunity to promote economic activity is un-exploited. In this chapter, we examine some select economic initiatives which will create growth opportunities, enhance employment, whose output is most likely to enjoy enough demand or is considered socially desirable. It is likely to be backed up with commensurate purchasing power and ability and willingness to pay or structures can be created which can recover the costs from the people who use the services and hence will not leave a dent on government finances.

There will most likely be more such growth engines. The examples have been chosen for their economic and welfare impact which might in some ways match the most visible and enduring growth engine during reform years India has created and nurtured—IT sector. The share of IT and ITeS sectors has grown from 1.2 per cent in 1997–98 to about 7.5 per cent of gross domestic product (GDP) by 2011–12, a stupendous growth indeed with an added bonus of being largely export oriented.

The next most successful growth engine we have created is the telecom sector which was slow to take off but fast to catch up in the last about a decade. The number of telephone connections[1] which were about 55 million in 2003, and 207 million by March 2007 is about 927 by December 2011—a near 17-fold increase in less than 10 years. But telecom is almost entirely domestically focussed—both provision and consumption of regular service (not the capital expenditure on setting up the network) completing the loop largely within India.

Of the three new growth engines identified, tourism is focussed both domestically and at international community, while dealing with wastes and building new cities are likely to be more domestically focussed. Even if the impact of these new engines are about half as strong as IT and telecom, it would still make a significant addition to our growth rates and make it stabilise at much higher orbit.

8.1 Developing New Capital Cities and Helping Urbanisation

As the economy grows, urbanisation increases. While the process may be inevitable, India seems to be lagging in this area both in the levels and the pace at which it is urbanising

[1] *Source:* Economic Surveys; section on Telecommunication.

as can be seen from Figure 8.1 which plots the per capita income (in current dollars) vis-à-vis the percentage of population (in select countries comparable to India) living in urban areas for 3 years, viz., 1990, 2000 and 2008 covering the breadth of India's reform years. It is clear from the picture that even when the income levels in countries such as Philippines, China and Indonesia were similar to India's current income levels, their levels of urbanisation were far higher. In these sample countries, as the income increased, their growth in urban areas was far faster than what is witnessed in India currently.

In India, urbanisation may be sluggish both due to lack of development of new areas and lack of opportunities within the existing urban centres which are bursting at the seams already. Both would need to be tackled simultaneously. In a country where the population itself is growing fast, urbanisation will

Figure 8.1 Progress of Urbanisation in Select Countries between 1990 and 2008[2]

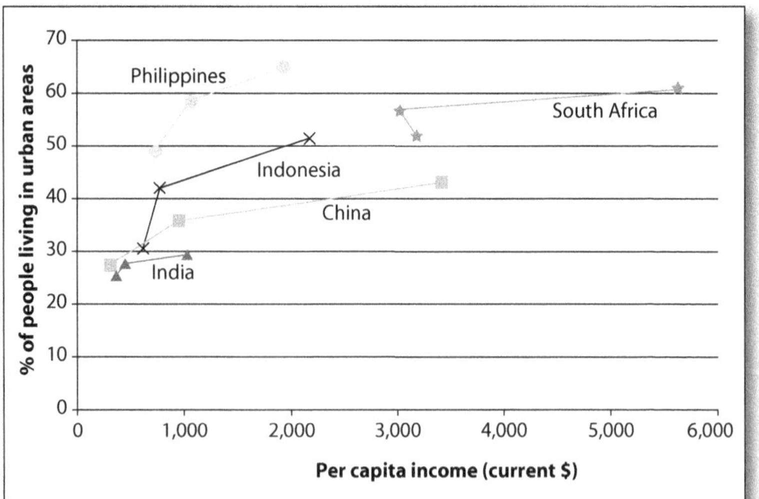

[2] Data for the graph have been sourced from USAID Country Compass.

involve geographical expansion besides accommodating more people within the confines of existing urban centres.

POOR QUALITY AND PACE OF OUR URBANISATION

The choice is between new geographical growth centres or enhancing the 'capacities' of the existing ones. Our overwhelming preference seems to be for the latter. Apart from the National Capital Region (NCR) comprising Delhi, Gurgaon and Noida and some new cities like new Raipur, there are hardly any new developments. In the last 60 years, Chandigarh, Navi Mumbai and Gandhi Nagar may be the rare exceptions of entirely new cities being built from scratch.

In most other cases, it is largely the existing cities taking the burden of increasing urbanisation. The newer areas absorbed to accommodate the growth have hardly been sufficient; nor has the development in these areas well planned or executed. It is quite common to see the very same 24-feet road created 50–60 years ago for a vehicular traffic[3] which was one-thousandth as is today supporting the increased traffic and six-floor societies (in place of the single-story buildings). Even in the NCR, it is not difficult to see such areas within a radius of 10 km from the seat of government and India Gate.

The only signs of futuristic thinking are the manholes and concrete drain pipes which project out dangerously half a foot over their surrounding road levels, probably constructed keeping in mind the next few years of road carpeting which will bring the road to the same level, inflicting a punishment on the users till parity of height is achieved. Perhaps no other country in our neighbourhood and even countries which have much lower per capita income than ours are guilty of such shoddy development and maintenance as our cities. Population is only one of the reasons.

[3] The number of passenger cars produced in 1950–51 was about 7,900 per annum while it was about 2.51 million in 2011–12.

Lack of planning, poor or non-existent quality or work execution standards, lethargy and overwhelming speed of growth besides apathy and corruption may be some contributing reasons. But there are also physical limits given our technology, law and order, helplessness of the government in enacting and enforcing laws relating to civic administration. With these constraints, it may not be feasible anymore to grow our existing cities to accommodate growing population besides upgrading the existing services to contemporary levels. An alternative is development of new cities and increasing their share in urbanisation.

HOW DO NEW CITIES HELP?

Developing infrastructure within the existing geographical confines of our urban areas imposes huge hidden or open but unaccounted costs. We try to squeeze in more and more infrastructure such as metros, overbridges, flyovers, monorails and ever-widening roads within the limited area but are awfully short on planning and shoddy in execution. There are road diversions, traffic jams which run for years on end, broken vehicles, frayed tempers and increased level of accidents and several person hours wasted on de-tours and traffic jams. None of these negative externalities seem to get built into our project evaluation.

It is almost impossible to achieve contemporary quality standards including time to execute with the plethora of constraints imposed by existing structures, infrastructure, vested interests, etc. A newer area developed from scratch or pulling down low-quality non-optimally sized structures may help us upgrade the quality substantially at same or lower costs—witness the planning in Chandigarh and Gandhi Nagar or even the upcoming new Raipur in comparison with Chennai and Bangalore.

Social services such as colleges and hospitals are spending a huge amount in creating infrastructure much of which is absorbed in land acquisition (whether they pay for it or government gives it to them at a subsidised rate, the total cost to society is high). The amount is better spent on other amenities instead of high-cost land, which will help create more hospital beds for a given level of investment.

In places like Mumbai, there is a degree of social tension due to influx of people from outside. While one may argue against these as being unconstitutional, it is inevitable when we pack such cities way beyond their carrying capacity. Newer cities may ease this somewhat.

The one major worthwhile argument going in favour of expansion in existing cities is 'proven demand'; a new city developed may not get occupied as people may not move into it which may affect investment paybacks. If the required amenities are created in new cities with some help from government fiats, it should be possible to tackle this issue. Once the initial tepid demand is overcome, growth and movement of people may not be difficult.

MODEL AND HOW TO MAKE IT HAPPEN

The government can identify new centres and make them the seat of administration and include institutions such as high end or specialty hospitals, higher education, research organisations, regulatory bodies, essential hospitality facilities and provide for services like schools. This will create the demand and shift the first wave of people into such cities. The government can acquire land, plan the layout, and develop the road, drainage and infrastructure and oversee rehabilitation work (including alternative skill development to existing residents for the new setting and to earn their livelihood). The investments in buildings, schools and hospitals, shops, hotels and residential colonies can come from private sector.

Out of the acquired land, the plan can provide for an additional 20 per cent for roads, parks, water bodies, waste treatment and other modern amenities to make them both functional and contemporary. If it is assumed that the land would have had at least 10 per cent in such works, the balance of 70 per cent can be developed for residential, commercial and government purposes. If the FSI is taken as 3 times on this one, we would be able to develop about 210 per cent of land area acquired. This can be used to pay the existing owners (for 90 per cent of land) and the new developers who can cover their costs of development by selling the balance.

OVERCOMING IMPEDIMENTS

The main impediments are likely to be (i) financing, (ii) shifting people and (iii) land acquisition.

Financing: The central government could allocate say, ₹40,000 crore per annum for the next 15 years and concentrate on basic planning, training and rehabilitation of project affected, the rest of development being left to private sector. The amount can come from employment and other loosely targeted subsidies and the various urban renewal programmes. At the societal level if most of these funds can come from savings otherwise going into gold and silver, it would have a salutary effect. Even if the investments come from savings which are otherwise going into real estate, it would still benefit the society in creating new additional 'capacities' rather than increasing 'capacity utilisation' of existing cities and stretching our cities beyond breaking strength. Once there is momentum, investment in real estate cannot be an issue; as seen before, it constitutes the main 'savings' method most of us are comfortable with and demand for real estate may be more than the demand for cricket and Indian Premier League (IPL) matches.

Shifting: The current wave of reforms has led to a lot of migration. One sees people from across the country working in far off places even at junior levels. Mobility for job sake is lot less of a stigma or constraint. Once a base level of economic activity is created, which can be done with government services, research, education, etc., other commercial activities will follow.

Land acquisition: The third and perhaps the most potent impediment is the land acquisition. We have discussed the issues and possible solutions in land acquisition in Chapter 2.

The government should start the exercise with re-training people in identified zones in skills that can sell in urban settings such as civic maintenance, road construction and maintenance, security, traffic regulation, running shops and establishments and the various gamut of services that go into it, micro entrepreneurial activities like running taxis. The compensation can be in the form of 40–50 per cent of constructed area in shops or commercial establishments and balance in residential space which will provide for both living and livelihood and continuing source of income. Replacing assets with which they are familiar instead of money will mostly overcome fear of unknown assets since real estate as a concept and asset has universal appeal.

BENEFITS AND IMPACT ON GROWTH

Assuming unproductive savings are diverted from gold and foreign direct investment (FDI) is about 25 per cent and private investments are twice for every rupee spent by government in such cities, for a yearly allocation of ₹40,000 crore, GDP can be better off by 1–1.25 per cent at current income levels.

8.2 Extracting Growth and Employment from Urban Wastes

KOLKATA WETLANDS

The wetlands in Eastern Kolkata[4] is a rustic, totally native bio-technical marvel which is a tribute to human ingenuity. It feeds the city's sewage to algae (algae is the largest global

[4] Most of the data quoted about the Kolkata Wetlands have been personally gathered by the author during a field visit in 2000 facilitated by IIM Calcutta under Environmental Capacity Building Programme of the World Bank.

producer of oxygen at 330 billion tonnes per annum[5]—nearly three-fourths of the total) grown in ponds and the oxygen—the universal cleanser—converts raw sewage into potable water in just 7 days. This is fed to downstream agricultural land. But the revenue of the occupants comes mainly from the fish that feed on the algae, which they supply to Kolkata along with vegetables. But the most interesting fact is that it has provided sustainable livelihood to about 60,000 people for well over a century.

Can we replicate this to 'extract' employment and growth from urban wastes? If reforms have to succeed and naxalism is contained, not by force but by winning over the disgruntled, we need to create lots of jobs at rapid pace absorbing existing skills.

We have scant respect for anything other than our immediate surroundings and use it a waste dump for just about anything from spitting to cigarette ash, used cars to sewage, plastics to used toothpaste tubes, various kinds of packaging material and wasted food. Our habits are not well formed and there is a lack of appreciation of how our behaviour and its resultant affect others adversely. So long as the stink or nuisance is out of our reach, the responsibility is divested. The same orientation has been aggregated at societal level and the government thinks of no measures to rein in this behaviour or manage its after effects.

There are several types of urban residential wastes including food left-overs, newspapers, construction debris, sewage, superannuated automobiles, etc. For want of space, let us focus only on some of the urban wastes such as plastic disposables, mineral water bottles and newspapers that litter our streets.

The chief beneficiaries of the litter are the fast moving consumer goods (FMCG), pharma, liquor, packaged foods, etc. companies who use sophisticated dispensers to deliver their products but have no clearly laid plans to deal with them once they have served their purpose. The consumers use

[5] *Source:* www.ecology.com.

Employment from Waste: A Case from Swaziland

Ngwenya is a village on the outskirts of Mbabane, the capital of Swaziland. A group of local craftsmen work on glass blowing. Their products include tableware, vases, jugs, decorative African animals and light fittings targeted at urban household show cases, high end hotel lobbies and corporate gifts. The raw material is 100 per cent recycled glass. Besides commercial arrangements and exchange of building material, there are student sponsorships of local foot ball for their efforts in collecting waste glass for the factory.

It employs about 70 people at the factory all trained in their art. The waste glass is heated in furnace up to 1,200°C and shaped into various articles while still malleable and hot. Each item is hand-made.

It is a great example of generating employment from wastes. The products are not marketed for their charity value—they compete with the best and are sold through high end malls and duty-free shops over southern Africa. The operations are environmentally friendly besides helping deal with waste glass from urban areas, safe disposal of drinking bottles, household glass, etc.

Swaziland is a country of a million people. Each city in India can develop and sustain a factory of similar size helping to deal with our wastes besides creating employment for urban unemployed without their having to undergo years and years of education.

these products but throw the waste around just about anywhere. We must make these two 'beneficiaries' bear the cost of 'clean up' between them in a sustainable way that does not create inconveniences to others or the government. There is no proper incentive structure in place now for collection and disposal of wastes; nor is there an effective deterrent law or enforcement.

CREATING AN INCENTIVE STRUCTURE

Littering is a kind of pollution and creates negative value for others. No one will willingly buy such negative values. Positive value has therefore to be 'created' by a creative reverse charge mechanism. The polluting beneficiary companies should be made to declare the complete recollection plan or re-cycling plan for all their waste products which are not physically consumed and which are seen littering our streets.

A pollution cess[6] of say 4 per cent (or other higher percentage where necessary depending upon the nuisance values) should be charged along with cenvat. This should be refundable to the producers based on actual re-use or recollection at designated re-use centres. The polluting company has to undertake re-purchase of wastes at the indicated values at their designated centres (whether owned by them or contracted) which should be properly notified. Any consumer or any one for that matter who presents the wastes at the designated collection centres should be able to claim refund of the 4 per cent or such amounts indicated.

There should be a minimum stipulation of recollection (say 80 per cent or so or initially lower but gradually increasing) which will help test whether the values specified are commensurate or not. If people find it cheaper or less bothersome to throw it around rather than reclaim the value specified (self or give it to as waste collector who collects the value from the redemption centres), it is a definite indication of inappropriate pricing. The benefitting companies should then dispose of the wastes collected either by recycling or otherwise disposing them in the pre-agreed manner. Hopefully over a period of time, most such wastes will find a value and will be recycled.

The refundable tax will create a base 'economic' value for the wastes. If a 4 per cent cess is levied on (say) mineral water bottles retailing at ₹10/bottle, used bottles will have a waste value of up to 40 paise at the designated collection centres. The bottles should be mandated to carry the 'redemption value' for which they can be redeemed. Even if the 'redemption value' is not lucrative for the actual consumer, there will be many waste collectors who will collect it from their doorstep (probably with other wastes), and reclaim its value from

[6] This can also take the form of pollution obligations. For example, the polluting industrial unit could be mandated to develop green cover at a specified ratio directly or indirectly by bearing the cost of such development done by third parties. This would provide employment in rural areas besides creating ecologically benefits.

the designated centres. Gradually, a reverse distribution channel will develop—from the end consumer of the original product back to the producer or recycler. If enforcement is tight, the redemption economic value will be shared by the various levels of waste aggregators, consumers, those involved in recycling and maybe the marketing companies themselves.

REVERSE DISTRIBUTION IS FAR LESS EXPENSIVE

Reverse distribution unlike distribution of products does not involve investment in stocks and working capital, shelf space rentals, air conditioned malls, cold storages, costly advertising or packaging and hence even a small incentive (and a lot of fines for pollution) is good enough. Most likely, the levels of skills required for carrying out the aggregating activity will not be of a high order and hence the wage costs (which is likely to be the single largest cost item) and the total cost of recollection will be low.

The yields (cash as well as energy) of Indian wastes are low since everything is mixed up. Segregation will improve it and attract commercial processors. Re-usable wastes have their own market value (like old newspapers) and hopefully originating factories will be hard-pressed to look at recycling alternatives if there is a stockpile of non-recyclable wastes at their gates. The balance of tax collected less refunds can be used by the government is creating and running waste receptacles as well as educating the public about safe disposal methods and fines attendant upon on improper disposals.

Similarly, producers of consumer durable, cars and automobiles, mobile phones, etc. should also be made responsible for taking back the used products for safe disposal. Since the demand for cars and durables are growing, there is likely to be a long gap in time between when the pollution cess is collected and the refund becomes due, locking up capital. The recycling cess so collected may be mandated to be invested in government bonds.

Fines and punishment, while difficult to impose and enforce in India, has achieved wonders in several other parts of the world. A threat of a fine of 500 dirhams (nearly ₹6,500) for an act of litter, spit, etc, keeps Dubai squeaky clean despite so much of floating population. We should make an earnest beginning and even with 20 per cent enforcement, it would still be a worthwhile.

EMPLOYMENT POTENTIAL

Statistics regarding wastes and their contribution to employment and GDP are not reported in a systematic manner either by Indian government or international agencies. Given the nuisance value of wastes and pollution, it is time that national level statistics are reported on these parameters. In the absence of such statistics, its contribution to growth and employment can only be a matter of guess work.

The total retail sales value of just packaged foods, FMCG, consumer durables and pharma products is over ₹300,000 crore per annum. A 4 per cent cess will yield ₹12,000 crore. Even if one-third is spent on wages, it would still leave about ₹4,000 crore for wages—enough to create more than a million jobs at ₹30,000 per annum. Hopefully with other wastes, the potential can be better. Most importantly, this may be highly manpower intensive and will sponge away most of the unemployed people with low skills or people who can be trained with minimum effort without having necessarily to be passed through the meaningless education grind.

It might call for a one-time investment of 8–10 per cent of current GDP to create the initial infrastructure required to deal with drainage, water treatment, incineration centres, etc. If one assumes that this is likely to take about 10 years and such spending will have multiplier effect of 2 times and 25 per cent of such expenditure will come through FDI or moneys which are otherwise low yielding, we should have 0.75 per cent to 1 per cent additional growth during the time of infrastructure creation. On a running basis, wastes may contribute 0.3 per cent to 0.4 per cent to our growth.

We need to create structures whereby private incentives and punishment can take care of wastes. If Lalit Modi and BCCI (despite the recent controversies) can create a super money spinner called IPL where none existed, and east Kolkata Wetlands demonstrate that there is enough employment and marketable output in sewage water, we should 'extract' employment out of wastes. Human ingenuity can be the only constraint in not doing it.

8.3 Travel and Tourism[7]

INDIA'S NOTABLE ACHIEVEMENTS

The government has rightly identified travel and tourism as one of the key growth engine, a foreign exchange earner and employment generator. Tourism can be the next big thing after software in many respects if we get our act together. The progress that has been achieved and where India stands today in tourism, while being nowhere near its potential or requirement, has to be classified as good given our income levels, constraints, stage of development, etc. Just a sample of indicators[8] to illustrate the good work done and efforts taken by the government are as follows:

1. India ranks 68th in the Travel and Tourism Competitiveness Index, 2011 (TTCI) (Brazil is 52nd, Russia is 59th and South Africa 66th). Given our problems, and relative rankings in many other economic and welfare parameters, this is a good rank.

[7] Most of this section has been written about leisure travel while business travel also forms a significant portion of travel industry. But it is a completely different 'product segment' altogether and the policy framework required and initiatives which will yield results are far different and hence not attempted here so as not to confuse matters.

[8] Most of the ranks and statistics in the following paragraphs have been sourced from The Travel & Tourism Competitiveness Report 2011 © 2011 World Economic Forum.

2. Tourism and travel rankings have a good correlation with the Human Development Index (HDI). This is only to be expected since the kind of factors that give a good HDI such as safety and security, health and hygiene and good sanitation are also what a traveller expects. Most countries in the world have TTCI ranks almost mirroring their HDI. India's TTCI rank of 65[9] is way over HDI rank which is 105—40 ranks better than its HDI. Only Thailand and China score better in this difference in relative positions. India perhaps takes better care of its tourists than its own citizens!
3. Even during the recent meltdown, India was one of the few countries which managed to grow in foreign tourist arrivals, amount of foreign exchange earned, etc.
4. India ranks 12th in premium tourists' arrivals. India perhaps gets the best receipts in forex per tourist.
5. In T and T investment spending as a percentage of GDP for the period 2006–10, India ranks second in the world (just behind Egypt)—a noteworthy rank indeed given our budget constraints and plethora of problems to be taken care by the government. Between 1995 and 2010, India has increased its investments in T and T by $37 billion. This is exceeded only by the US.

It is an irony, however, to note that the state which has the highest potential for tourism (at least by popular perception), Rajasthan has lost out the maximum during reform years. Its growth rate which was 8.3 per cent in the decade before reforms came down to 6.1 per cent in the two decades after—puzzling indeed!

EMPLOYMENT POTENTIAL

As per the estimates (for 2010) by The World Travel and Tourism Council TSA research, 2010, the tourism industry has contributed $41 billion to our GDP (directly) and $117

[9] The ranking is for the year 2010.

billion (both direct and indirect taken together) and has employed 18.6 million and 49.1 million, respectively. The high employment generated per dollar of GDP is the main feature of the travel and tourism industry on why it should be accorded a better priority than perhaps even the software sector and why it holds a promise to take care of many of our problems.

Travel and tourism has a lot of forward and backward linkages and hence creates a lot of income and employment in related sectors. When someone moves from his base place of residence especially on overnight trips, he has to provide for all daily needs including food, stay, entertainment, local movement, travel between source and destination, money transfer, connectivity, just to sample a few. This creates opportunities for food and hospitality industries, taxis, airlines, banks and money changers, etc. Thus, the demand for allied industries gets built up leading to growth in these sectors.

Apart from its ability to generate income and employment, it also helps by-pass (in a relative sense) several other intermediate development requirements and engages us with others; India does not need to solve its hunger, rectify its laws, modernise all its airports or achieve a certain percentage literacy before it hopes to have foreign tourists or domestic tourists. In many other industries, we need to go through several grinding steps which may themselves involve investments and skill development of a high order requiring a lot of time before it is mature enough for exporting its goods or services or even attract investments. This chain is likely to be far shorter in T and T industry. People may still visit India even while it is busy solving its multitude of problems.

COMPARISON WITH THE REST OF THE WORLD AND LESSONS

According to the World Travel and Tourism Council (WTTC) estimates, the T and T sector now accounts for a remarkable 9.2 per cent of global GDP, 4.8 per cent of world exports and 9.2 per cent of world investment from direct and indirect activities combined. In India as per the Economic Survey

2011–12, tourism has contributed 5.92 per cent of GDP and 9.24 per cent of organised employment. While this looks gratifying, statistics of some other nations which have similar experiences to offer the tourists, points to a scope of a vast increase in size of this industry. Just like in IT and ITeS where India enjoys a disproportionate share of world markets, tourism also has to be viewed as a sector where we can have a far greater share. Table 8.1 summarises the key performance parameters relating to tourism for India and select countries.

While there are many redeeming features, there are still gaps in our overall infrastructure and scope for improvement indicating a lot of potential. The number of tourists arriving

Table 8.1 Tourism: A Comparison between India and Others

	T and T Competi-tiveness Index 2011	Int'l Tourism Receipts (ITR) 2009	ITR/ GDP (%) 2009	Foreign Tourist Arrivals 2010	FTA/ Popula-tion 2010	ITR Per Tourist
Country	**Rank/139**	**Billion (US $)**	**%**	**Mil**	**%**	**$/Tourist**
India	**68**	**11.1**	**0.9**	**5.8**	**0.5**	**1,914**
Switzerland	1	13.8	2.8	8.6	111.7	1,605
Singapore	10	9.2	5.0	9.2	184.0	1,000
Malaysia	35	15.8	8.2	24.6	89.5	642
China	39	39.7	0.8	55.7	4.2	713
Thailand	41	15.9	6.0	15.9	23.5	1,000
South Africa	66	7.5	2.6	8.1	16.4	926
Indonesia	74	6.3	1.2	7.0	3.0	900
Egypt	75	10.8	5.7	14.1	17.0	766
Philippines	94	2.3	1.4	3.5	3.8	657
Jordon	64	2.9	11.6	4.6	76.7	630
Cambodia	109	1.1	10.1	2.4	16.2	458

Source: Travel and Tourism Competitiveness Report, 2011 of World Economic Forum. Foreign Tourist arrivals from World Bank, World Development Indicators. ITR per tourist is calculated by Receipts of 2009 and Arrivals in 2010.

in India is rather low and hence the forex receipts from tourists. But it appears that once they arrive in India, most travellers spend enough money (and maybe time) within the country. The way forward is clearly to make more people try out India for tourism and get it into the consideration set of countries for travellers.

Table 8.1 shows that the tourist arrivals in Egypt and Jordon countries which are nowhere near our geographical size were 14.1 and 2.6 million in 2010 compared to 5.8 million in India. Egypt is known largely for its historic monuments and ancient civilisation. All the monuments from Aswan to Luxor to Edfu to Cairo and Alexandria if, hypothetically speaking, compressed may not even match India's monuments between Delhi to Agra. But while they have the Nile Cruise to offer, our rivers are being used as dumps for raw sewage and industrial wastes, even as we have plenty more rivers which if prepared and maintained well can offer cruises in a variety of areas. The level of training of the guides and the cleanliness at the monuments is way above our standards even if other areas within Egypt may present a different picture, pointing to the special efforts taken to accommodate the wishes of visitors.

Switzerland which has more visitors per annum than its population has everything tailored to make the tourists comfortable even if its offering is largely unidirectional—scenic beauty. Even the citizens at large who may not be employed by the travel industry seem trained to help and facilitate the tourists. It may be difficult for any visitor to Switzerland not to recommend it to others who ask for their opinion. The response of public service personnel involved in other tourist friendly countries has lessons to offer. India needs to do a lot of fit-for-purpose training to at least the people directly involved in the industry if not others to reach the standards of at least Egypt and Cambodia if not Switzerland.

Thailand whose population is about one-fifth India's attracts nearly 3 times as many tourists as India. Cambodia has GDP which is roughly 1 per cent India's but its tourists arrivals are about 41 per cent India's. This is only to show what can be achieved with proper policies, focussed attention and action on the ground.

INDIA'S USP

India's diversity itself can be its unique selling proposition. India has more history and monuments of different dynasties and kings and regimes spread all over. It is an amalgam of various cultures. A person travelling the length or the breadth of the country by road or rail can come across a bewildering range of languages and dialects, local customs and practices each having no semblance of connection or relationship with the others. Our temples, mosques or churches or places of worship of other major religions offer a rich diversity that is not found elsewhere—not even in Syria and the Middle East—the cradle of two of the most widely followed religions. India boasts of some of the finest hotels, some wild life and beaches to people from cold climes seeking winter warmth. Of late, India has also become known for medical and wellness tourism. India given its sub-continental size and peaceful co-existence and diversity has a lot to offer to satisfy the curiosity of most travellers. It has an aura and mystic that is capable to attracting a wide variety of travellers with many differing tastes. What is perhaps lacking is our approach,

The Kangra Fort

The Katoch dynasty, erstwhile rulers of the Kangra valley, is arguably the oldest in India dating back to days earlier than Ramayan and Mahabharat. King Porus known for his bold encounter with Alexander the Great belongs to the dynasty. There is a ruin of the fort built by them which was substantially destroyed in an earthquake in early 1905—more than a century ago. There is also a museum of the family's history and articles used by the royalty.

The presentation of artefacts and the story and preservation of the ruins of the fort offers perhaps some best in class lessons. There may be many beneficial lessons to be learnt for other sites.

some vital missing links, lack of seriousness, lack of nation-wide psyche (like one sees in Switzerland), and some last mile but vital infrastructure, and constraining airports like Goa—one of the main tourist attractions for foreigners.

IMBALANCE IN INFRASTRUCTURE AS AN OPPORTUNITY

On a comparative scale, India is perhaps better placed with tourism today than IT and software in 1991 when reforms started. India should aim to double its foreign tourists arrival (FTA) in the next 5–6 years, along with the forex receipts from them. It should also aim to double the employment in this sector. Perhaps incentives in this sector will achieve much more mileage than most other industrial activities.

Fortunately, there are many imbalances in India's overall infrastructure and facilitation as seen from the ranking on individual parameters that go to make the overall T and T competitiveness index. While our rank in Human Development Indicators may be 105 and TTCI may be 68, there are several essential aspects facilitating travel on which India's score is way above what anyone can expect a developing country to have. Hopefully in those areas we do not have to make much investment. We need to be selective in our remedial efforts and focus on the balance areas. Investments in the missing links and last mile connectivity investments will have positively disproportionate returns compared to when all round infrastructure is required, which is the case with several other efforts and industries or initiatives.

Summarised below are some factors where India's rank are overwhelmingly favourable (when viewed from the overall rank) and where some further efforts will have immediate and quick payoffs.

Fortunately, most of the factors on which we need quick improvement are the softer less investment intensive varieties which may need only training, and education of staff involved and balancing investments. Hence, a quick response to initiatives and investments can be expected.

Many of the factors which need upgradation (apart from those listed above) are also essential for day-to-day living of our citizens and domestic travellers. Hence, any improvement even if focussed on areas frequented by foreign travellers will benefit the local residents and hence resistance is likely to be less and allocation of resources may not be politically inconvenient (Table 8.2).

Himalayan Tourism

India has a long northern shoulder in the Himalayas—perhaps the longest range with many of the tallest mountain peaks, very scenic and right through the year covered with snow. There is a great potential for developing it on the lines of Swiss tourism. We can develop specialised mountain trains and infrastructure right from Kashmir to Sikkim or perhaps even beyond. It can be thrown open for development by private hands and attract both domestic and foreign tourists. This alone has the potential to duplicate India's current traffic and earnings from leisure travel.

Table 8.2 India's Ranks on Various Sub-factors of Travel and Tourism Competitiveness

Favourable Ranks	Rank	Factors Which Need Improvement	Rank
Transparency of government policymaking	42	Visa requirements	135
Air travel infrastructure		Pollution (suspended particulate matter)	105
- Airport charges and ticket taxes	18	Reliability of police services	68
- Available seat km, domestic	7	Road accidents	73
- Available seat km, international	16	Sanitation	118
Quality of railroad infrastructure	23	Hospital beds	112
Road density	31	Govt's priority for travel industry	80
Purchasing power parity	2	Hotel rooms available	136
Taxation on travel	36	ATMs accepting visa cards	100

(Table 8.2 Continued)

(Table 8.2 Continued)

Favourable Ranks	Rank	Factors Which Need Improvement	Rank
Number of world heritage natural sites	7	Overall ICT infrastructure	111
Biodiversity (total known species)	10	Attitude of population towards foreign visitors	81
Number of world heritage cultural sites	6	Staff training	59
Number of international fairs and exhibitions	31	Overall ranking (out of 139 countries)	68

Source: Report on Travel and Tourism Competitiveness, 2011, World Economic Forum. The numbers in Rank column are India's rank out of 139 countries who have reported data.

ACTION PLAN

The action plan for achieving doubling incomes from T and T could revolve around the following suggested measures:

1. *Training of personnel:* Travel is an experiential product or service. One bad experience will translate to many lost customers especially in this age of facebook and internet. It is necessary to train the entire army of people involved in the delivery chain—from the ticket conductor, to the airline staff to the security staff at airports, the taxi drivers and porters, guides at the sites, police personnel, banks and money changers and many others involved.

   Just an example of guides to illustrate the point. Our guides are largely self-trained and run out of material quickly and within a short time their attention is more towards catching the next customer rather than satisfying the existing customer. Probably for many of them, it is hereditary and there is hardly anything that they can say that you would not read in the published literature. In many countries including the likes of Egypt, Myanmar, Syria, leave aside Switzerland or Estonia, the guides are specialised graduates and professionals who seem capable of answering competently most queries of visitors and capable of throwing in enough to satisfy the curiosities besides keeping them engaged for long hours with their knowledge. Many of them take the pains of finding and reporting back if they do not have immediate answers. Their attention levels and ability to take care of the customers seem far superior by training. Harassment for tipping is another annoyance in India.

Guide services is a specialised profession and requires as much depth and skills as the computer operator or bank professional in operations, if we are to treat travel as a serious business. We simply do not give it the same importance and the delivery of this most important link is shoddy with insincerity and competence way short of expectations. We should quickly re-train those already in the profession even if at governments cost and allow only the serious minded and specially trained personnel henceforward.

2. *Sanitisation of tourist areas:* The areas and factors which we are lacking currently may take a lot of time and efforts and investments to improve on an overall nationwide scale. But the areas of interest to tourists are much smaller. It may be better to focus quick improvement in such geographic pockets and service areas and create separate track for dealing with tourists. Egypt has special coaches in their overnight trains for tourists which makes it easy for them to take care of tourists, even while the other coaches carry their domestic passengers.

   It is better to demarcate such areas and provide for better security, safety, sanitation, health and hygiene and hospitals where required. Civic maintenance should be better and can be funded by fees collected. These areas should be off for littering, begging, unauthorised parking, way laying, unauthorised solicitation for services, etc. with heavy fines if necessary. Tourists—domestic or overseas—should feel secure and safe and should have a quick source of remedying any grievance.

3. *Encouraging domestic tourism:* Domestic travel and tourism can also have the same impact if enough people can be cajoled to make it as an alternative to international travel (to whatever extent). Domestic tourism will help in better distribution of incomes and create employment especially if the tourism is in remote areas. It will also facilitate infrastructure development by private sector if tourist volumes build up. Domestic tourism remains a largely neglected area and the local tourists should be treated on an equal footing as foreign tourists. Low-cost hotels, better connectivity, tax offs for travel, etc. can be some measures for encouraging domestic travel.
4. *Governance infrastructure:* Specialised police who are not just policemen but capable of helping along the tourists with directions, things to see, and areas and annoyances to avoid, local news, shops to visit as and when approached (even within the existing set up) may be helpful. Each such area if the numbers justify can have fast track courts to deal with annoyances and safety and security issues which should be summarily dealt with. Even the existence of such facilities will in most cases act as a deterrent.
5. *Separate services:* Tourism is an important industry which has its own nuances and requires specialised knowledge of technology, comparative advantage, market intelligence of developments elsewhere, training of user friendly systems and procedures and protocols, constant connect with the end-users and travellers, quick action for remedial measures, specialised tourist promotion activities from time to time or periodical basis (such as car races, shopping festivals, event promotions). It will perhaps be better to have people with long-term commitment and passion for such activities (like our forest service or foreign service or police services) instead of general purpose administrators.

As said in the preamble, travel and tourism is for several purposes. Focus on missing link areas and bottleneck areas promises a quick return on investment and reduction in employment deficit.

CONTRIBUTION TO GROWTH AND EMPLOYMENT

For reasons argued in the earlier paragraphs, doubling GDP contribution from tourism may not be difficult. Investment fatigue may not set in at least till we achieve 3–4 times the current levels of activity. The government should carve such funds out of other subsidies or if inevitable even by increasing the taxation levels by 0.5 per cent GDP. The payoffs are well worth the sacrifices.

If employment and travel GDP double, it means an additional direct employment of 19 million and direct and indirect employment of 49 million (Table 8.3). Things may not be this linear due to technological changes and even if 20 per cent of these numbers come true, it would substantially solve our unemployment problems and reduce excessive dependence on IT and ITeS sectors.

Table 8.3 Tourism Industry: Contribution to GDP and Employment (2009)

Country	Tourism GDP ($ bn)	Tourism GDP/GDP (%)	Employment (Million)	% in Total Employment	Tourism GDP ($ bn)	Tourism GDP/GDP (%)	Employment (Million)	% in Total Employment
	Direct				*Direct + Indirect*			
India	**42.0**	**3.1**	**18.6**	**3.8**	**117.9**	**10.0**	**49.1**	**10.0**
Switzerland	31.1	5.8	0.35	7.8	72.4	13.6	0.79	17.5
Malaysia	11.1	5.1	0.59	5.3	29.0	13.4	1.33	11.9
Thailand	17.2	6.2	1.88	4.9	38.4	13.9	4.00	10.4
Egypt	14.4	7.0	1.39	5.9	26.7	13.0	2.54	10.9
Cambodia	1.0	8.9	0.51	6.8	2.1	18.4	1.07	14.3
Jordon	2.2	9.0	0.13	8.6	4.9	20.5	0.29	18.3

Source: Travel and Tourism Competitiveness Report, 2011 of World Economic Forum.

Doubling of income from tourism sector (overall) means an additional GDP of $120 billion, i.e. nearly 8 per cent of the current GDP levels. This means an additional growth rate of 1.5 per cent per annum over the next 6 years.

There are several countries which have tourism's share in GDP 2–3 times ours and employment levels 1.5–2 times indicating that we may not be pushing practical limits. Travel industry itself may have to grow by 13–14 per cent to achieve doubling of incomes in 6 years which has earlier been achieved by IT sector and in some years by travel itself.

Chapter 9

FEASIBILITY AND THE GROWTH POTENTIAL OF SUGGESTED ACTIONS

Economic growth without social progress lets the great majority of the people remain in poverty, while the privileged few reap the benefits of rising abundance.

—John F. Kennedy (1961)

Reforms sound progressive and connote change in the existing order of things and a sense of urgency to overcome obstacles. Hopefully, this is about accelerating the rate of growth of the economy and delivering better benefits to the citizens and pulling out those who are stuck below the poverty line. But it also connotes that it is predominantly about undoing or rectifying what has been done in the past.

The initiators and the neo-converts of reforms proclaim its efficacy and success by pointing out the increase in growth rate from 4.2 per cent pre-reforms to the 6.5 per cent since reforms began. Several large states have exhibited increase in their growth rates by significant percentages as is shown in Figure 9.1. Surprisingly, the state which has gained the maximum between pre- and post-reform years is West Bengal while Rajasthan has lost out the maximum with growth rates coming down steeply during the reform years.

While any growth in the growth rate is welcome, it is a rather weak and inappropriate way of evaluating or benchmarking. We should more appropriately focus on the potential for growth rather than the past actual. Using the performance parameters of the past (pre-reform period) to

Figure 9.1 Growth Rates of Select States—Pre- and Post-reforms

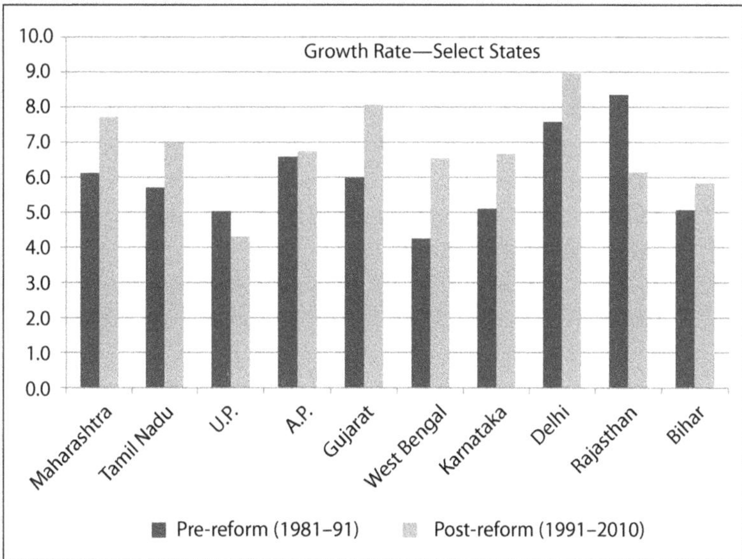

Source: Reserve Bank of India, *Handbook of Statistics on Indian Economy*, Table 5 (Growth Rates calculated from Net State Domestic Product numbers).

evaluate the success of the reforms is self-deception, especially when we are so busy decrying the past policies and proclaim to be freeing ourselves from it. Especially when our northern neighbour (China) has shown consistently over a sufficiently long period of over two decades that 10 per cent growth rates are not unattainable on sustained basis, what could be the big point in being satisfied with 6 per cent and 7 per cent even if it is 2 per cent or 3 per cent over the so-called 'Hindu rate' of growth. Even when some other Asian countries whose per capita income levels are many times more than ours are still clocking 6 per cent and 7 per cent annual growth rates, given our low base, benchmarking against the past bases itself becomes the first sin.

HOW DO REFORMS INCREASE GROWTH?

In a centrally planned economy, the economic decisions are mostly taken centrally without the aid of independent price signals arrived at by the market based on wishes, desires backed by purchasing power of consuming citizens, even if the execution of those decisions itself may be left to private initiatives. In the pre-reform period what capacities to create and what price to sell were largely dictated by the licensing authorities or mechanism.

This has a chance of creating a gap, significant sometimes and not so at other times, between what exactly the end consumers and citizens want and what the centralised system produces. This can create wasted production if the people do not consume what has been produced. This might result in wasted standing capacities as well leading to poorer incremental capital output ratio (ICOR). Likewise, the people may not get what they desire to consume and thus save more or made to settle for something other than what they like best. This will result in welfare loss. It cuts at both ends.

If markets are made to play their due role, both of these can be avoided to a great extent. This will itself add to the gross domestic product (GDP) and growth rates, depending on the effectiveness of the steps taken to remove various constraints and creating conditions for proper operation of markets. Efficient functioning of markets would require (i) facilities for proper enforcement of contracts, (ii) clearing information asymmetries, (iii) proper rules and regulations, (iv) control over certain kinds of market structures like monopolies, which itself distorts choices, etc.

Reforms have also aimed at removal of constraints of various kinds. Markets largely function within the limits set by the existing available skill levels, technology, infrastructure, government system and governance standards, risk taking ability, knowledge of production methods, social aspirations, culture, etc. These become constraints at various levels and different points in time. Growth requires that these constraints are identified from time to time and relaxed. The capacity and oftentimes the willingness of markets to change these to more productive levels or levels socially desirable are sometimes limited. Removal of such constraints creates conditions for better growth. Liberalisation of foreign exchange markets, reduction of tariff levels, removing of convoluted structures in taxation will all lead to further capacity to grow. Invitation of investments from abroad relaxes the capital constraints for funding growth.

INDIA COULD GET BETTER YIELDS FOR ITS PAINS

Within the democratic structure (where economic decision making is often painfully time-consuming and politically risky), what we have achieved by way of reforms may be worthy of celebration. Developing a more functional yet democratic structure may perhaps lead to further improvement and faster growth. But there are also several things that we could have done better, as has been illustrated through the book.

Irrespective of the political structure, several other countries have done remarkably well and sustained such growth and momentum over a much longer period of time. As we have seen in Part II of the book, India's growth rate has gone up by 2.3 per cent during reforms compared to 4.7 per cent in China. This can make one wonder whether all the pains of adjustment under reforms have been worth it. It is imperative to increase the returns to reforms (by way of enhanced growth rates distributed equitably) so that the pains are felt to be a fair price for the compensation received. The signals received from the political system often indicate that the balance has not yet been found; pains seem perhaps more than gains on balance. There are also fears that we may have created whatever gains at the expense of future putting the government's finances at a great risk or created some dysfunctional structures which are not easily altered in the future (such as National Rural Employment Guarantee Act [NREGA], minimum support price [MSP] and land acquisition measures).

9.1 Feasibility: Lessons from Other Countries and Indian States

Before we summarise the action plans which may facilitate a 12 per cent growth rate, it would be ideal to see other countries and states within India which have traversed that path earlier and the consistency and longevity of such high growth rates, to gauge both the feasibility of achieving and sustaining high growth rates. This will set at rest sceptical and debilitative arguments like 'no one has done it; no big country like India has done it before'. This is done by looking at other countries over the last 50 years (1961–2011) and the Indian states from 1961 to 2010.

EXAMPLES FROM OTHER COUNTRIES

There are several countries which have demonstrated double digit growth rates for long periods of time before and will give us company in the future. This includes small economies like Botswana, Angola; Oil economies like Oman; big ones like China; war-ravaged economies like Rwanda and Ethiopia; countries on which economic sanctions have been in operation intermittently or continuously like Myanmar and Iran. China and Korea have demonstrated high growth with consistency. In the list, India and South Africa stand out as countries which have not yet clocked a 10 per cent growth rate.

Table 9.1 lays out some countries which have achieved or maintained high growth rates of 10 per cent and 12 per cent. BRIC (Brazil, Russia, India and China) countries have been given for reference.

It is possible that the natural resource endowments, political systems and other exogenous factors which have a bearing on the functioning of the economy are vastly different in these countries. Perhaps this should be a source of hope. The varied nature of countries should perhaps convince us that there is no single formula for success as well as that

Table 9.1 Countries Which Have Seen More Than 12 Per Cent Growth Rates

Country	Average 1961–2011	Years for which info Reported	No. of Years with Growth Rates		Maximum Consecutive Stretch with	
			>10%	>12%	>10%	>12%
Botswana	8.9	51	20	13	6	5
Oman	9.3	51	16	13	5	4
China	8.3	51	24	11	5	3
Iran, Islamic Rep.	4.7	46	12	9	4	2
Singapore	7.9	51	20	9	9	6
Myanmar	5.0	51	10	7	6	3
Ethiopia	4.8	30	8	4	5	1
Jordan	6.1	35	5	5	1	1
Korea, Rep.	6.9	51	9	3	3	1
Brazil	4.5	51	5	2	3	2
Thailand	6.3	51	7	2	3	2
India	5.2	51	0	0	0	0
Mexico	4.1	51	1	0	0	0
Russian Federation	0.7	22	1	0	0	0
South Africa	3.3	51	0	0	0	0

Source: Compiled from data from World Bank, Development Indicators.

the solutions need to be country specific, even while we make efforts to draw appropriate lessons from them.

INDIAN STATES WITH HIGH GROWTH

Several Indian states have grown at 10 per cent and 12 per cent in pre-reform as well as post-reform periods. Table 9.2 summarises the number of times select big states have grown at rates in excess of 10 per cent and 12 per cent during the pre- and post-reform period, respectively. The table lists all states with a yearly state NDP of over ₹175,000 crore separately.

Table 9.2 Growth Rates of States

States	Pre-reforms 1981–82 to 1990–91 (10 Years)		Post-reforms 1991–92 to 2010–11 (20 Years)	
	No. of Years with Growth Rates			
	>10%	>12%	>10%	>12%
Maharashtra	2	1	8	4
Tamil Nadu	2	1	5	3
UP	1	1	1	0
AP	3	3	4	1
Gujarat	2	2	8	6
West Bengal	1	0	0	0
Karnataka	0	0	6	3
Delhi	2	2	11	6
Rajasthan	3	3	8	4
Bihar	1	1	9	7

Source: Table 5, *Handbook of Indian Economy*, RBI. (Calculated from Data on Net State Domestic Product.)

Bihar has been given for reference even though it does not have a state GDP of ₹175,000 crore per annum.

The table shows some surprises. With all the constitutional and political constraints imposed by India, many states (whether of party ruling at the centre or otherwise) have grown at 12 per cent and 10 per cent. Delhi has clocked the maximum number of above 10 per cent growth years and Bihar the maximum with over 12 per cent growth years.

This only highlights that 10 per cent and 12 per cent growth are definitely feasible. In reform years, we have 146 times out of 517 (28 per cent) above 10 per cent growth years and 85 instances (16 per cent) of 12 per cent and above growth rates. The way forward may be to study and standardise the best processes and policies, as much as feasible, across other lower growth rate states and pull them over. Even the high growth states may have a few lessons to learn from such a process.

LESSONS FROM CHINA

China presents the best example that a large country can grow consistently over a long time and that size does not need to impede growth. China embarked on reforms post its totalistic communist regime which eased up considerably after 1978 when the new economic policy was ushered in. Its track record with democracy and civil rights may not be as good as India's. India embarked on reforms post-1991 forex crisis. Our track record on poverty removal or governance has not been as impressive as China's. China has gained significantly due to reforms; its average growth rate has grown from 5.2 per cent (between 1961 and 1978) to 9.9 per cent—an increase of 4.7 per cent per annum, post-reforms. India has not gained as much and its growth rate has grown from 4.2 per cent to 6.5 per cent an increase of 2.3 per cent—just half of China's gains. Both have become much more consistent with growth, with the difference between the best and worst years within each decade coming down sharply over the last 50 years although China again has been able to achieve better results (Table 9.3).

IT IS POSSIBLE TO ACHIEVE 12 PER CENT GROWTH RATES

All these examples and past results should be a definitive indicator that 12 per cent growth rates are possible with purposive policies, better governance and meaningfully designed reform programmes. People quite often blamed the difference between China and India on democratic handicap of India and tight policing in China. Even Singapore has tight rules and regulations so very strictly enforced as to look like a military regime, even if it allows for democratic elections. The difference is one of discipline, training, respect for rules

Table 9.3 Decadal Growth Rates (Average)

Years	China				India			
	Average	**Best Year**	**Worst Year**	**Difference**	**Average**	**Best Year**	**Worst Year**	**Difference**
1961–70	4.7	19.4	–27.1	46.5	4.0	7.8	–2.6	10.5
1971–80	6.3	11.7	–1.6	13.3	3.1	9.1	–5.2	14.4
1981–90	9.4	15.2	3.8	11.4	5.6	9.6	3.5	6.2
1991–2000	10.5	14.2	7.6	6.6	5.6	8.5	1.1	7.4
2001–11	10.4	14.2	8.3	5.9	7.4	9.8	3.9	5.9
1961–2011 (51 yrs)	8.3				5.5			
Pre-reforms	5.2	19.4	–27.1	46.5	4.2	9.6	–5.2	14.8
Post-reforms	9.9	15.2	3.8	11.4	6.5	9.8	1.1	8.7

Source: Data compiled from World Bank, Development Indicators.
Note: China Reforms have been taken as started in 1979 and India's from 1991.

and regulations, fear of law and in general attitudes than one of political decision-making systems. India itself has demonstrated wonders like its election systems under the very political system which gets blamed for many other ills. Yes a faster decision making can be facilitated by changes in system and easier ways of building consensus, but that is the art our politicians are supposed to bring to the table and convincing them should be the art that our economists should master.

9.2 Pros and Cons of Existing Reforms

While we may have achieved some results with our reforms, duly sterilised by our democracy, these have not all been a success. Some have shortcomings even as they seek to do some good and some have been stellar successes like our handling of foreign exchange liberalisation and careful calibration of capital account convertibility, others like our approach towards regulation, civic planning, public distribution systems, minimum support prices, NREGA scheme, etc. seem more to lean on the negative impact either in their long-term impact and sustainability or damage of government finances for a given level of goals and achievement.

Table 9.4 summarises the pros and cons of some of the key reforms already implemented. While perceptions will vary, there is a definite need for initiating further studies on most matters and taking a dispassionate view on course correction measures or outright jettisoning some of them.

In summary, while we should celebrate our successes we have left out a lot to be desired. Reforms do not seem to make definitive impacts where necessary, do not seem to keep in mind the social processes and likely reception. Prioritising of measures and target beneficiaries seems to have gone awry at several places. The overall master plan of our reforms does not seem as clear-cut and defined as is necessary. Our economists may do better with greater sensitivity to people's expectation, pains and aspirations and perhaps learn a few lessons

Table 9.4 Pros and Cons of Existing Reform Programmes

S. No.	Reform measures	Pros	Cons
1	Removal of licensing	Has freed up entrepreneurial energy which is an essential requirement for growth.	Without licensing from time to time capacity creation has far exceeded demand or lagged creating price pressures and wasted investments.
2	Dilution of import curbs and reduction of customs duties	Made import of goods easier. Increased competition and efficiency of domestic manufacture.	However, with several handicaps imposed by government services and infrastructure, domestic manufacturing seems to be in serious trouble.
3	Free markets for Forex. Liberalisation of all current account transactions	Made imports a lot easier. Made exports a lot more profitable. Generally, the process has been handled admirably.	The recent free trade agreements are a cause of worry. The impact from these on domestic employment, competitiveness of various industries has not been reckoned properly in signing these agreements.
4	Capital account convertibility	Helped in sourcing FDI.	Has made our financial systems more vulnerable to currency attacks, wider fluctuations than can be under the control of RBI as recently seen.
5	Reduction of income tax rates	Ensured better incentive for compliance.	Lowered government revenues, prevented expansion of government services in line with growth in economy and has worsened the service levels of most government services. Left a huge employment backlog.
6	Simplification of tax rules and structures	Compliance made easier.	Equitable distribution could have been done a lot better with differential rates. Has equitably distributed the burden instead.
7	Introduction of state VAT	Will facilitate integration of India as a common market. Will ensure that production is done at the most cost competitive location. May also curb generation of black money.	

(Table 9.4 Continued)

(Table 9.4 Continued)

S. No.	Reform measures	Pros	Cons
8	Slow dilution of fiscal incentives	Enables and furthers the markets being able to decide with lesser say of government.	The effective reach of our monetary policy is far too low given our monetisation and poor financial inclusion. Distributing the fruits of growth in a more equitable manner would have been far more easier with fiscal policies.
9	NREGA and Food Bill	Has provided immediate succour for millions who did not see any line of sight for removal of persistent hunger.	In the long-term imposes severe burden on government finances, increases 'net effective' wages in rural areas and is highly detrimental in the long term to the beneficiaries. Politically impossible to withdraw whatever the state of government finances.
10	Right to education	If the curriculum had been designed better, it could have been of help.	Does not appreciate the reasons behind poor attendance at schools. Money should have been better spent on skill development.
11	Land acquisition	Might prevent land grabbing and concentration of this key resource.	Does not seem to grasp the psychological fundamentals clearly. Will increase prices steeply and nullify the effect of reforms along with labour.
12	Market access to foreign goods and services	Better goods and services available within country. This may have promoted domestic manufacture in select areas.	India does not seem to have negotiated reciprocal access well.
13	FDI	Provides the much needed financial capital accompanied oftentimes by technology and physical capital for growth.	We have to cede market access. Leads to rapid replacement of manpower-oriented technology with machine-oriented technology and hence slows down job creation.
14	Road construction	Has changed much of India with better connectivity and faster movement of vehicles. May have promoted domestic tourism.	Poor execution and delays in completion. During construction phase inconveniences imposed on users are far too much. If these are duly accounted for returns may be considerably less. It may be better to develop new urban centres and new cities.

(Table 9.4 Continued)

(Table 9.4 Continued)

S. No.	Reform measures	Pros	Cons
15	MSP	Has achieved better distributive justice. Shifted a lot of purchasing power to rural areas thus developing rural consumption and markets.	In the long term farmers will look at MSPs to decide what to grow rather than what suits the soil and blunt his skills in reading the situation on the ground, weather conditions and planning. Has been the main reason for food inflation, wastes of a high order. Benefits only the land owning class and may have benefitted only the top third of the target agri-producers.
16	PDS	No meaningful measures have taken place here.	Corruption is still widespread. Poor systems and incentive structure.
17	Direct transfers of cash	Decreases leakages.	The recipients will follow his hierarchy of wants, whereas the government might want him to consume goods and services which are not strictly in the same order. Money meant for food might, for example, get spent on marriages, intoxicants, IPL matches, etc.
18	Reforms in equity markets	India has one of the finest functioning equity markets today in the world.	Poor contribution to growth in terms of mobilisation of risk money. Structure may have run far ahead of requirements.
19	Reduction in public sector employment		Has been the chief reason for jobless or job loss growth. Has prevented government services from expanding in line with requirements.
20	Increase in pay for public sector employees	Growth in line with private sector was necessary.	However, select sections of private sector ran way ahead creating ideal conditions for jealousy and temptation for corruption has been the main reason for shrinkage of employment (as recommended by fifth pay commission).
21	Futures and options for agri-commodities		How exactly it will benefit the end producers instead of speculative elements does not seem to have been thought through carefully.

on social marketing and design of programmes so that they are received well.

9.3 Action Plan for Growth Summarised

The overall strategy for reforms and growth should be (i) improve skills and capabilities and thus enhance competitiveness. This will be most required for achieving equitable growth so that more people can participate in growth and its dividends rather than see most of growth going to a select few percentage of people. Skewed distribution and development have long-term social risks. (ii) This will bring down the 'effective wages per unit of production or service' even if the money wages keep going up. With this we should create more employment, (iii) grow government services and other employment opportunities and (iv) create new avenues of growth (growth engines) and create market structures where existing consumption is lower than socially desirable. Growth in employment will create the market demand which will attract private investment for fulfilling the demand.

The process has been examined and detailed in the previous pages. The likely net impact of these on employment and growth rates has also been detailed. Together with optimisation of our ICOR and culling unproductive savings, we should be able to add 4–4.5 per cent to our annual growth rates. On a base of 7.5 per cent based a savings of 32 per cent, we should see growth of 12 per cent and above. If history is any lesson it is not impossible to sustain it over a period of time, particularly for India which depends mostly on domestic demand where imported disturbances to growth are much more limited than in most other export-oriented economies including China (Table 9.5).

The government has a leading and pivotal role to play in 'causing' growth to happen. It needs to enact appropriate laws for new growth engines to emerge, provide for appropriate governance mechanisms, rules and regulations but leave

Table 9.5 Action Plan for 12 Per Cent Growth

S. No.	Action	Effect on Employment	Effect on Growth Reason	Increase Growth % Per Annum
1	Growth of plantation	Can create up to 2 million jobs at the low skill end	0.1 per cent to 0.2 per cent including follow on consumption	0.20
2	Lowering the savings rates by selective targeting	Shift from manufacture of investments goods to consumption goods which have a higher employment intensity can add jobs	Negative effect on growth; however, GDP will itself raise by 0.11 per cent for each percentage drop in savings due to multiplier effect	0.25
3	Improving ICOR by 0.5 times from 4.25 to 3.75 (or whatever the starting ICOR)	May have negligible impact; however, if the action which improves ICOR has a rub off impact on overall existing capital as well, it can perhaps take away some jobs	Given a savings rate of 30 per cent, an ICOR of 4.25 yields 7.05 per cent growth and ICOR of 3.75, the growth rate is likely to be 8 per cent	0.95
4	Urbanisation and development of new cities	Will create employment in creating cities	This as explained before can create growth of 0.5 to 1.0 per cent	0.5–1.0
5	Tourism development	5 million (assuming travel volumes will double in 5 years)	As explained in Section 8.3, India has the potential to enhance growth by 1.0 to 1.5 per cent in tourism	1.0–1.5
6	Waste collection and recycling system set-up	Initial addition of about 1–2 million jobs	One time addition of 8–10 per cent to GDP over the initial 4–5 years from the capital investments made and the systems to be set up	

(Table 9.5 Continued)

(Table 9.5 Continued)

S. No.	Action	Effect on Employment	Effect on Growth Reason	Increase Growth % Per Annum
7	Waste collection (running the systems)	2–3 million jobs	Accretion to growth rates can be 0.3 to 0.4 per cent	0.40
8	Expansion of government services in line with growth and closer to world standards	10–12 million additional employment	if government services grow in line with GDP growth rate, it can add 1 per cent to growth, besides the one-time impact and huge welfare enhancement, better sense of security, justice, policing and better ranks on HDI and social services in world Ranking; this can perhaps improve ratings and cut down borrowing costs for India	1.00
	Incremental employment and growth	**15–18 million jobs**		**4.4–5.4**
	Existing growth at 32 per cent savings and 4.25 ICOR			**7.50**
	Total			**11.35–12.35**

the actual action to commercially oriented private sector. If something is not commercially viable probably it is not worth pursuing in the first place, with possible exceptions which arise because of mismatch in timing of investments and related returns, where this is long given the investment profile, private sector often shrugs its shoulders.

9.4 Action Plan for Distributing Growth and Enhancing Welfare

After over a couple of decades of reforms, it is not possible for India to continue promising but not delivering. Let us create growth and distributable kitty and will talk of distributing it once we have enough in the kitty is an argument whose time is well past its due date. For people whose discounting rates are closer to 100 per cent and the society itself aims for 12–14 per cent nominal growth (which is a close approximation of the society's ability to wait for future gratification instead of present) which implies a maximum 6–7 years wait or payback. Having waited almost four decades till reforms and a further two in heightened hopes, it is foolish to expect further patience from a majority of low-income people. This is already showing in growing protests and unrest with select reform programmes. It is necessary to consciously plan for distributive justice instead of leaving it to the market alone or throw inane promises like wealth distribution will automatically follow wealth creation. The steep increase in our savings rate and the high rate of savings itself are symptomatic of a highly skewed distribution. In the last few years, this has become more pronounced. Corruption of mega scale and skewed distribution has blunted the marketability of reforms.

Table 9.6 lists some measures to promote employment and better distribution of wealth.

Table 9.6 Action Plan for Enhancing Employment, Equity and Better Distributive Efficiency

S. No.	Action Plan	Effect on Employment and Distributive Efficiency
1	Investment in skill development and reduction in expenditure on education	Will supply skills to industry and reduce 'effective productivity adjusted cost' of labour. This might improve India's competitiveness and open up more sectors for export growth. Will create employment opportunities and reduce dependence on agriculture.

(Table 9.6 Continued)

(Table 9.6 Continued)

S. No.	Action Plan	Effect on Employment and Distributive Efficiency
2	Increasing tax GDP ratio by about 2–3 per cent	Will reduce government's deficits and improve rating and aid better FDI inflow. Government can improve its staff strength and improve efficiency of its various services. It has to improve the 'quantity' of its various services for maintaining governance standards.
3	Letting banks increase interest rates to rural and agricultural sector, engaging with micro finance initiatives, providing insurance to moneylenders and absorbing them within the formal system	Will reduce interest rates to disadvantaged sections and aid better financial inclusion. Will improve effectiveness of social interventions.
4	Freeing up fuel pricing controls	Will increase prices and reduce qty consumed and reduce import bill and may help reduce current account deficits. Will reduce subsidy burden and help government tackle deficits and improve ratings.
5	Recovering proper prices for all economic services rendered by government. Subsidies only for bottom 30–40 per cent, cost recovery for the next 30 per cent and commercial prices or prices based on 12–14 per cent nominal return on investment for the rest	Will focus subsidies and enable expansion of economic services of government in line with economic growth.
6	Setting up an effective Lokpal or any other system of surveillance and control	Might ward off parties relying on money power or substantially dilute the power and restrict the number of parties which can aid consolidation of power and facilitate faster legislative decision making including reforms measures.
7	Re-directing resources for intermediate markets in education, medical care, equity markets, legal services, etc. to end use markets	Will deliver better end use benefits, increase augment supplies of essential services.
8	Develop alternative ways of using forex reserves	Better returns on our reserves, lesser dependence on FDI, faster removal of infrastructure constraints.

(Table 9.6 Continued)

(Table 9.6 Continued)

S. No.	Action Plan	Effect on Employment and Distributive Efficiency
9	Privatising public distribution	Better delivery efficiencies. Reduction in subsidy burden. Enable private players to integrate their services into rural and agri-sector. Huge stock in FCI godowns even while there are shortages and hunger all around will be handled more efficiently.

Table 9.6 lists some measures that can pave the way for a more egalitarian society not by social security and freebees but by way of economic inclusion where productive efficiency of individuals increases. The beneficiary individuals can contribute meaningfully to society to earn their livelihood in a respectable and secure manner. The government should play a facilitative role. At this juncture, it looks like improving the gini-coefficient by deliberate action is vital; leaving it to casual determination may be a huge risk.

Conclusion

The most fatal illusion is the settled point of view. Life is growth and motion; a fixed point of view kills anybody who has one.

—Brooks Atkinson

When a socialist and of late the officialdom see a hungry man—they see an empty belly. The reaction is one of patronisation and benevolence to feed him. The alternative is to see a set of hands that are idling, to train them so that they contribute to the national kitty of goods and services.

The latter approach will not only provide income for him and his family in the long term, but from what he earns and spends create employment for someone else as well. Such an approach will essentially be expansionery in nature. The current benevolent approach is contractionary and hence will in the long-term impede inclusion. It also dilutes individual initiative, drive and ambition so vital for personal growth and makes him settle at a low individual economic equilibrium.

Firstly, GDP is just the quantum of goods and services produced by the country. If more people work, producing socially or economically desirable goods or services, the society's GDP should rise. India has a high unemployment rate of 30–35 per cent (hidden though in an official unemployment of 10 per cent). If only we can find some way to productively employ all those—even if by contrived mechanisms or induced demand—over the next 10 years at our average income levels of ₹5,000 per month, it will mean a 30–35 per cent increase in our GDP.

Secondly, our skill sets and levels are rather low when compared to several comparable countries. If the productivity is improved by appropriate training and skill development, it is inconceivable why we cannot achieve an additional GDP of 30–40 per cent over the next decade. Development of skills and improvement of productivity together should give 60–75 per cent additional GDP in about a decade. This implies an additional 5 per cent per annum growth.

A 12 per cent growth is feasible. There is sufficient material in economic history to prove it. But to attain it we have to first start thinking about it. We need to overcome the mental blocks and self-imposed restraints so that we can design programmes without being saddled with the baggage of the past. Informed debates will definitely open up more possibilities.

We need to think employment instead of growth alone. For example, can we make people pay for clean surroundings and deliver the same by training people? How do we ensure better road safety—another concern of citizens—by employing more people? Can we reduce our road accidents by better discipline which can be brought about by increased policing? We need greater green cover. Can we deploy more trained resources to develop it and deliver commercial value to willing users? If we train and deploy even 1–2 million in each such activity, it would do a great deal more to reduce poverty than the Food Security Bill kind of schemes which are highly ineffective in delivery and have limited long-term potency. Creation of 20–30 million low-skilled jobs for the tribals, poor and landless labour promises faster reduction of poverty than dubious schemes.

Estonia, a part of erstwhile USSR, was one of the most crime-prone areas in the world. But in 15 years since the early 1990s, it has become one of the least crime-prone and safest places. While there are social problems in Estonia—marriage rates are falling and divorce rates are increasing alarmingly and one sees signs of drugs on the streets of its capital Tallinn, the crime as we know it has largely (if not fully) been controlled.

Closer home we witnessed Surat being transformed after the plague in the early 1990s from being one of the dirtiest cities to being one of the cleanest within the decade itself.

Recently, when gold prices were plummeting, there was a long queue in front of a particular shop in Chennai. This shop had guaranteed its buyers price protection for the next 3 months, i.e. any customer who bought gold was promised reimbursement of the difference in case the prices fell. What perhaps would have happened is the owner would have bought equivalent 3-month options for selling gold from which he would have recovered the difference for reimbursing the clients. Thus, what was an adversity was made use of by him for gaining long-term loyalty of the customer and establishing his name firmly in the minds and psyche of his existing and new clients.

These only indicate that with appropriate plans backed by official will it is not difficult to achieve transformational growth rates. This seems applicable for cities as well as nation states, not just corporates. Constraints and impediments are mainly between our two ears.

The difference between 8 per cent and 12 per cent growth means leaving twice as much to the next generation; in 20 years, our incomes would be twice as much with 12 per cent growth as it is with 8 per cent growth—a very enticing prospect indeed. That should be enough motivation and reward to give it our best.

If an individual is regular with his exercise, takes care of his diet, follows hygienic habits and avoids harmful addictions, his health will most likely take care of itself. Sound health cannot be achieved by regular monitoring of blood pressure, ECG, cholesterol, or by taking medicines, scanning, etc. These are just checks that can help with course corrections. Most of the intensely debated topics in our economic spheres such as Current Account Deficit (CAD), CRR, Sensex, inflation, forex rates or reserves are just like health check indicators. There is unfortunately excessive concentration on these. Instead our debates should be to get our micro-level initiatives right and generate several creative alternative programmes and designs and implement them with regular course corrections to fine-tune them for better results.

Epilogue

Economics is extremely useful as a form of employment for the economists.
—J.K. Galbraith

It appears that economics as a discipline requires serious cross pollination with creativity, ground-level realities and social circumstances. Most of our economists are urban trained and most of economics as a subject of study has evolved in the last century or two in the Western social and industrial settings. People who have been trained in these surroundings seem to miss some vital links of native logic and domestic compulsions with the result we end up with ineffective programmes and difficult-to-market policies.

Sure they are at least as patriotic as the political class. Their inability to appreciate the ground realities leads to raucous arguments where the well-meaning economic designers call to question the wisdom and financial discipline of the political class (as indeed anyone who stands in their way) and stand in an intellectual island of their dreams and theories. Sure, our political class instead of engaging with them and finding viable solutions in the long-term interest reciprocate with equally vicious arguments or defeat economic reforms on the floor of the house wherever feasible.

It looks like there are two distinctly separate good Samaritans guiding the country these days—the reformists/economists and politicians, and the distance between them seems to be increasing day by day. Marriage between the socially desirable and the economically viable is seemingly becoming increasingly unattainable: witness the petrol price scenario, debates on NREGA, land acquisition reforms and the fate of the railway minister presenting a reformist budget.

The most basic unit of economic action is the individual—his actions and his motivations. By a proper understanding of these, it is possible to come up with solutions of a far wider depth and breadth than the current state of macroeconomics would suggest.

Macroeconomics as a discipline looks too bereft and unimaginative, still thriving on ideas thrown at it more than half a century ago and some intellectually incestuous breeding thereon. If socialism as a dogma is dead or dying, macroeconomics increasingly looks as dogmatic even if it exhibits far less moral overtones. It looks more like a king who has lost touch with his subjects. It needs to go in disguise amongst its subjects to understand their travails, ground-level reality, their aspirations, hierarchy of wants, the way people think, social, psychological, and physical settings, their chain of action–reaction, causality, etc. and get to grips with the real problems afresh and reboot itself.

India somehow seems wedded more to theories than its own ground realities unlike many East Asian countries. Programmes designed as a consequence are struggling to deliver the kind of superior results as in other East Asian countries.

Bibliography

Bhaduri, Amit and Nayyar, Deepak. 1996. *The Intelligent Person's Guide to Liberalization*. New Delhi: Penguin Books.

Bhagwati, Jagdish and Panagariya, Arvind. 2012. *India's Tryst with Destiny—Debunking Myths That Undermine Progress and Addressing New Challenges*. New Delhi: Collins Business.

Bhatt, Mahesh P. and Mehta, S.B. 1996. *Planned Progress or Planned Chaos—Selected Prophetic Writings of Prof. B.R. Shenoy*. Madras: East West Books.

Bhaumik, T.K. 2009. *Old China's New Economy—The Conquest by a Billion Paupers*. New Delhi: SAGE Publications.

Chelliah, Raja J. 1999. *Towards Sustainable Growth—Essays in Fiscal and Financial Sector Reforms in India*. New Delhi: Oxford University Press.

Cummins, Barbara J. 1990. *Dam the Rivers, Damn the People*. London: Earthscan Publications.

Dantwala, M.L. (ed. Pravin Visaria, N.A. Mujumdar, T.R. Sundaram), 1996. *Dilemmas of Growth—The Indian Experience*. New Delhi: SAGE Publications.

Desai, Ashok V. 1993. *My Economic Affair*. New Delhi: Wiley Eastern.

Jalan, Bimal. 1996. *India's Economic Policy—Preparing for the Twenty-First Century*. New Delhi: Viking, Penguin Books.

———. (ed.). 1992. *The Indian Economy—Problems and Prospects*. New Delhi: Viking, Penguin Books.

Joshi, Vijay and Little, I.M.D. 1996. *India's Economic Reforms 1991–2001*. New Delhi: Oxford University Press.

Lucas, Robert E.B. and Papanek, Gustav. 1989. *The Indian Economy Recent Developments and Future Prospects*. New Delhi: Oxford University Press.

Mills, Greg. 2010. *Why Africa Is Poor and What Africans Can Do about It*. Johannesburg: Penguin Books.

Sachs, Jeffrey. 2005. *The End of Poverty—How We Can Make It Happen in Our Lifetime*. London: Penguin Books.

Stiglitz, Joseph. 2003. *Globalization and Its Discontents*. New Delhi: Penguin Books.

Swaminathan, M.S. 1996. *Sustainable Agriculture—Towards Food Security.* New Delhi: Konark Publishers.

Yunus, Muhammad. 2007. *Banker to the Poor—The Story of the Grameen Bank.* New Delhi: Penguin Books.

Index

About the Author

V. Kumaraswamy did his schooling in Chennai and later graduated from IIM Ahmedabad in the 1980s, where he studied under some of the leading economists of India. The institute encouraged freedom of thought by its unique system of pedagogy. Both the tutelage under illustrious teachers and the system have encouraged him to experiment boldly while writing his columns in economic newsdailies.

He has been working with the industry since the mid-1980s. His corporate work in search of natural resources takes him to several remote rural areas in India and abroad. The unconventional ideas and insights in several parts are born out of first-hand experience during such sorties. He enjoys travelling and loves talking to people at various strata in remote areas here and elsewhere which has given him unique insights and helps him get into the core of some of the key issues affecting them.

He has been writing on reforms and economic policies in economic dailies such as *Business Line* and *Business Standard* for well over a decade which has honed his skills as a writer.

This is his second book. The first book *Corporate Insurance* published by Tata McGraw Hill was co-authored with his wife Sharada. Both his wife and daughter have dabbled in writing for magazines.

He can be reached at blueprint12percent@gmail.com.

www.ingramcontent.com/pod-product-compliance
Lightning Source LLC
Chambersburg PA
CBHW041258210926
51847CB00009B/65
* 9 7 8 8 1 2 6 9 4 3 6 2 3 *